AF433604

HOW TO BUILD A NEW BLACK WALL STREET

By Kyle Davis, Megan Swann and Benjamin Wheeler

Dedication

This Book is Dedicated to My Grandchildren: Milan, Kennedy and Julian

"June 1, 1921, an African American community of Greenwood within the city of Tulsa, Oklahoma, was burned to the ground by a mob of racist white people and bombed by airplane, resulting in the massacre of hundreds of black people. This community was known as Black Wall Street because of it's prosperity in having a bank, insurance companies, a hospital and 600+ businesses. Subsequently in 1982, a music group The Gap Band, named after Greenwood, Archer and Pine Streets, published the song: You Dropped a Bomb on Me," based on the events of 1921."

" Who We Are... is What We Do! "

Contents

Introduction

The contributors to this Step-by-Step Guide for Building a New Black Wall Street: Kyle Davis, Megan Swann and Benjamin Wheeler, have years of worldwide and local Experience developing, consulting and marketing commercial enterprises and economic initiatives.

We are a great people with a great and lustrous African Heritage. We built the Pyramids, which cannot be duplicated with current European knowledge of engineering. Slavery is not our history, and beginning in 2016, our children will be motivated and inspired by our actions with the development of Legacy Black Economics.

Children look up to and admire leaders that have an impact upon their lives. Who we are, is what we do as leaders within our communities. Leadership within the Black Community will not be dictated by the media identifying Black People as God Fearing, with the Black Church nor Black Mega Churches as controlling forces of the Black Community.

Leadership within the Black Community will be defined by the actions we take in creating job opportunity for our youth, and eliminating the unemployment of our youth. Leadership within the Black Community will be defined by our HBCU graduates running and managing businesses developed and financed by the Black Community. Leadership will be defined by our children's children, because we laid the foundation and infrastructure for their continued success.

Black Wall Street is not a particular or specific location, but is a network of like minds implementing and sustaining economic leverage for the benefit of Black Communities Nationwide.

We want Black Power and we say #BlackLivesMatter, so let's do what it takes to have actual power and to make our lives matter.

To help facilitate the Building of a New Black Wall Street, a universal platform has been established to maintain focus in advancing economic development for African People Worldwide: www.TheBankOfTheWorld.org

Moving forward, we foresee growth and development of culture and trade between African Americans and Our Brother and Sister Nations in Africa and the Caribbean.

Nothing is stopping us from achieving Greatness, except Ourselves.

So let's stop with the complaining and go make some money and build legacy economics...

Together as a People... Together as The New Black Wall Street !!!

Part I: Opportunity is Everywhere

9 times out of 10, great black-owned business opportunities are right in front of our face. Nevertheless, we still need reminders to open our eyes to routinely overlooked opportunity. Even work experience can be developed into a business opportunity.

Then on the other hand, we refuse to seek help. You may have the idea and the money to finance a business startup, but we do not always have the experience. That's where our children can help, which should be the number one reason we send them to college. To run these black-owned businesses that we develop and finance for their legacy.

Keep in mind at all times, that a corporation is the only type of business entity that will accomplish the development of legacy black economics. As a corporation, the black community can buy into the various enterprises through stock purchases. Such a share of ownership cannot be done as a sole proprietor or cooperative enterprise. Partnerships have limited value and still do not offer tangible ownership as a shareholder through the purchase of stock from a black-owned corporation.

Below is a list of a variety of businesses and activities, that can be used as reminders of everyday activities that we routinely overlook as a black--owned business opportunity. Even if it appears that there's saturation of a particular industry, realize that there's always an untapped niche market available to be exploited. A niche market exists as a sub-category of any given industry or market. Take for example, a large number of people like blue sneakers, but some people like red sneakers. The red sneakers are the niche market, where actual buyers exist, but without much competition.

Carpentry & Construction:

Lawn Mowing Service, Snow Removal, Garden Tilling, Window Cleaning, Deck Cleaning, Landscape Designer, Deck Construction, Storage Sheds, Playhouses, Doghouses, Children's Outdoor Playset Installer, Low-Voltage Outdoor Lighting and Electrical Wiring, Stonemason and Decorative Brick Worker,

Maintenance:

Handyperson, Errand Runner, Vacation Home Caretaker, Vacation House Watcher, House Painting, Chimney Cleaning, Pool Service, Firewood Delivery, On-demand Trash Removal, Christmas Tree Service, Small Engine Repair (Lawn mowers, snow blowers, snow mobiles, jet skis), Housecleaning, Rug Cleaner, Interior Decorator, Upholstery and Slipcover Maker, Wallpaper Hanger, Specialty Indoor Painting, Furniture Stripping, Furniture Repair, Closet Organizer, Bookcase and Shelf Builder, Indoor Plant Care, Custom Silk and Dried Flower Arrangements, Computer Buying Consultant, Computer Repair and Upgrade, Web Design and Maintenance.

Entertainment:

Food (Fish Fries, church cooked meals), Party Planner, Children' Event Organizer, Party and Special-Event Rentals, Catering, Visiting Chef, Specialty Cake Baker, Prepared Custom-Meal Service, Freelance Bartender, Entertainer, Holiday Decoration Service.

Childcare & Family Services:

Babysitting, Babysitting Agency, Children' Night Out, Vacation Child Care, Dog Walking and Vacation Pet Visits, Pet Sitter and Doggie Day Care, Senior / Elder Companion, Senior / Elder Care Consultant, Genealogical Research, Family Biographer,

Education:

Homeschool consultant, Tutoring, Language Instructor, Music Teacher, Computer Instructor, SAT or ACT College Test Preparation, College Selection Advisor, College Application Consultant, Instructor at Community School, Webinar Developer, Webinar Instructor

Design & Decorations:

Alterations, Custom Tailoring, Custom Knitting, Sweater, and Afghan Design, Custom Quiltmaker, Jewelry Making, Portraits from Photographs, Custom-Built Dollhouses, Musical Instrument Tuning and Repair, Graphic Designer, Freelance Photographer, Film to Digital Scanning, Photo and Document Restorer, Videographer

Transportation:

Car Service (Driver on-call), Independent Delivery Contractor, Auto Detailing, Mobile Auto Repair.

Professional Services

Virtual Office Resource, Temporary Secretary, Transcription Services, Temporary Worker at Conventions and Business Meetings, Bookkeeping, Billing Service, Resume Design, Business Plans and Letter Writing, eBook editor, eBook conversion.

Sales

Cold water bottle vendor, Yard Sale Organizer, Consignment Resale, Thrift Store, Antiques and Collectibles Wholesaler, Used Book Reseller, Tool and Equipment Rentals, Newspaper Delivery Route, Online Auctions: EBay, Online sales: Etsy, eBook distributor, Author: Urban Literature and Children's Books.

NOTES

<u>NOTES</u>

<u>Chapter 1: Show Me The Money</u>

To Build a New Black Wall Street, we need access to a money transfer system.

Commercial Bank Accounts are not the only way to deposit money from your
business enterprise.

Consider using debit cards: Greendot or even a Rush Card, these two have reasonable fee schedules. In addition, debit cards offer a safety cushion, where you should only leave not more than $10 in the account in case of online theft and lost or stolen cards.

Debit cards also come with a checking account number, which is used for direct deposits and PayPal verification. When opening a PayPal account, PayPal will make two small deposits that you have to verify to raise daily access amount limits.

After (60) sixty days as a seller of products or services, you will then be eligible for a Paypal merchant debit card, which gives you direct access to your PayPal cash.

Now that you have access to a cash transfer system, let's start making money.

<u>NOTES</u>

Chapter 2: Never Miss Opportunity

How many opportunities have you missed?

In America's black communities nationwide, there's a selfish mentality that's preventing our creatives from realizing their fullest potential.

Take for example, black graphic artists who perceive a value for their work, where no value exists because there is no market for such artwork. Not because their work is without public appeal, it's just the simple fact that black artists refuse to create and establish a value based market for their artwork.

Black artist cannot establish themselves, if they continue to watermark artwork that they post online. Today, for something to become viral, it has to be shareable, and watermarks stop a viral opportunity dead in it's tracks. Black graphic artists, to develop a fan base, you have to be engaging with the public and realize that the public is your best friend. Stop taking offense when you find your artwork being shared or fan versions created. Otherwise, you're losing out on creating actual and unforeseen value for your work.

Nevertheless, to Build a New Black Wall Street, we must collaborate across industries. Poets should work with graphic artists, and graphic artists should develop advertising and sign companies that can produce the display work for new businesses that we open locally and nationwide.

On the other hand, if you're an entrepreneur who has come up with a good idea, protect it like it's your child. Don't let some theif steal it from you. I'm amazed when I see entrepreneurs share their precious ideas with strangers or potential investors. It's as if they've got thousands of other good ideas in their brain for backup. Share your ideas with others cautiously.

It's easy to play devil's advocate when it comes to the evaluation of ideas. We've all come across people that are fantastic at playing this role. They believe they are doing you a favor thinking up every possible reason why an idea won't work. "It's too narrow." "It's too ahead of its time." "The product is too expensive to produce." These are the same people that have never come up with any ideas of their own. I don't mind someone providing feedback on an idea, but please don't just knock it down. Try to improve it or provide some solid advice.

However, to Build a New Black Wall Street, we have to be open to criticism, and realize these are not personal attacks to ones character, or ability. It's just plain old criticism.

And don't downplay the power of idea generation. The process of coming up with a great idea is fuzzy, unpredictable, chaotic and at times difficult. Your mind is a complex, adaptive, non-linear system. There are days when the mind flows freely with so many ideas that we have difficulty writing them all down. But on some days you have to get into the idea zone to allow yourself to Inspire your mind, and guard new ideas carefully.

Treat your ideas with the utmost respect. Ideation is an unpredictable process. It's hard to predict when you'll come up with that "big idea." Everyone enjoys thinking of big ideas, but ideas are only the beginning of an entrepreneur's journey. You might have to add, modify or edit your idea to make it workable in the marketplace.

Beware of idea Wolves. Sharing ideas with everyone is not a good thing. And in business, never share ideas with people outside the contractual circle within your company. You never know who might be an idea wolf. When you share your ideas, you risk having them stolen from you.

Don't let social media bamboozle you either. You see share buttons everywhere on the internet because social media companies encourage people to share their thoughts, advice and ideas. My advice: don't be so social when it comes to sharing your ideas before they're hatched. When you're business is up and running, with product ready for the marketplace, share your idea to the utmost.

Otherwise, guard your idea like a top military secret.

Silicon Valley does a good job of keeping ideas below the radar until it's time to build the market hype. You see this with startups and established companies. Nobody does it better than Apple. Apple guards its product ideas like the gold at Fort Knox (except for the time one of their employees left the iPhone 4 prototype at a bar). You should too.

Chapter 3: Leverage Advantage From Disadvantage

In Building a New Black Wall Street, we have to recognize the value within our community and exploit that value to the fullest extent.

Take gentrification for example. Instead of protesting and making superficial noise, demand that your local mega church finance job creation industries that will prevent gentrification, where white flight from the suburbs will not have the ability to take root in a misperceived disadvantaged community.

The Black Community must realize that, profits on sales and profits on investment are not merely different concepts. They can move in opposite directions. One of the keys to the rise to dominance of the A&P grocery chain in the 1920s was a conscious decision by the company management to cut profit margins on sales, in order to increase the profit rate on investment.

Lower prices were possible by selling with lower profits per item, to which, A&P was able to attract a greatly increased numbers of customers, making far more total profit because of the increase in sales volume. This low price and high volume strategy set a pattern that spread to other grocery chains and to other kinds of enterprises as well. In a later era, huge supermarkets were able to shave the profit margin on sales still thinner, because of even higher volumes, enabling them to displace A&P from industry leadership by charging still lower prices.

Conversely, a study of prices in low-income neighborhoods found that there were larger than usual markups in prices charged their customers but, at the same time, there were lower than usual rates of profit on investment. Higher profits on sales helped compensate for the higher costs of doing business in low-income neighborhoods but apparently not completely, as indicated by the lower rates of profit on investments and the resulting avoidance of such neighborhoods by many businesses, including supermarket chains.

A limiting factor in how high stores in low-income neighborhoods can raise their prices to compensate for higher costs is the fact that many low-income residents already shop in stores in higher-income neighborhoods, where the prices are lower, even though this may entail paying bus fare or taxi fare.

The higher the prices rise in low-income neighborhoods, the more people are likely to shop elsewhere. Thus stores in such neighborhoods are limited in the extent to which they can offset higher costs and slower turnover with higher prices, often leaving them in a precarious financial position, even while they are being denounced for "exploiting" their customers.

It should also be noted that, where there are higher costs of doing business in low-income neighborhoods when there are higher rates of crime and vandalism, such additional costs can easily overwhelm the profit margin and make many businesses unsustainable in such neighborhoods. If a store clears a penny of profit on an item that costs a quarter, then if just one out of every 25 of these items gets stolen by shoplifters, that can make it unprofitable to sell in that stolen by shoplifters, that can make it unprofitable to sell in that neighborhood.

However, if black communities leveraged the wealth of our mega churches and developed industries that created a labor force, then low-income neighborhoods would become a thing of the past. Thereby reversing the trend that made it uneconomic for stores to flourish in such neighborhood.

<u>NOTES</u>

<u>NOTES</u>

Chapter 4: Right vs. Wrong Perspective

How can you refresh your perspective and see things in a new light?

Put something or someone in an unusual place. Looking at your subject in an unexpected location throws off the preconceptions and stereotypes you have of that subject, revealing its extraordinary potential.

The expression "The Real McCoy," validates a counterfeit from an original. Elijah McCoy was a Black Inventor who in 1872, patented an "oil-drip cup" used for lubrication within the railroad industry. Railroad engineers would inquire if
a locomotive was fitted with "the real McCoy system," to avoid inferior copies of the oil drip-cup design.

Owen Maclaren designed the undercarriage of the Spitfire, the British fighter plane that dominated the skies during the Battle of Britain. Its undercarriage folded up in a neat but complex way.

In 1965 Maclaren invented a collapsible stroller inspired by this folding mechanism, and it revolutionized the transportation of babies and small children; previously, carriages and strollers had been heavy, rigid and impractical. Owen went into production with the new lightweight aluminum Maclaren Baby Buggy in 1967. It sold millions in dozens of countries. Maclaren also inspired other collapsible objects, such as the Strida bicycle.

At Microsoft, Bill Gates liked to transfer employees to completely different departments for a while, to see what new ideas might result. Sometimes it produced nothing, but occasionally it produced amazing results.

To Build a New Black Wall Street, we must realize the creative dynamic in putting disparate people and things together, and see what happens. We cannot continue being self-controlling in everything that we intend to develop and establish. Otherwise, the *Black Business Community is Limiting Our Commercial Potential.*

Chapter 5: Good Ideas vs. Bad Marketing

Something done badly always has opportunity. Such as being uncool or nerdy has hidden long-term value.

In the Black Community, we must develop tough skin, in order to show people that you don't care what anyone else thinks, be it friends or family.

The Black Community here in America, even African Communities in Africa, are full of people who dedicate their lives to seeking approval. They chase after vindication from White Society and White Institutions, and lose themselves in the process. Aiming for such critical credibility or commercial success can be vastly more limiting, than relying on your own passion and enthusiasm, which powers creativity.

Then there are those, with too much self-criticism, which can paralyze and stop you from moving forward. On the other hand, people with mediocre ideas and poor taste often achieve exceptional success because they don't know when to stop. Better the errors of enthusiasm than the slick competence of the cool.

With the foregoing in mind, let's consider AuctionWeb, which was a bad website. People posted badly about it, with unfocused photos of junk the site wanted to sell. It was a 24/7 worldwide garage sale, even with it's horrible, visually appalling photos. One of the first items sold was a broken laser pointer•for $14.83. Astonished, the founder of the site, Pierre Omidyar, emailed the winning bidder to ask if he understood that the laser pointer was broken. The buyer explained in his reply, "I'm a collector of broken laser pointers." That's when Omidyar realized he was on to something.

Pierre Omidyar founded AuctionWeb in California in 1995. It soon changed its name to eBay. eBay became one of the great new technology companies of the last twenty-five years.•Initially, it was bad and unashamedly uncool. Omidyar poured his enthusiasm into it and made it work well, but he didn't try to make it chic or sophisticated.

Experienced and newbie entrepreneurs alike are susceptible to the mentality that a great idea is the only thing they need to achieve guaranteed success.

But business is business. And in addition to that great idea, you need management experience, market luck and timing, sufficient capital, quick consumer adoption, press acceptance, and many other variables you may not even think about when you launch your idea.

Nevertheless, ideas, especially great ideas, are not easy to generate.

The idea is just the beginning of your entrepreneur journey. You will also go through the journey of assembling a management team and board of directors for your Black Owned Corporation. Your entire founding team must buy into the idea if they're going to take the risk of going down that entrepreneur highway.

You may have to modify your *Great Idea* in order to make it investor friendly.

You may need to build your idea into a product or service, market it, sell it and support it.

The potential is always just below the surface. But the choice is yours, in realizing that every new black owned business, automatically becomes part of a New Black Wall Street.

Working together, we can make every bad opportunity a great opportunity.

<u>NOTES</u>

<u>NOTES</u>

<u>Chapter 6: Challenge Your Competition</u>

"If ignorant both of your enemy and of yourself, you are certain in every battle to be in peril."

Sun Tzu, in•The Art of War•on Offensive Strategy.

It doesn't matter who you are, how successful you are, or how dominant you are, you have to watch what your competition is doing, even if you fully understand or think you understand your customer.

To Build a New Black Wall Street, we have to know our customers, and we also have to know the competition better than they understand themselves. Startup founders are lazier than people at Fortune 500 companies, when it comes to analyzing the competitive marketplace.

Entrepreneurs rely more on their intuition than on competitive analysis. I was guilty of this myself in my earlier entrepreneur days. To a certain extent, intuition
is extremely valuable, but you need to thoroughly understand the competitive landscape, whether you're burning your own money or getting investment dollars from elsewhere.

As an entrepreneur, you need to analyze the competitive space from standpoints of both direct competition and indirect competition. Develop your competitive overview by looking at the following key variables played out in the marketplace:

A) Competitive Rivalry

How many companies are competing in your sector at the local, regional, national and global levels?

Are Fortune 500 companies already fighting it out in the sector, or is it mainly startups or emerging companies? Do they know you're in the game? Are you even on their radar? The less they notice you in the beginning, the better.

B) Competitive Size

How big is the market sector in terms of current and potential users?

Is it a 100 million dollar market? If not, is it forecast to be a billion dollar market soon, and over how many years? How do you know the industry is growing fast? Are VC-funded companies already in the sector? Are any divisions of Fortune 500 companies in the sector? How big are the competitors? Does the market consist of mom and pop companies? Is there a clear leader or a few still fighting it out? Is there a clear follower? Is the market still young enough for new entrants? What is the largest company in the sector in terms of revenue? How much money has the sector received in investment dollars? Who has received the most funding?

C) Competitive Leverage

Are there companies in the sector that are leveraging their assets from different industries?

Are there line extension brands from other related or unrelated categories? Are there any companies, especially Fortune 500, using profits from other markets to build their brand in your market?

D) Competitive Substitution

What is the substitution offering for this sector or market?

For instance, in the entertainment film business, Hollywood competes against gaming video titles such as Counter Strike, NFL Madden Football, etc. Hollywood also competes indirectly with Facebook, Twitter, Instagram, SnapChat and other social sites; not for money but for the customer's attention.

You have to understand the customer's bandwidth. Teenagers can't watch TV, go to school, text 24/7, go to theaters, chat on the phone, sneak out of their room at three in the morning, listen to music, walk the malls; play video games on the computer, Wii, Nintendo, Xbox or on their cell phones, play sports, study, sleep, go out, have personal relationships, chew gum, bicker and fight with their parents; all in a 24-hour period.

That's what is meant by bandwidth. Something's got to give.

E) Competitive Differentiation

How are you different from your competitors?

Find out if the variables or differentiation vectors, actually make a difference to the consumer, not just your company.

Consider the automotive industry, where GM went sour due to lack of differentiation in some of their product lines. For instance, Pontiac, Chevrolet, Oldsmobile and Buick models looked somewhat the same. And with all things being equal, was one of the reasons why GM went bankrupt, and Uncle Sam had to bail them out.

Toyota has been much better at differentiation, until recently. They separated their luxury brand, Lexus, successfully, despite recent quality issues. One could forecast a branding and positioning problems if they continue to come out with lower-priced Lexus models. Because, at the lower end of the spectrum, do you buy the Toyota Camry or the Lexus series?

F) Competitive Goals

Have you figured out the competitive goals of your competition?
Are they trying to build the market, focus on growing the market, or suck out as
determine how their strategy might affect yours. Dumb competitors, especially
well-funded ones, can throw a monkey-wrench in a sector, because they confuse
the potential customer of a new market segment with various value propositions.
One example is when a company sells products below cost, thinking they can
make it up in sales volume.

As you can see from these competitive considerations, knowing your customer
is important, but it is not enough. You can't put on blinders and hope nobody will
notice you until you get big. You have to understand where you fit, in the
competitive landscape.

On the other hand, having competition doesn't mean you can't succeed. Look
at how many restaurants open every year. In any competitive marketplace, there
is always "churn and burn" between winners and losers. Today's leaders may
be tomorrow's goners.

G) Competitive Localization

How many ventures are in your space at the regional, national and global level?

Does geography matter or is some other competitive variable more important?
Localization works in retail and with the internet.

For instance, Costco Wholesale started on the West Coast while Sam's
Wholesale Club started in the Southeast. It took a decade for them to cross paths.
Zynga social gaming started in California and Wooga started in Germany. Today
they compete head-on.

H) Competitive Intensity

This is when a sector heats up in a hurry with new entrants, a proliferation of
new products launched into the marketplace, and an intense increase in venture
capital funding. When a specific sector becomes hot, VC-funded companies come
out of the woodwork.

Competitive intensity differs from competitive rivalry.

With competitive rivalry, there could be a bunch of competitors milling around
in a stagnant industry, boring the consumer to death. Then an eruption
occurs, usually caused by the release of a product innovation by a startup or
follower.

Customers are mesmerized and rapidly buy the new product or service. The
competition also experiences a ramp up in sales. When the entire category heats
up in a hurry, you have competitive intensity.

For instance, Coca-Cola or PepsiCo did not invent the energy drink sector. Red Bull, out of Europe, single-handedly created this monstrous category. Even though there was already competitive rivalry in the beverage sector, the competitive intensity was low or non-existent in a new category. This allowed Red Bull to take over a large market share before the rest of the industry woke up and smelled the coffee, in this case, the energy drink. You have to be in tune with the level of competitive intensity in your sector because you have to know how to ride the market. The time you choose to get on the train or get off, due to competitive intensity, could make a difference between being acquired, going IPO, going bust or not even getting into the game.

Psychology tells us that rivalry has the potential to both help and hinder creative success; it all depends on how we handle the competition. Whatever your field, embrace competition: it can make you strive to be better, to go that extra mile.

Chances are, you too have at least one close rival. Monitor that rival's achievements with admiration, and a touch of envy. Then get back to work.

<u>NOTES</u>

NOTES

Chapter 7: Failure is Success

To Build a New Black Wall Street, we must overcome the blame game, as well as, not justifying everything based on learned behavior influenced by the Black Church. Praying will not resolve bad business practices or decisions.

Nevertheless, realize this, If you fail in your venture, people will look at you differently.

No matter what they say or don't say, some of your friends and business associates will think you're a loser; at least until you get another venture going and become successful. You can try, try again; but it's not as easy as it sounds.

What can you do when you fail?

First, re-frame your mind. How you treat your current failure affects your future success.

Failing is not the end of the world, but it is harder to pick yourself up if you're not psychologically ready. Don't beat yourself over your head, because plenty of other people will do it for you. Don't let your subconscious call you a loser or sucker. You must protect your mind from negativity, words have power.

In one of the Batman movies, the Riddler kept telling himself, "I am a winner. I am a winner." Be like the Riddler. Repeat this morning and night, I am a winner!

Second and the most important, is to review the reasons for the failure. There are always reasons, but you must be honest and admit to yourself, the actual and factual reasons.

Finally, surround yourself with people who support you, such as your friends or family. Don't listen to psychological mumbo jumbo. But when you fail, talk to someone who understands and loves you. That flow of human interaction and energy will recharge you like a battery.

Failure is the beginning of something else that could be big, as long as you learn from your mistakes and never repeat them. Stay committed to trade and commerce, and you'll find the one idea that you can turn into a successful reality. It's simply a matter of when. Never forget that.

Another view is productive failure, strive for imperfection.

Miss deadlines, get lost on the way to the airport, forget to reply to emails and show up at parties a day early. It's more interesting. If it's broke, don't fix it; if it ain't broke, break it.

The coffee chain Starbucks embraced imperfection. They introduced new concepts quickly. Whether an iced caramel macchiato or a new store design, these concepts were launched before they had been perfected and then improved as they went along.

Sometimes, it's simply a matter of a procedural failure that led to loss of opportunity.

Consider that an innovation process that is trying to achieve something faultless, is too slow and restricted. Innovation requires errors and failures because they lead to new ideas. The conundrum for organizations is how to foster an innovative culture, with all the messiness and faults that come with it, while the perfectionists in an organization work to reject imperfection.

Perfectionism can be a roadblock to new ideas; it can bring you to a full stop, whereas imperfection can lead somewhere unexpected.

High standards are worthwhile, but perfectionism is another story.

Chapter 8: Create Positives From Negatives

A Black Owned Startup has great potential, and if others respond strongly to something you've done, that's a positive, even if the reaction is negative.

What should really concern you, is not having any reaction at all.

In every culture, there's a history of negativity towards new new ideas, and therefore, to be a successful person you often have to build a strong foundation with the bricks others throw at you.

Another thing, business is not a personal endeavor, and the Black Entrepreneur must understand this fact. And you cannot rely on your friends or family to validate your business ideas. It just doesn't work. So stop getting upset with friends and family for not purchasing your products or services. Friends and family are Not your customers, the public is your customer base. Of course, your supporting mother will always say your idea is great. On the other hand, your father, may think you should stop fooling around with being an entrepreneur and it's a horrible idea; that you should come back to the real world and get a real job. Your spouse or significant other, depending on your relationship, might be supportive, depending on their risk appetite.

But at the end of the day, it shouldn't matter what anybody thinks about your business venture, because it's your dream and it's up to you to make it happen. You are the one that'll be running your business and you cannot allow anyone to get in the way of your success.

However, as an entrepreneur, you must realize the actual value of your spouse. Be sure your spouse supports your venture when you're out for dinner with a potential investor or business partner, otherwise, your spouse may inadvertently share negative or potentially harmful information. Always consider that there's a due diligence reason behind a dinner invitation for you and your spouse.

When starting a new business, you'll find out who your true friend are. Get rid of any friends that do not support you emotionally while starting your venture. You don't need anyone telling you you're not going to make it, especially anyone who
doesn't have the guts to try being an entrepreneur themselves.

Consider that it really doesn't matter what your friends, family, spouse or significant other thinks about your idea. First, what matters is what you think. Second, what matters is what the market (aka customer) thinks about your product or service. The third thing that matters is what a potential investor thinks.

If you're reading this book, you've heard it before. Friends will give you a million reasons why it won't work. And if you're successful, those same friends won't have anything to say for your benefit, but you'll hear and see the disbelief in their words and actions. Nevertheless, don't be arrogant about your success, because it's a waste of the energy that should be directed at growing your business.

Girlfriends or boyfriends can have a positive or negative effect on the ventures as well. Be careful that when you start a venture your relationship is on solid ground. Entrepreneurs work hard every day, and some relationship cannot withstand that loss of personal attention. They might not tell you the truth about your venture either. Not that it matters but it's always nice to have some mental support. You have to be cognizant that you're around positive people when you launch your company. You don't need your significant other telling you how your idea sucks, or how it's not going to make it or how you're going to go broke.

Startups are hard enough. If the person is negative, then either get rid of the venture or get rid of your significant other. It's that simple.

<u>NOTES</u>

29

Chapter 9: Weapons of Mass Creation

The key to Building a New Black Wall Street, is taking action, and taking action that will have mass effect within and across the black community nationwide. This is an Industrial Endeavor, that must be addressed with creative but practical ideas that disrupt the current status quo.

All around us is opportunity that can become large scale enterprises based on a simple principle: teamwork. The black community is always stating that it takes a village to raise a child. Well, now is the time for the actual application of that principle. But that ideal can only be accomplished by using a legal entity for commercial for-profit purposes. The entity to be used is that of the corporation. A corporation can be as small as a single person owner, but can grow to become massive with hundreds of thousands of owner stockholders.

Mass creation is the abandonment of selfishness; the abandonment of the ego; the abandonment of pride of ownership, to the reality of having pride in accomplishment. There is nothing greater than having pride in a successful black community that has created job opportunity for our youth on a massive scale.

Our reality is not fiction. Therefore, realize the potential of your circle of influence by networking at a commercial level with other outside circles of influence. Again, the structure of the corporation entity allows these networks to have commercial relationships as stockholders in each other, as newly created corporations. With the structure of a corporate entity, your opportunities are limitless.

No matter the size of your idea, big or small, it can become massive by extending opportunity to potential partners, investors and business owners as stockholders in a new corporate entity. The potential of any business idea, can easily be realized with value added relationships by use of the corporation structure. Stock ownership in a corporation is tangible, compared to an agreement by handshake.

Consider individual fashion designers coming together to open a retail store, as well as manufacturing their designs. The idea may sound great, but who will be the owners of the designs, who will sign the lease and any other contract agreements. The corporation is now the owner and the corporation signs all contracts and agreements. If the business grows or closes, each designer as a shareholder, is compensated based on stock ownership. The same can apply to barbershops,beauty salons, natural care products.and any other business idea you have in your mind.

Industrialized countries have averted disaster by following the counterintuitive advice of economist Paul Samuelson, by raising spending on infrastructure projects, cutting taxes, allowing imports to flow in and driving interest rates down to near zero.

Samuelson's economic theories were inspired by concepts from medicine and physics. For decades he read medical journals in search of ideas that could be transferred to economics, such as Mendelian dynamics. He also applied the equilibrium principles of•thermodynamics to economics. He had such a huge impact because he applied creative thinking to economics when everyone else was applying logic.

Applying creative thinking in an "uncreative" field gives you an advantage.

Like the one-eyed man in the kingdom of the blind, if you think creatively where no one else is, it gives you the edge.

With all of this in mind, we cannot do it alone in Building a New Black Wall Street, and that lone wolf mentality will only get you but so far. Recognize your own limitations and admit it... you'll be a more successful factor in Building a New Black Wall Street.

<u>NOTES</u>

__Part II: Pride of Ownership__

Bill Gates doesn't own controlling shares of Microsoft, however he's the second richest person in the world (Carlos Slim of Mexico is first). Steve Jobs
doesn't own the controlling interest in Apple either. These are public companies. When you go public, you lose control but gain wealth and influence.

Look at Groupon during its IPO filing. The largest equity shareholders are investors and founders. Eric Lefkovsky cofounded and funded ThePoint, which later become Groupon. Lefkovsky owned 21.6% of the company. NEA (New Enterprise Associates), a prominent Venture Capital firm, owned 14.7% for investing into ThePoint and following up with an investment into Groupon.

CityDeal Management owned 10.3% after Groupon acquired them in May 2010. Bradley Keywell owned 6.9%. The other cofounder and CEO, Andrew Mason, owned only 7.7% of the company.

Tally them all up, and the above members owned a total of 61.2% of the company. It doesn't stop there. Groupon had Class A and Class B common stock. Class B shares, while making up a small percentage of the overall shares, received higher voting rights to continue the management, control and influence. The founders were smart. Both Lefkofsky and Mason had 41.7% of Class B shares. Bradley Keywell had 16.7% of the Class B Shares.

Therefore, to Build a New Black Wall Street... Pride of Ownership is Not a Priority. Job creation and developing an influential tax base is Our Priority.

Chapter 10: Black Corporation Stockholders

A corporation is given authority to operate as a legal entity by a charter issued by the state. As such, a corporation exists independently of the people who invest in it, manage it, and share in its profits. The corporation, owned by its shareholders, can raise funds through the sale of additional stock; depending on the type of stock sold, shareholders may receive partial, majority, or total control over operations.

Although it is possible to set up a corporation without the involvement of an attorney using do-it-yourself kits and Internet sites, you may benefit from the advice of an attorney, and you'll want to coordinate such efforts with an accountant.

The principal advantage of a corporation is that its owners (the shareholders / stockholders) are personally liable only up to the amount they have invested in the corporation.

However, a board of directors with just a single seat held by a licensed professional, allows that corporation to operate in otherwise restricted areas.

Consider nationwide pharmacy companies, which are required by state laws to be a licensed pharmacist.

When it comes to taxes, the corporation reports its own income, expenses, and profits to state and federal authorities and pays its own taxes and fees.

NOTES

Chapter 11: Black Franchise Dealmakers

Over the last two decades, franchising has emerged as a popular expansion strategy for a variety of product and service companies, especially for those smaller businesses that cannot afford to finance

internal growth. Recent International Franchise Association (IFA) statistics demonstrate that retail sales from franchised outlets make up nearly 60 percent of all retail sales in the United States, estimated at over $1.5 trillion, and the outlets employed more than 17 million people in 2009.

There is a wide variety of reasons cited by successful growing companies as to why they have selected franchising as a method of growth and distribution. These reasons include:

1) Obtain operating efficiencies and economies of scale.

2) Achieve more rapid market penetration at a lower capital cost.

3) Reach the targeted consumer more effectively through cooperative advertising and promotion.

4) Sell products and services to a dedicated distributor network.

5) Replace the need for internal personnel with motivated owner/operators.

6) Shift the primary responsibility for site selection, employee training and personnel management, local advertising, and other administrative concerns to the franchisee, licensee, or joint venture partner with the guidance or assistance of the growing company.

In the typical franchising relationship, the franchisee shares the risk of expanding the market share of the growing company by committing its capital and resources to the development of satellite locations modeled after the proprietary business format of the growing company. The growing company' risk of business failure is further reduced by the improvement in competitive position, reduced vulnerability to cyclical fluctuations, the existence of a captive market for the growing company' proprietary products and services (because of the network of franchisees), and reduced administrative and overhead costs.

Regulatory Issues

The offer and sale of a franchise is regulated at both the federal and the state level. At the federal level, the Federal Trade Commission (FTC) in 1979
adopted
its trade regulation rule 436 (the FTC Rule), which specifies the minimum amount of disclosure that must be made to a prospective franchisee in any of the 50 states. In addition to the FTC rule, more than a dozen states have adopted their own rules and regulations for the offer and sale of franchises within their borders. Known as the registration states, these states generally follow a more detailed disclosure format known as the Franchise Disclosure Document (FDD).

Each of the registration states has slightly different procedures and requirements for the approval of a growing company before offers and sales are authorized.
In all cases, however, the package of disclosure documents is assembled, consisting of an FDD, a franchise agreement, supplemental agreements, financial statements, a franchise roster, an acknowledgment of receipt form, and the special disclosures that are required by each state, such as corporation verification statements, salesperson disclosure forms, and consent to service of process documents.

The specific requirements of each state should be checked carefully.

<u>NOTES</u>

NOTES

Chapter 12: The Existing Business Option

If you're interested in entrepreneurship, but lack ideas or time to create a new business, buying an established company may be a wise alternative. You'll inherit a working infrastructure complete with resources you'd otherwise have to secure on your own, such as equipment and employees. You'll also ideally be taking over a known brand built on a positive reputation over many years' time.

Buying a business typically does require more capital upfront than if you were to build one anew. But asking prices have been on the decline in recent years due to the weak economy. And sellers are increasingly offering to finance a portion of the price for buyers who are unable to obtain bank loans.

The median asking price for a small business was $239,000 in the second quarter, down from $249,000 a year earlier, according to BizBuySell.com, a global online marketplace for small business acquisitions based in San Francisco.

For businesses sold in the quarter, the median selling price was $150,000, down from $155,000.

If you are considering working with a business broker, here are some things to consider:

What's the cost? Business brokers are typically hired by the seller so there is normally no cost to the buyer.

Do your homework. Before contacting brokers, determine the kind of business you'd like to buy. Research different industries and business types.

Where to look. The website of the International Business Brokers Association, ibba.org, has a free broker directory. You also can look for brokers' contact information in listings at business-for-sale websites such as BizBuySell.com and BusinessBroker.net.

Be honest. Let brokers know what you realistically can afford. "If you dance around finances, it's a waste of everybody's time," says Scott Evert, president of Sunbelt Midwest, a business brokerage. Besides, brokers and sellers "are going to do due diligence on you anyway."

Joint Venture or Strategic Alliance

Another strategic alternative to an acquisition that is available to today' small and growing companies is a legal structure known as a joint venture. A joint venture is typically structured as a partnership or as
a newly formed co-owned corporation where two or more parties are brought

together to achieve a series of strategic and financial objectives on a short-term or a long-term basis. Emerging growth and middle-market companies that want to explore this strategy should give careful thought to the type of partner they are looking for and what resources they will be contributing to the newly formed Entity. As in the raising of a child, each parent will be making its Respective contribution of skills, abilities, and resources.

Joint ventures, strategic partnering, cross-licensing, and technology transfer agreements are all strategies designed to obtain one or more of the following: (1) a direct capital infusion in exchange for equity and/or intellectual property or distribution rights, (2) a "capital substitute" where the resources that Would otherwise be obtained with the capital are obtained through joint venturing, or (3) a shift of the burden and cost of development (through licensing) in exchange for a potentially more limited upside.

Embarking on a search for a joint venture partner is a bit like searching for a spouse. Care should be taken to truly conduct a thorough review of prospective candidates, and extensive due diligence should be done on the final few that are being considered.

Develop a list of key objectives and goals to be achieved by the joint venture or licensing relationship, and compare this list with the objectives and goals of your final candidates. Take the time to understand the corporate culture and decision-making process within each company. Consider some of the following issues: (1) How does this fit with your own processes? (2) What about each prospective partner' previous experiences and track record with other joint venture relationships? (3) Why did these previous relationships succeed or fail?

Why Consider a Joint Venture or Strategic Alliance?

1) Develop a new market (domestic or international).

2) Develop a new product.

3) Develop or share technology.

4) Combine complementary technology.

5) Pool resources to develop a production or distribution facility.

6) Acquire capital.

7) Execute a government contract.

8) Access a distribution network or sales or marketing capability.

NOTES

<u>NOTES</u>

<u>Part III: Don't Worry About Taxes</u>

Black entrepreneurs suffer from a fear the paying taxes syndrome, and believe that the non-profit business model is the answer to tax free wealth.

Open your eyes, people. Looking around any black community, we see 501(c)(3) Mega-Churches that have yet to create wealth or jobs for the communities that these churchs serve, using that tax free business model.

There are no secrets to making money, but paying taxes is a reality that cannot be avoided. Therefore, the more black business owners focus on making money versus avoiding paying taxes, the easier it is for a business to be profitable and taxes then become a non-issue.

To build a New Black Wall Street, we must stop making the mistake of getting trapped in the details, spending hours, days, weeks or longer perfecting the percentages before we do anything.

Worse, some entrepreneurs who get stuck in minute detail never get around to doing anything. It's our old nemesis: analysis paralysis. So, if at any time you think you are lost in a research rabbit hole, stop and move on, perfectionism kills every dream and it's better to just start your business and tweak it along the way.

Chapter 13: Cash Flow Techniques

To ensure success with your business, setup multiple checking accounts for maintaining expenses. At a minimum you'll have separate accounts for the following: Sales, Operating Expense, Payroll and Taxes.

Identify Profit Target Allocation Percentages

Target Allocation Percentages (TAPs) are goals we have to set for distribution of a businesses revenue (sales) based on percentages. We want to ultimately be banking a minimum of 20% of accumulated deposits for Profit. We won't necessarily start there, but we will build to it.

Now you need to do a little bit of research to set specific target numbers. There are a few ways to approach this:

1.   Research public companies: Look at the financial reports public companies are required to make available. Do a quick Internet search using the term "financial market overview" and you will find dozens of websites that report the financials for public companies. Look up at least five companies in your industry, or a similar industry. If you don't find your niche, try expanding. For instance, if you find no public DJ companies, expand to entertainment companies and select five that come close. (Tip: Marketwatch is easy to navigate for these reports. You might also try Yahoo! Finance and Google Finance.)

For our purposes, look up the income statements for the last three to five years. If you really want to dig in, check out the balance sheets and cash flow statements for these companies, too.

For each year, divide the net income (profit) number by the total sales/revenue number. Do this for each year and then come up with the average. This is how you find the profit percentage for any public company. Do this for each of the five public companies you look at, and you will find the overall industry profit average.

Use that overall industry profit average as your Profit TAP as mentioned above.

2.   Review your tax returns for the last three to five years and determine your most profitable year (based on percentages, not on dollar amounts). Why do we want the percentage? Because a billion-dollar company that only reports a million dollars in profit is in big trouble. Even if they only had one bad day, a million bucks wouldn't be enough to bail them out. But a five million-dollar company that reports a million in profits is kicking butt and taking names. That company spits at bad days.

3. Or, the easiest way, just pick your profit percentage number based on your projected revenue for this year, using revenue for the last twelve months.

If more than half the stuff your company sells comes from materials rather than labor or software, as happens with manufacturers, restaurants and retailers, use the gross profit (sometime called gross income) as the Real Revenue number, and you need to evaluate your business based on that. Whenever you run the numbers for your business, or evaluate others, you will always base it on Real Revenue (gross profit).

Consider this, if your sales were to stop completely, with not a single deposit coming in, here's a good longevity rule of thumb:

1. •5% profit allocation = 3 weeks of operating cash

2. 12% profit allocation= 2 months of operating cash

3. 24% profit allocation = 5 months of operating cash.

Why is it that, as the percentages basically double, longevity almost triples? The math doesn't seem to make sense at first glance. But it does make sense. The bigger your percentage, the more efficiently you are running your business, which means less in operating expenses. So not only do you have more saved up with a higher percentage, you spend less, which affords you even more time.

The goal is to make your profits as high as possible. However, super-high profit percentages are not sustainable. At least not for long, and definitely not if your revenue stays stagnant. The reason for this is, if you can pull off consistently fat profits, say 50% and your Operating Expenses for only 10% of revenue, your competitors will figure out what you're doing. Then, to get more business, they will drop prices (they likely have the profit margins to afford it). When that happens, you will have to drop prices too in order to stay in business. For competitive sharks, fat margins can be like blood in the water. The only way to keep big margins is to milk them for all they're worth when you have them and keep innovating to find new ways to bump up profitability.

Business Owners Pay:

Gone are the days when you paid everyone but yourself and had to support your life with credit cards and loans from the in-laws. Remember, your business is supposed to serve you; you are not in service to your business! No more leftovers for you!

Owner's Pay is the amount you and the other equity owners take in pay for the work you do. (Equity members of your company who do not work in the business just get a profit distribution.) Your salary should be on par with the going rate for the work you do, in other words—the salary you would have to pay your replacement.

There are two options to consider when choosing your Owner's Pay number. *Either:*

1. Take a realistic look at the work you do. If you have a small•company with, say, five employees, you may call yourself the CEO, but that's just the title on your card. Likely, you are doing a lot of other work. You probably spend a lot of time selling, completing projects, handling customers and dealing with HR concerns. In reality, around two percent of your time is spent actually doing

job of CEO, but that's just the title on your card. Likely, you are doing a lot of other work. You probably spend a lot of time selling, completing projects, handling customers and dealing with HR concerns. In reality, around two percent of your time is spent actually doing the; vision planning, strategic negotiations, acquisitions, reporting to investors, addressing the media, etc. Determine your salary based on what you are doing 80% of the time, and what you would reasonably pay employees to do those jobs.

2. Evaluate pay for all equity owners who work in the business. Add up the salaries that represent your Owner's Pay draw. The percentage of revenue must, at minimum, cover Owner's Pay draw. Remember, you will likely get raises, maybe even a bonus for a job well done. So make the percentage one-and-a-quarter times the amount you determine for your salaries, so you can adjust for revenue fluctuations.

Or, pick the percentage based on your revenue range. This money is divided among all equity employees. It does not have to be split up equally, nor does it have to be split up based on your equity percentages.

This is why you should have a separate account even if you and the other equity owners working in the business are just employees, but you are the most important employee. If you had to fire people, I suspect you would fire everyone else before you fired yourself. Think about your very best employee. I'll bet you take extra steps to ensure that you are taking care of your best employee. I'll bet you would do everything in your power to keep your best employees happy, including paying them what they're worth, right? Well, there you have it, you are your best, most important employee. We must take care of you.

When it comes to pay, different business formations require you to take Owner's Pay in different ways. An S -Corp is treated differently than an LLC or a sole proprietorship, which are both treated way differently than a C-Corp. The Owner's Pay allocation still works the same way; you just need to work with your accountant to make sure the money flows out properly and legally. (I strongly recommend an accountant who knows exactly how to support your business.)

Tax Allocation Percentages:

The first step is to determine your income tax rate. Taxes range all over the place, depending on your amount of personal income and corporate profit and the area you live in. As of this writing, many entrepreneurs have an average income tax rate of 35% or so; for others it will be less, and in some countries is can be more.

Taxes vary from country to country, income bracket to income bracket, and surely change everywhere every year. But regardless of what the numbers are, you need to prepare for them.

One goal in building a New Black Wall Street is that the company takes care of all forms of tax responsibility. It's mandatory that you research your tax laws and talk with your accountant so you can understand and be advised on all the

Here are four different approaches for determining your Tax:

1. Look at your personal and business tax returns. Add up your taxes and then determine the percentage of taxes you paid compared to your real revenue. Do this again for the prior two years. Looking at your taxes as a percentage of real revenue for the last three years will give you a good sense of your ongoing tax responsibility.

2. From your accountant get your estimated tax responsibility for your business, year-to-date (YTD), and then determine your tax percentage of your YTD real revenue.

3. Do a search for "tax rates" + "your country" + "tax year."

For example, "tax rates United States 2013" returned the following results on Google:

Tax Rate Schedule Y-1, Internal Revenue Code section 1(a)

10%•on taxable income from $0 to $17,850, plus

15%•on taxable income over $17,850 to $72,500, plus

25%•on taxable income over $72,500 to $146,400, plus

28%•on taxable income over $146,400 to $223,050, plus

33%•on taxable income over $223,050 to $398,350, plus

35%•on taxable income over $398,350 to $450,000, plus

39.6%•on taxable income over $450,000.

Then, pick your likely income range, which depends on the type of company formation you may have and the combination of your Owner's Pay and Profit contributions and you have your federal tax rate. Now do the same thing for state taxes and add the two.

4. Or simply use 35% as your tax number. It may not be perfect, but it's usually pretty effective. And while the optimal number will have you neither paying additional taxes at the end of the year nor receiving a refund, it is better to guess a little too high, get a refund and consider what to do with the extra cash than to get a call from your accountant, because you don't have enough money, and have to ask your son or daughter for a loan.

Therefore, reserve not less than 15% for taxes. Let's do a little simple math.

Determine the percentage that stays in your Operating Expenses Account, after you move money to your Sales Account, your Owner's Pay Account and your Tax Account. The amount left over for expenses is likely going to be somewhere between 40% and 60%. This is the money you have available to pay all your expenses.

Next, subtract that percentage from 100%. So, if your total Operating Expenses

Next, subtract that percentage from 100%. So, if your total Operating Expenses

Account is at 55%, you're left with 45%. That 45% is the amount you will be taxed on. (More often than not, expenses are not taxed. This is why some accountants encourage you to buy equipment or make other large purchases toward the end of the year.) Now, multiply your non-operating percentage (in this case, 45%) with your taxable income percentage (in this case, 35%). You end up with a percentage of approximately 16%, which is your Tax percentage.

Now that you have a more accurate picture of your actual percentages, let's focus on profits and build a New Black Wall Street.

But first, open a separate business account for depositing your profit percentages before all other expenses.

And remember to always·move money to your *Profit Account* first, then to your *Owner Pay Account* and then to your *Tax Account*, with what remains to expenses.

Always in that order. No exceptions. Move it, stash it and let it accumulate. And if there isn't enough money left for expenses? This means you can't afford those expenses and need to get rid of them. This will force you into running a leaner business without unnecessary expenses.

<u>NOTES</u>

<u>NOTES</u>

Chapter 14: Cash Flow Revenue

Focusing solely on top line thinking (sales, sales, sales!) does not lead to profitability and will not contribute to Building a New Black Wall Street. In fact more sales, without efficiency, can lead to further inefficiency. In other words, more sales make you less profitable. It's a vicious cycle. So before you can focus on sales, you must first nail Efficiency 10.

Efficiency increases your profit margins, or, the amount of money you earn as profit on each product or service you offer. It's basic logic, increased profit margins will boost your company's profits without the need for increased sales. So the method is simple, achieve greater efficiency first, then sell more, then improve efficiencies even more and then sell even more. Over time, speed up the back and forth between efficiency and selling until the two happen simultaneously.

Making your company more efficient is more than just eliminating extra coffee breaks and redlining your expenses. To tap into that potential stream of profits flowing under the surface of your company, you need to look at efficiency in every aspect of your business.

Serving the same types of clients with the same or very similar problems, using one consistent solution to fix the problems, is the path to efficiency. You want to duplicate your best clients, because that means they have a consistent need; and in turn, you want to reduce the variety of things you do to the fewest that will best serve your best clients' needs. Think McDonald's. That company is a moneymaking machine because they feed hungry people who don't care about their health as much as their hunger, with a few products: fries, hamburgers and breaded chicken. The fewest things you can do repetitively to serve a consistent core customer need spells efficiency.

If you want to actually Build a New Black Wall Street, take a look at every aspect of your business and determine how to get two times the results with half the effort.

How do you get two times the results with half the effort?

Effort is financial cost and time cost (your time, your people's time, your software's time, your machine's time). For example, if you own a Snowplowing company and currently plow one parking lot per hour, ask yourself to figure out how to plow two parking lots (two times the results) in thirty minutes (half the time). Huge profits can be had if you can pull this off.

Your first thought might be, "That's impossible!" If you believe that it's impossible to increase efficiency in this way, you are trapped in "let the other guy figure it out" mode. If instead you say, "Hmm. . . let me think about that. Let me find a way," you will fast forward to profitability. Why? Because innovation occurs in small steps, big leaps and everywhere in between. To double the results with half the effort is an initiative that forces big thinking, and it brings about small and big changes which can effect the bottom line.

The biggest innovators ask big questions. Do you think Elon Musk asked, "How do I get a few extra miles per gallon?" when he thought up Tesla? Or, "How can people transfer money a little bit faster than a bank wire?" when he started PayPal? As he worked on his Hyperloop supersonic speed-train concept, the one that travels through a complete vacuum system running from LA to San Francisco, do you think he was considering how to be a little bit faster than the Greyhound bus? Hell, no!

Innovation in business and innovation in efficiencies comes from big, bold questions, which we need to Build a New Black Wall Street.

Most entrepreneurs focus only on tiny improvements, "How do I do this a couple of minutes faster?" Small questions yield small answers. Plowing a parking lot five minutes faster is not going to make much of an impact on your bottom line. Just skip the coffee break, or just "hold it" when you need to go to the bathroom.

But the more you focus on substantially improving efficiency (like with a design for a plow that can move snow twice as fast), the closer you'll get to achieving double the results with half the effort. This gain in efficiency is amplified the more you sell. That is the power of percentages. Since you now plow every parking lot more efficiently, every new account is an opportunity for increased profit.

Did you know that United Parcel Service (UPS) trucks almost always take right turns? In 2006, UPS dared to ask the efficiency question about fuel costs. They discovered that the less time UPS drivers spent in left turn lanes, the less fuel they burned waiting at lights and to cross traffic, and the less idle time there was for each driver. UPS is now experiencing a savings of $6,000,000 a year from the change.

The "brown truck" company didn't stop with their first efficiency discovery. Next time you see a driver delivering a package, look at him and try to spot his keys. Let me give you a hint: They are not in his pocket (that's a banana).

UPS drivers found that fumbling for their keys in their pockets when they got back into the truck cost them five to ten seconds (or more) every time. UPS figured out that it is more efficient to keep their keys hanging from their pinky fingers. Now, a UPS driver makes a quick flip of his wrist and the keys are in his hand. Multiply that saved five to ten seconds by fifty stops a day and five gazillion drivers and you have a very huge savings indeed.

UPS also found that they could save millions by washing their trucks once every two days rather than every day. Over time, this gave them huge savings in time, energy and water, and the trucks looked just as shiny.

Look, if you've never asked yourself, "How can I get two times the results with half the effort?" how will you know if you can? You might be missing your own efficiency miracle and not even realize it.

Fire Your Bad Clients:

Letting go of clients who suck your business dry and eat up profit margin, is a way of making space for clients an enterprise can serve exceptionally well, by doing what the business does best with fewer resources. It is all about improving both, the top and bottom line.

A study by Chicago-based growth-consulting firm Strategex, analyzed the revenue, cost and profit breakdown for a thousand companies. What they found was nothing short of a "duh" moment, as in, I already knew this but I still haven't done anything about it in my own business.

Strategex sorted the clients for each company into four sections, in descending order based on revenue. For example, if a company had a hundred clients, the twenty-five clients that generated the most revenue were put in the top quarter, the next twenty-five highest revenue-generating clients in the second quarter, and so on. Strategex found that the top quarter generated 89% of the total revenue, while the lowest quarter only accounted for a meager 1% of total revenue.

The study also found that each group of clients required pretty much the same amount of effort (cost and time). This meant that it took the same amount of effort to serve a big-revenue client as it did a client who barely affected revenue at all.

Then came that awkward moment. Strategex's profit analysis showed that the top quarter generated 150% of a company's profit. The two middle quarters were effectively break-even, and the bottom quarter, the one that generated 1% of the total revenue, resulted in a profit·loss·of 50%! In the end, the profits generated from the top clients are used, in part, to pay for the losses accrued in serving the bottom clients.

I'm sure you know this scenario all too well. Those clients who barely pay you peanuts, yet constantly complain about how much you charge and how you do nothing right; the clients who demand you rework everything you've done for the third time and then never pay you for your work, or never pay you on time, are the clients costing you money. Get rid of them. Fast!

Dumping your worst clients may seem counterintuitive at first. But, if you remove your worst, unprofitable clients and the now unnecessary costs associated with them, you will see a jump in profits and a reduction in stress, often within a few weeks. Equally important, you will have more time to pursue and duplicate your best clients.

I know how scary it feels to dump any client when you are scrambling to cover this week's payroll, especially if you fought hard to get that client in the first place. But remember, profit is about the percentages, not a single number. So take it easy on yourself. Start by dumping one rotten little apple at a time. The emotional distraction that client caused you and your staff will disappear immediately. The profits you earned from other clients and were spending to keep this bad client on board will now stay in your pocket. And since those special requirements are no longer need to be serviced, you now have time and headspace to find another, better client, an ideal client, a clone of your very best clients.

Duplicate Your Best Clients:

Just for a moment, I want you to think of your favorite client: the call you will always take, the person or company you say yes to without hesitation. This is the client who pays you what you're worth, on time, without question. This is the client who trusts you, respects you, and follows instructions. This is the client You love, and they love you. Now imagine if this client had five identical twin companies that all wanted to work with you. Wouldn't that boost your business? Wouldn't it be easy to serve those clients? Wouldn't it help you keep your bottom line healthy? Now imagine ten clones, or a hundred clones.

For almost any B2B business in the world, landing a hundred clones of their best client would put them at the front of the pack. They would dominate. The same is true for B2C businesses. If just a mere 10% of their clients behaved like their number one client, those businesses would rule, too.

Having clients with similar needs and very similar behaviors offers a few magical profit-making benefits:

1.•You will become super-efficient, because you now serve very•few
but consistent needs, rather than an excessive array of varying needs.

2. You will love working with your clones, which means you will naturally and automatically provide better service. We cater to the people we care about.

3. Marketing will become automatic. Birds of a feather flock together (for real) and that means your best clients hang out with other business leaders who have the "best client" qualities you're looking for. Your best clients are awesome,
remember? You love them and they love you, and that means they will talk you up every chance they get.

Clones of your best clients are the very definition of efficiency, which is why they are like gold. Find them. Nurture them. And then find out where even more best-client clones hang out and cultivate them, too.

Consider this story, it speaks to how fast things can go down the "upselling" rabbit hole. In the fall, I pay a lawn service (XYZ Landscaping) to clean up all of the leaves in the yard. This past year, the owner of the business, knocked on the door after finishing the leaf clean-up and said, "I noticed that there are leaves in the gutters." He offered to remove them, for a fee.

XYZ Landscaping had just expanded his service offering. Easy money, right? To complete the job, the owner had to run out and buy some ladders to do the job. He came back thirty minutes later and got right to work. Because he pulled out the leaves by hand, he wasn't super efficient, but he got it done fast enough. However, he didn't have the tool to snake out the downspouts, so he made a note to buy it and come back at a later date to finish the job.

While the owner was up on the roof, he spotted another opportunity, fixing

damaged shingles. More easy money! More revenue! Again he asked and I agreed, and again he ran out and picked up some roofing tools. He came back an hour later, replaced the shingles, cleaned the downspouts, and, while doing that work, noticed a crack in the chimney and a soft spot on the roof, a sign of rotting wood. When the owner approached me about it, I asked him to fix those things, too. This time he went out to get more tools, band saws, cement, brick supplies and temporary labor. XYZ Landscaping came back near the end of day and pushed through to get it finished. He even bought floodlights to keep the work area lit as dusk approached.

At the end of the day, I paid $1500 for all the work. Not a bad deal, considering XYZ Landscaping "only" gets paid $200 to clean the lawn. But, the $1500 he earned cost the owner an investment of about $2000 for tools and supplies that day, plus a lot of driving back and forth and the cost of hiring a laborer.

XYZ Landscaping lost money on me, but grew his sales by a lot. Tomorrow he intends to use his new equipment and tools to take care of other clients and in theory, will earn his money back and then some. The problem is, that rarely happens. As the bills mount, the pressure grows to sell more and more; and you end up working on projects in which you have limited experience and sometimes little interest.

As the variety of things you do increases, you need to buy more tools and equipment and hire more specialized labor. And none of this gets used to its maximum potential, because you do many different things, not one thing. Your stuff sits there unused. While you rake lawns, your ladders just lie there. As you fix roofs, the leaf blowers just sit in your truck.

You get stuck in the Survival Trap and end up not doing a very good job at any one thing. For example, when the owner wrapped up for the day he said, "I'll be back early tomorrow to clean the lawn again." Why? Because he threw the leaves from the gutters onto the lawn he had just cleaned, as well as shingles and other things. His additional work required that he actually•redo•his original work, while all that new gear he bought just sat on his truck, not being used. What's efficient about that?

Across the street, my neighbors hire a different guy (ABC Landscaping) to clean up their leaves in the fall. He also charges $200. On the same day XYZ Landscaping worked on my house and earned $1500, my neighbors guy serviced four more properties and also knocked on the doors at two other properties that, needed his help.

I suspect that if the two business owners had had a beer together that night, XYZ Landscaping would have boasted about doing one-and-a-half times the sales the other one pulled, but the ABC Landscaping would have ended up paying for the drinks. ABC Landscaping achieved efficiency, and recognized the profitability of efficiency, in getting more of the same things done with better and better results, using fewer and fewer resources.

Selling more is the most difficult way to increase profits, because in the best-case scenarios, the percentages stay the same; and in the worst-case, the more common scenarios, expenses generated to support sales increase•faster,•resulting in smaller percentages and a smaller profit margin.

NOTES

<u>NOTES</u>

Chapter 15: Cash Flow Management

The Best Way to Manage Your Cash Flow is with a spreadsheet software, such as Microsoft Excel.

Whatever your business, you'll need to establish multiple accounts and keep track of when, where and why money will flow between certain accounts.

Create a single-page document that defines the function of each account. Explain what purpose each account serves, and the process you will follow. For example, document that, on the 10th and 25th of the month, all the money in your Income Account is distributed to the Profit, Owner's Pay, Tax, and Operating Expenses Accounts based on the respective percentages. Then, the specific dollar amounts— $75 for Petty Cash and $1500 for Employee Pay—are transferred from the Operating Expenses Account into the respective accounts. Finally, the total money in Bank 1's Profit and Tax Accounts are transferred to Bank 2.

This process is a system, so it needs to be documented. Your bookkeeper might have to take this over for you, if it becomes too much to manage.

You should have *five principle bank accounts* open: *Sales (Income), Profit, Owner's Pay, Taxes, and Operating Expenses,* with the Profit and Tax Accounts in a separate bank. Looking at the numbers using the spreadsheet, you will be able to see instantly where your business stands at any time.

The following are additional accounts, contingent on your business needs, that are recommend for you to consider opening:

Income Account

In this account, you collect all of your income deposits so that you can clearly see how much cash you collected. This will separate incoming from outgoing cash, both of which are managed by the Operating Expenses Account.

An Income Account will give you an accurate picture of how much money you collected during any period of time. And the Operating Expenses Account will transition to only paying the expenses for operations, so you will have an accurate picture of how much money is flowing out of your business at any given time.

It's critical that you adjust to your actual revenue. If you have material and subcontractor costs, allocate these fixed amounts first, then allocate all remaining money in the Income Account to the other accounts: Profit, Owner's Pay, Taxes and Operating Expenses. And possibly a few others suggested below.

Reserve Account

The reserve account is an ultra low-risk, interest-bearing account that you can use for short-term emergencies. At a certain point, leaving 50% in your Profit
Account to act as a rainy day fund is not prudent since the money flow is a little unpredictable. A bad quarter won't contribute much to the Profit Account. Then

you take 50% out for a profit share, and now that Profit Account reserve might be too small for a big business. Every business should have a three-month reserve, meaning that, if not a single sale came in, all costs could still be covered for three months (a quarter). The question isn't•if•you will have a dark day (your supplier goes out of business, your biggest client goes bankrupt, your best employees leave to start a direct competitor and your clients decide to go with them, etc.). The question is,•when•will your dark day come? The reserve account is there for that.

When you set up a reserve account, you•must•also establish certain rules for its use. What I mean is that, when you have a situation so dire that you need to access this money, you also have instructions written in advance on how to proceed. For example, if the money is pulled due to a drop in sales, you will pre-plan that, besides just trying to get more sales, you will also cut all the related costs in your business within two months if things haven't improved. Few people have the discipline to think clearly or act appropriately in times of panic, and that's why we document a simple set of instructions for ourselves in advance.

Stocking Account:

This is an account for big purchases and to pay for stocking your inventory. For example, a roof decking company, RoofDeck Solutions, Ltd., sells the materials contractors need to complete their projects. And you, the contractor, includes some basic nuts and bolts with each order, usually fifty or a hundred of each; yet his supplier requires a minimum order of ten thousand at a time, which costs you roughly $5000. Each order will last ten months or longer, so you set up what is called a "large purchase account" into which you allocate 1/20th (that's $250 each time) of the funds needed for the next big nuts and bolts purchase. Why 1/20th? Because you know you'll need the next order in ten months, and your on the 10/25 Rhythm. Ten months, two times a month, equals twenty allocations before the next big purchase. By doing this, you'll be able to chip away at the big bill•before•it happens. Then, when it's time to cough up the $5000 for the next big nuts and bolts order, you're ready. If not, this bill might catch you off guard and then have to scramble to cover it. Now, you'll barely feel the $250 allocated to this Stocking Account twice a month.

Pass-Through Account:

Some businesses receive income from customers that is not to be allocated for Profit or Owner's Pay. Sometimes you may provide a service or a product to your customer at cost (or near cost), and other times you may be reimbursed for costs outright.

For example, travel expenses reimbursed by clients. That income is not allocated to cover payroll or added to the Profit Account. It's a pass-through and goes directly into this account, and then off to the corresponding vendor to pay the bill. If you paid the bill in advance, the money is deposited into the Pass-Through Account and then transferred to the Operating Expenses Account, from which you paid the initial bill. For accounting purposes, the name you give each is entirely up to you, such as Reimbursement Account.

Materials Account:

If most of your revenue is pass-through revenue and the core of your business is basically the management of that pass-through, set up a Materials Account for the money that is allocated specifically for purchase of materials. Do not allocate it for anything else. (Ever!) If for some reason there is money left over at the end of the quarter (in other words, you had a larger profit margin than you expected), you can move that balance to your Income Account and make the allocations accordingly. The Materials Account functions in the same way the Pass-Through Account does, but it is broken out separately so that you know its exclusive purpose is for materials.

Subcontractor / Commissions Account:

If your business does not purchase materials, but uses contractors or sales people paid on commission instead, this is where you allocate the funds to pay these people. Treat it just like the Materials Account, but apply it to contractors and commission-based employees.

Employee Payroll Account:

Employee pay is relatively predictable, full-timers are on salary and part-timers, for the most part, work an average number of hours per week. This means you can look at the cumulative gross pay for your employees plus the payroll taxes you'll incur and allocate funds from your Income Account or Operating Expenses Account to the Employee Payroll Account. If you use a payroll service, set them up to pull the payroll from this account (not your Operating Expenses Account).

Major Equipment Account:

Similar to your Stocking Account, this account is for big purchases you may need to make farther down the road, such as new computers or high cost capital purchase. Estimate how much you might have to spend on future equipment purchases, divide it by the number of months you have to save up for it, divide that number by two and allocate that amount twice a month to accumulate enough money for that big purchase.

Drip Account:

This account is for retainers, advance payments and pre-payments on work your company will complete over a long period of time and for which you have yet to expend resources. Say you get a big project and you receive $120,000 from the client up front for work you will complete every month over the period of a year.

That means that each month, you will really be earning $10,000. So when you get that check, put the $120,000 into the Drip Account and then automatically transfer $10,000 to the Income Account every month (or better yet, $5,000 twice a month). Don't touch any of the balance in the Drip Account. You only make allocations when you drip a portion of the funds, in this case, the $10,000 each month, into the Income Account.

The Drip Account helps you manage the true cash flow of earned money, so that you can manage your expenses and costs. For example, the labor doing the work
will be paid monthly.

Petty Cash Account:

Set up a bank account and get a debit card for petty cash purchases, such as client lunches. Then, allocate a regular dollar amount from your Operating Expenses Account to petty cash. For example, allocate $100 every two weeks for the office and a few employees who need it. These funds cover gifts, lunches and other small purchases.

Sales Tax Account:

If your business collects sales tax, every single penny of the sales tax you collect is immediately allocated to this account. For example, if you sell something for $100 and sales tax is 5%, you will deposit $105 into your Income Account. First, transfer that $5 into your Sales Tax Account; then allocate the remaining $100 to the various account. The Sales tax isn't even legally your money; you are just acting as a collection agent for the government, so never, ever treat that money as income.

<u>NOTES</u>

NOTES

Part IV: Who We Are is What We Do

The world views African Americans without value.

However, the opportunity to change that view has been ours for a long time. We must demand more from our local financial institutions: Black Churches and Black Mega-Churches are the Major Financial Institutions within the Black Community.

Demand... Demand... Demand...!!!

Demand, Legacy Economic Commitments from Local Black Churches. At a minimum, your local church should develop local businesses based on a percentage of it's congregation.

We cannot continue to have the Black Church identified as a source of leadership, when there is no commitment by these financial institutions to develop legacy black economics within our communities.

Consider this... If a Church as a congregation of 5,000 (five thousand) members, then 10% (ten percent) of that membership should represent a minimum of 500 (five hundred) local businesses to be created and maintained. The sole purpose of those businesses are job creation opportunities for local unemployed black youth.

These are Not training programs, but actual jobs with actual pay with a minimum pay rate of $30,000 (thirty thousand dollars).

Building a New Black Wall Street requires absolute change and commitment, without reservation.

Chapter 16: Black Wall Street is Our New Brand

Black Wall Street is Our New Brand.

However, it is completely wrong to have branding as your primary marketing goal. Branding should be a byproduct.

Austen Riggs, a famous psychiatrist said, "Happiness is only a byproduct of successful living."

Well, so is branding. You cannot "buy" happiness, and you cannot "buy" a brand.
It's impossible to have a good brand without all the other elements in place. Branding is the personality of your service or product. It is created through the interaction with your customers and prospects. It's the result of a relationship.

Whether you are a person or a company. It cannot be created using billboard advertising bragging that your business is the best. You have to deserve it. Your relationship should focus on providing substance and qualitative value, not on image building.

So why do people love branding so much?

In commerce, industry loves branding for two reasons. The first is because it's what everyone does and thinks they should do. Advertising agencies are continuously stalking to try to fill some space in newspapers or television. So as a marketer it is the obvious way. If you don't spend money on branding and the product doesn't work you might get blamed that no one knows about your product. This leads us to the second reason: The most positive effect of "traditional" branding is the effect inside the company. All employees love branding, because it makes them feel more important. Employees might call their relatives or friends to ask if they saw their brand campaign.

Many companies have gone bankrupt because they felt they needed to build a brand in order to sell. But on the other hand, even in the off-line world we see great brands that achieved the branding through the creation of excellent customer experiences. Take Starbucks, for example. They created what they call the "third home," and spent a lot of time and money, not on pure branding, but on the relationship. Through this relationship building, a brand was born.

You cannot create a brand before you create a business: Your business creates your brand.

Chapter 17: African Governments

Establish relationships with African governments.

We cannot Build a New Black Wall Street without relationships with our homelands. Therefore, take advantage of your status as a United States Citizen and register as a Foreign Agent for African governments.

The Foreign Agent Registration Act, is a federal statute that gives authority to solicit, lobby and receive funds on behalf of any African government.

FARA also creates transparency as to who and which groups have actual and legitimate relationships with African governments.

For additional information: https://www.fara.gov

FARA was enacted in 1938. FARA is a disclosure statute that requires persons acting as agents of foreign principals in a political or quasi-political capacity to make periodic public disclosures of their relationship with the foreign principal, as well as activities, receipts and disbursements in support of those activities. Disclosure of the required information facilitates evaluation by the government and the American people of the statements and activities of such persons in light of their function as foreign agents.

<u>NOTES</u>

Part V: Making Money

Every business today requires a website, which gives you a public face even if you don't have a physical address.

When purchasing a domain name, never ever, buy from the same vendor that is hosting your website. There may come a time when you want to move your domain from one web hosting company to another, at which time, there are always problems.

Buy your domains from either GoDaddy or DynaDot. Average price for a domain is $15 (fifteen dollars).

In Building a New Black Wall Street, it is recommended to use Wordpress as the platform of choice for setting up your website. If you can use Facebook, you can use Wordpress, and without the need of a webmaster to manage your website once setup.

It is recommended that you use HostGator for Website Hosting. Hostgator has great packages with unlimited bandwidth. The best starting package is the "Baby Plan" at $12 (twelve dollars) per month with the ability to host unlimited domains on a single account. HostGator has great response times for websites, due to their infrastructure of more than 10,000 servers at your disposal. Over 9 million websites use HostGator.

The key to using HostGator, is that they have a Free one-click install for Wordpress.

After installing Wordpress, you can use it straight out the box, or upgrade with professional themes for any type of business category. Themes install on the fly. Just upload the theme into the Wordpress Theme Folder and Click Activate from
the Wordpress Control Panel. Easy as 1-2-3.

To preview available themes, go to: https://www.premiumwp.com

To further upgrade your Wordpress install, there are a variety of plugins to take your website to the next level: Memberships, e-Commerce, Auto-post to Social Media, event Calenders and event Management, website Ad managers, etc... But for e-commerce, try the WooCommerce plugin, which is Free and contains all features necessary to have your online store up and running.

Download the WooCommerce plugin directly from Wordpress.org:

https://wordpress.org/plugins/woocommerce

Now that you're online and have a great online presence, let's change the world and together build a New Black Wall Street.

Chapter 18: Target Audience

To Build a New Black Wall Street, we need to reach a target audience, the game-changers!

Imagine you have a headache and enter a pharmacy to find some medication to relieve your pain.

You have a choice of Aspirin, Ibuprofen, or "Algipain" medicine that says: This pill relieves all possible pains. Would you even consider this last one? Of course not. It's too broad. Even if this medicine has the same chemical composition you would not buy it.

The big companies like Procter & Gamble have applied this for decades and created billion-dollar brands by narrowing their target groups.

Take cosmetics, for example. There is not one type of makeup that will work well for all women. This is definitely not a mass-market product. You want to divide this large market into relatively homogeneous segments of customers, so that you can fully satisfy needs with a different product. In this case, for instance, you may want cosmetics for different skin needs, such as dry, normal, or oily skin. Or, you may want to have ethnic products for African Americans, Asians, Caucasians, and the variations in between.

Instead of conducting promotions in all these markets at the same time, you should be addressing them one at a time. Even dry skin can be divided into smaller variables, such as a woman's age, coloring, and daily activities. Even if the composition of most of these cosmetics is fairly similar, packaging them differently and targeting those groups will be the key to success.

This does not mean that you will ignore the other niches, but only that you take one niche at a time. You choose your particular niche, optimize the best way to promote it, and then go on to another niche. This is a difficult exercise, because it takes a lot of patience. You want fast results and are used to the old marketing "numbers game." The more people you reach the more you'll convert. But this hypothesis is purely based on the assumption that the conversion is the same when you target a big audience or a small-niche targeted audience that you understand, know their fears, problems, and how to speak to them.

If you were a photographer and had the choice between promoting yourself at a seminar with a thousand people or getting the list of twenty who are getting married this year, what would you choose? I hope you've chosen the latter. This option allows you to focus on their needs, not "photography," but wedding photography, where you can show them your expertise and what you can do, not bothering them with other kinds of photography they might not be interested in. Being "laser-focused" you can adapt the marketing sequence to the end user's interests.

Before the internet and online existed, the main direct-response marketing medium was direct mail, and marketers had to do this narrowing exercise.

They had to limit the number of targets, because there was a cost linked to them: printing and postage. Paradoxically there were fewer options to segment but the marketer was forced to do a better job at understanding and segmenting.

In fact the narrowing effect has proven to be very successful even in situations that are not so obvious. When a sales area is too large, it is difficult for the salespeople to focus on all the smaller opportunities that may arise. They often get better results in a reduced area than in a larger one, because they can focus, to better understand and serve their customers.

Narrowing the focus does not mean leaving the other segments behind, not at all.

Always choose the best target, be laser-focused and then start with another one.

But you do this one at a time! Not only will the prospect relate more to your offer but you can also charge more. Think of where the highest tickets are paid: general products or tailor-made ones; general practitioners or specialists?

Finding and Prioritizing Niche Markets

How do we come up with these different niches and how can we prioritize them?

You might know your product and have an idea of some niches but there is a logical way to identify and rank them:

Here is a *seven parameter* framework (A - H), that will help you with this. On one hand it will help you with prioritizing your niches, but will also be a guide to better understand your niche.

The Google Keyword Planner tool is great for finding niches. Even though there are other keyword tools available, Google's tool is readily available. With the Google Keyword Tool, you can find related words, searches for that keyword, and get an idea of different niches.

(A)   Number of People

Try to estimate the total potential niche. The bigger the niche the more potential and possibilities you will have. But be aware that a sub-sub-niche is always better than a broader niche. In this process you will also identify niches that are too small to be targeted.

The following tools are recommended to do this exercise:

Google AdWords Keyword Planner. Here you can evaluate the number of searches a certain keyword gets per month in a specific language and or territory.

Facebook: You can simulate an ad and see the number of people that might be interested in your topic.

Twitter Analytics: You can check the number of tweets that you get for a certain keyword related to your niche.

78

Look at your competitor's sites and analyze them. Find out how many visitors they have and their demographics. Some useful tools are: Quantcast.com - Alexa.com - SEMrush.com.

Are there forums for that niche? Are there magazines on that niche topic?

With all this information give your niche a score between 1 to 10, based on the number of potential buyers you estimated from your research.

(B)   Competition

How many competitors are out there? Do they own the space? It is important that there is some competition, however, it should not be saturated. Look at their websites, the number of visitors. What keywords are bringing people to your competitor's website?

Look at the AdWords and their bid prices. The higher the prices, the more competition but this also means that there is money to be made.

(C)   Potential Profit

Analyze the AdWords bidding prices. You should look at the offers of the competitors. These are an excellent indicator whether people are making money on them. The higher the bids, the more money can be made, but the negative side is that there is also more competition for these. So you'll have to pay more to get them too.

(D)   Time Frame

How actively is your prospect looking for a solution? Is the need very urgent.

Is he waiting for the ambulance or is it something that can wait? Do you need to educate them a lot; do you have to show him his problem? An important point here is that you should avoid educating the market yourself. Many companies have failed because they chose to open with educating a market. Of course you have the iPads and iPhones, but as a general rule, if there is no competition, prospects need to be educated. Be very careful!

(E)   Opportunity or Problem Solving

If your product or service solves the problem there might be no business afterwards, unless it is a recurring problem. Typically you will see that problems are more time critical. However, having a solution to answer an opportunity might be a lot better. People buy services or products to pave the way to their dreams. With opportunities, you can always expand and have changes that transform. In most instances, solutions for opportunities can be sold at a higher value.

(F)   Reach

How easily can I reach my audience?

Can you reach them on one of the five online traffic highways:

1).   Google
2).   Facebook
3).   Youtube
4).   Amazon
5).   iTunes (Podcast, Apps)

What keywords can I bid on and what will be the total volume?

Can I target them on Facebook? How many?

Do I have an e-mail list? Can I buy or rent one?

Is it easy to get the data of potential contacts? B2B data is normally easier to get.

(G)   Passion

How much do you like this niche or what affinity do you have with this niche? This is the only subjective parameter, but it can be an important one. If you are passionate about something you will be eager to learn more about it and will also communicate better with your niche.

(H)   Ranking

When you score the *seven parameters*, you add them, and the final score is the niche score.

If you do this for all the niches that you see potential of opportunity, you'll generate a ranking that you can use to prioritize these niches.

Never overlook existing customers.

If you already have customers, you have gold in your hands that you might easily overlook.

Do some data mining to identify your best segments. Try starting with two data mining exercises:

1) 80/20

Here we look at the 20 percent of customers that are bringing in 80 percent of profit, revenue and growth.

Look to see if there are some common factors.

If your business is a Busines-to-Business (B2B), you might analyze these top groups and try to find the main industries, the size of the company or top location and define your target company profile.

If your business is Business-to Consumer (B2C) look at the data you have: If you don't have these so called DNA data (gender, age, marital status, number of children, hobbies, education level, income level, type of employment) you mightconsider mailing them a survey. SurveyMonkey.com is a great tool to do this.

What you are doing is identifying the common elements of your target market or ideal client and establishing a simplified image of this person.

2.) RFM

This methodology is the old solid way to get your best customers.

You will rank them based on three parameters:

* Recency (R): last buying data
* Frequency (F): how often did they buy
* Monetary Value (M): how much did they spend in total

You then take this data and divide your customers into percentiles of 10 percent (so group them in 10) where the top tier receives 10 points, second tier 9 points, third tier 8 points and so on. You do this exercise for each parameter. And then you add the three scores together. The highest points are the ones to analyze. These are your best customers you should focus on this niche.

NOTES

Chapter 19: Focus on Audience Interest

Building a New Black Wall Street is Not for Everybody. On the one hand, it doesn't take a million people to run a business. And on the other hand, a business doesn't even need millions of customers buying it's products or services, but it does need a consistent source of customers.

Now that you have identified a "potential" niche, you should focus "only" on that one. Ideally this will be a sequential process, where you identify various other niches by repeating the exercise over and over again. But as with most things in life, success will come if you focus your full attention and energy on this ideal niche.

The next step now is to understand your ideal niche's desired end result. What you should do is try to put yourself in the shoes of your ideal prospect. "The secret of the best fishermen is not to know how to have and use the best fishing gear, it is to think like the fish." You'll be able to understand your prospect better and realize the advantage in speaking not to a group, but to an individual as if it were on a one-to-one basis!

Begin with the end in mind: what is the desired end result and find the path to arrive to that result. Can you identify different milestones?

These milestones will usually be the steps in resolving obstacles or problems that one might encounter in achieving the end result. In other words, each step means bringing the prospect closer to their desired end result.

You might think, "How do I find these steps?" Compare it to a chess master who knows his end goal: "checkmate king" and goes backward to understand the steps in achieving this.

Ideal ways to understand your prospect and what is going on in his mind is going to both, YouTube and Facebook, and look at posts and videos. Sign up on forums and see what your niche prospects are talking about and questions being asked. Do a search on Twitter and find the burning topics and questions. Look at what your competition is offering. What products are being sold on Amazon; look at the comments.

The better you understand your target audience and their objectives, the better you will be able to map out their journey. You have to go as deep as you can to know what the conversations are, that they are having in their mind.

If you have them, survey some of your best customers or some prospects. Organize a face-to-face appointment or call them, otherwise you can do an online survey with Surveymonkey. Then expand this "core" information to other topics that support this core information. Ideally you should identify the top topics for your niche. This will be important for the next steps in developing a sales funnel. The better you know your target niche, the better you can compel them and speak to them in order to dominate that niche!

The objective here is to lay the foundation for all your next marketing and sales activities.

Once you have identified the various milestones, identify how to help your prospects move closer to the first milestone. You will create the "bait," "bribe" or lead magnet, as some call it. These are valuable pieces of information or items that we will give for free.

This can be: information, a test, results of a questionnaire, a cheat sheet with key steps, a price calculation or a framework. They can be given in various formats such as a PDF, audio, podcast, a video or membership only website. But you can also give free software. This generally works very well. Some lead magnets or bait is better than others.

In order to be successful, your lead magnet should have the following characteristics:

1. It should be easily consumable and give immediate gratification.

2. It should be very specific to help your prospect reaching his first milestone.

3. It should also have a high-perceived value.

4. Ideally it should be incomplete.

Immediate Gratification and Easily Consumable:

The prospect does not know you and will not want to spend too much time to consume your bait. Bear in mind that his time is even as valuable as his money. So the key here is to develop something that can be read, watched, or used quickly, in 15 minutes or less, but at the same time will give the prospect great value. Think about TED•talks: great value and less than fifteen minutes.

Most people will not consume your bait, but those that will are your best prospects.

Books or mini-courses for example are not good lead magnets. The value can be enormous, but very few prospects will consume the information. Rather, give them a summary or quick report.

Very Specific Information or Help: Don't give theory away. Your bait should be of direct practical value, it should really help the prospect get closer to an end result. Moving your prospect closer is the key to success. Get the prospect moving, and if he sees the value, he'll be open for more. One of the biggest mistakes is to make the information not specific enough and fall into the "generalization" trap. Too often sites give away a general report or white paper about a topic. Your piece should answer a specific question.

High value Traps: The information or item you give away should be of the highest value. You should not give "crappy" stuff away. The perception of the customer of your value to him will be based on this first interaction. If you give great value, he'll think, "

If this great value is for free, the paid value will have to be excellent!" Many marketers have problems in giving great stuff away, but this is what you have to do. This is the way to break through attention filters. We are living in a freemium economy. The bait should also not be seen as "bait" or "a bribe" as such. People are way too sophisticated these days. If they perceive your "value piece" is bait or a bribe, they will quit immediately.

Here's a great analogy about cheese and whiskers. You need a "more cheese, less whiskers" approach at lead generation. A mouse is programmed to sniff out and follow the cheese. However, if it sees the whiskers of the cat; just the barest notice, the mouse will run away. We react like these mice, when we see the least sign of advertising, we are repelled instead of compelled. We have to make our first piece so valuable that it is perceived as 100% pure value for the prospect. So ideally, don't brand it!

Incomplete Information: After the prospects consume the lead magnet, they should have that "wow" effect, but the lead magnet should not resolve all steps to get to the desired result, but should open the way to a next step, so that they'll want more of what you gave them.

<u>NOTES</u>

Chapter 20: Leverage Competition

Analyze in detail your competition and define how you can be better and unique.

Often people see innovations and new developments as ideas coming "out of the blue." Someone wakes up and has a great idea and implements it, but the majority of the big innovations are improvements of already existing products or services.

Creating new markets are difficult. Many companies that thought they had a good innovative idea, wanted to be the first on the market, and most of them, not all of them failed. It is important to look at what the competitors are doing and analyzing what is working, if people are spending money on their services or products. If some services do not work there is a huge risk that if you launch them, they won't work either.

A huge mistake for instance is to rely on some market study where people are asked their intentions. Most people would like to change or quit their jobs, but how many do? How many people want to lose weight and even show the intention to start, and go to the gym in January, but how many follow through?

Don't be the first, be the best!

So what you have to do is analyze what is working for your competitors and what isn't. Copy and improve what works! The big advantage today is that we have so much competitors' data available: the best keywords, the campaigns that are working for them. What kind of visitors they have, etc..

What is also key here, is to really find out how you can differentiate your content in a better, more appealing way. How can you add more value than your competitor is giving?

Here's a few sites that can help you to get this information: www.alexa.com, www.semrush.com, www.quantcast.com, and www.compete.com.

To find out more about their visitors and traffic, you can see which keywords people are typing to get to their website; what paid keywords they are bidding on.

All this information is crucial to set the foundation for developing a sales funnel. Most often people jump into setting up a sales funnel without doing their homework properly. If you have defined your niche, know the desired end result, the stepping-stones to achieve it, defined the bait to compel your prospects so that they'll identify themselves, and know how you can differentiate yourself, you are ready to set up a sales funnel.

Chapter 21: Buyers are Not Equal

Realise that all prospects are not equal, and that these techniques work offline as well.

Avoid the temptation of using a fresh prospect's email for pitching offers or dumping it into your sales channel. This could be a possibility if your product or service is solving some urgent need, but even when you think they are ready you might want to "warm up" your lead.

When I worked for corporate companies, I also made the big mistake of getting leads and handing them directly over to the sales teams and wondering why they were complaining about the bad quality. I had not figured out the concept of "lead readiness." Other marketers might speak about lead scoring. Today it is one of the fundamentals of an online Marketing strategy. It saves sales cost and improves efficiency and effectiveness. To really understand this concept, consider analysing two parameters: Whether they will buy and When they will buy

For simplicity let's only take two choices: They'll buy or not, and they buy now or they buy in the future, but the reality is often that only a very small amount will buy and is ready to do it now. However, you have a very large amount that will eventually buy in the future but are just not ready now and need some time. It might be that they have to inform themselves more, evaluate choices, or find that the need is not there at the moment.

Studies have shown that 50 percent of the people that showed interest in a product but did not buy sixty days after showing interest did eventually buy it. You have to acknowledge this and build your marketing activities around it. Your role is to educate them and prepare them to decide to choose your product or service, when they will be ready to buy.

You have to create trust and show your expertise. The golden rule is never to pitch before you feel that the prospect is ready to buy. We would love to know when our prospect is in this ready-to-buy mode, and this is our task now to find this out. When you set up your sales funnel properly and start to get data of the full funnel, you will be able to perfectly forecast how long you'll have to nurture your leads before they will become customers.

This is how to turn a slot machine into a vending machine! What will also happen in the process is that you will also "disqualify" some prospects. Nevertheless, take into consideration that 30 percent will never buy. They might be "interested" in your product, but not have the money or the "authority" to buy, mainly in a B2B environment. So don't waste very expensive sales time with them.

There is a concept often used in lead qualifying and lead scoring that is called BANT. This is an acronym which B stands for Budget, A for Authority to purchase, N for Need, and T for Timeframe.

B - will be difficult to have an impact on, unless you are willing to drop your prices dramatically. But as a Ferrari dealer, would you drop your prices 90 percent so that most of the interested people "are able" to buy from you? Interest is not a synonym of the ability to buy. There is a fine line between what someone is prepared to pay for something he's interested in and what he actually will pay. Your role will be to increase his desire.

The Authority level is something you have to identify as quickly as possible. If someone is not "authorized" you should ask that person to pass the information to the "authority."

The remaining parameters, Need and Timeframe, are the ones that you can have a impact on through education. Your prospect might not be "really" interested or interested enough in order to buy from you? There is no connection, no trust. Building trust takes time.

The Emotional Bank Account

The emotional bank account concept is simple: The relationships you have with other people can be seen as a bank account, in which you can deposit money or withdraw money. Every positive interaction adds value, and being kind is like a deposit to the account. Every negative interaction or pitching, can be seen as a withdrawal from the bank account. These deposits are the trust you build in your prospect's mind. The more deposits you make the easier it is to withdraw money,
the easier it will be to pitch. Without a certain trust level or money in the bank account, you cannot pitch or withdraw money!

Every positive interaction over time will grow the trust or goodwill. Every pitch lowers it. At a certain point you can really pitch without jeopardizing the trust you have built! Therefore, the more value you provide, the less impact negative pitching has.

The question now is: what type of content should you deliver?

Having narrowed down the niche and identified the bait, you should also have identified the different steps to achieve the desired end result that your prospect is looking for. Break down these steps like playing chess in reverse, from the last move to checkmate. What are the obstacles your prospects have to overcome? What is the information they need? Educate your prospect how to overcome the obstacles and solve his problems. Make a plan. The sequence is crucial. You have to make a calendar and based on the "educational" stages your prospect is in, you give him the appropriate content. Each prospect has another agenda so the content that you deliver should be individualized. This can easily be done if you automate the process.

Anticipate the top needs that your prospect will have and make it easy for them to take the next step. Every prospect will receive pieces of the educational value in a sequence and at a pace that they choose! Here you can use the power of technology and the available tools.

Every time you send something to the customer you should consider that trust building has three main parts that are:

90

1. Creativity: the "value pieces" you create for the prospect
2. Relationship: the act of giving free content and building reciprocity
3. Leadership: helping your prospects head in the right direction

If you are providing good content that moves the prospect closer to his desired end goal, then you are developing trust, which eventually creates your brand within the prospect's mind, but not shouting how great your product is! Consistent contact will increase the trust factor. More contacts increase "liking." The magic thing about trust is that, if you have built enough trust you can even sell products that are not exactly in your field. Who you do usually ask for advice: real pitching experts or your friends?

The Tools

If you have content and the e-mail of your prospect, you are good to go. The easiest and best way to educate your prospects is to send them e-mails in a sequenced manner.

Never make the mistake thinking that we can use and abuse e-mail because it's free.

E-mail is indeed free if you look at it technically, but sending people unsolicited or too frequent mails might not be depositing value in the emotional bank account, but perceived as withdrawals and might create rejection. It is therefore important to segment your prospect list based on some triggers and adapt your e- mail frequency per segment.

You can create segments based on the click activities; you can ask your prospects if they want more or fewer e-mails from you. You can ask where they are in the process of getting to their end results. You can also ask what they want to know. Your communication should be split into segments.

Remember that the more "niche" we can go the better. Wouldn't it be ideal to have one-on-one e-mail? That is indeed the ultimate goal, but if you want to scale your business this will be unsustainable. That is why you need marketing automation, and there are readily available tools that you can use for this. These tools allow you to build e-mail sequences based on triggers or what is most commonly named 'tags'. Tags can be anything like opening a certain e-mail clicking on a link, attending an event, filling in a survey, buying a product, or simply answering a question.

Will these e-mails reach all your prospects? If half of your prospects open your mail you are lucky or have done an excellent job. The hard reality is that you should expect that less than 50 percent will read your e-mail due to technical factors such as the deliverability and psychological factors: e-mail overwhelm.

Often people fill in fake addresses fearing the spam follow up. But even if you have the right e-mail address, some of your mail will not be delivered due to the deliverability score of your mailing and end in the junk folder. Every e-mail is linked to an IP address, the "@yourdomain.com." You can get your IP address from whatismyipaddress.com. This IP address has a "reputation" score that is created based on criteria like the bounces, un-subscription rates, and the frequency you send mailings, number of mailings.

The better the score the higher your chances of arriving in the inbox of your prospects. Do you get a lot of complaints when sending out e-mails? Do you end up with a lot of people that get to your page and quickly link away, is a high bounce rate. E-mails also don't reach their destination because the address is no longer good. How many e-mails do you send out that are returned? You can actually see your reputation at senderscore.org. The very bad IP addresses get even blacklisted and always arrive in the junk. These can be found on senderbase.org.

You can improve your score by cleaning your database: Remove the inactive and bounce e-mails from your list. If possible ask for double opt-ins when asking for their e-mail so the probability of getting in to spam is lower. With a double opt-in your subscribers will receive an e-mail after they have given their e-mail or filled in a web form and have to confirm that they really want to be on your list.

Another more technical thing you can do to increase the open rate is to choose the best days of the week and hours of the day to send your mailings out. Typically mid-weekdays are great: from Tuesday to Thursday. The best time of the day you send out your e-mail is usually the beginning of the day or right after lunch.

However these are averages, you have to test what works best for you because every audience is different. Don't forget to segment by geographic location and think also mobile! More and more people are reading their e-mails on mobile, so make your e-mails mobile friendly! When you design a website you have the advantage of custom tailoring your content for mobile and for desktop, however with e-mails you don't know how your prospect will read your e-mail. Therefore it should be readable regardless of the device.

If you make html e-mails I'd recommend following some tips:

* Use body text no lower than 13px
* Use only one column
* Don't use images. Most Android devices will turn it off.

You should really do these technical improvements, but they are only the starting point. The biggest leap to make your way through the clutter of distraction and get the reader's attention is psychological. To get people to read our mail out of maybe, the hundreds they receive each day, consider these two elements to increase your e-mail open rate: build intrigue and anticipation into your e-mails and speak one to one!

The subject line is the most important piece of your e-mail. People will decide to open or not open, based on that subject line. Is the subject intriguing? Raising questions? Here are some proven subject line examples that work in many industries and get high open rates:

* Top 10 . . .
* 7 Secrets of . . .
* How to . . .
* Quickly and Easily . . .
* . . . in 24 hours
* . . . Step by Step

Branding or having a corporate style guarantees a low-open rate, because these elements will activate your prospects "human spam filters." Instead place a question that relates to the desired outcome. Have a pattern interrupt, confuse your prospect or just put their name as the subject. I've struggled in the corporate world to have this understood. People are so tied to the neat corporate styles. It is similar to the off-line world when you open your mailbox you sort the letters in two piles: the branded ones and the ones that you'll read.

If you have a great subject line, do follow up on that in your body copy, do not make the big mistake of not aligning the body of your mail with the subject. Your prospect will feel cheated. If you asked a question, answer it, and elaborate. Do not use the fancy templates of your mail provider; they will trigger the "spam" filter of your prospects. They might look pretty nice, but do you send your friends e-mails with a template? Perhaps you'll do that on their birthday, but not in conversational e-mails. Even worse is to brand your e-mails. These are again the biggest mistakes in design that most big companies make.

Simply send a plain e-mail with white background. The language should be conversational, no ego-tripping. Your prospects want e-mails with good value helping them. A good format is plain text including a picture with a play button, as if it were a video, and linking it to the main article, a video or whatever you want to give on a webpage. Make sure that your prospects consume the content. Do not overwhelm them. Cut your content in small easy consumable pieces. It's like the bait, if they don't consume your content you might lose them in the next steps. Include anticipation in every piece. Prepare your prospects for the next mail.

A great way to do this is to build your e-mail sequences like a Soap Opera Series. The success of the soap operas series lies in the open endings. Unless it is the last episode, all the series have an open end: creating anticipation, leaving a Question in your mind. Our mind is very bad at coping with this. We want to close the loop; we want to know what happens next. It's like an unfinished music tune.

Try this out: stop one of your favorite songs in the middle, you'll keep it in your head and hum it during a couple of hours. The same can be done with e-mails. Create a flow of stories with open endings. Leave your reader with some questions and anticipate you'll answer them in the next e-mail. Your open rates will dramatically increase. Try not to have too big of an interval between your e- mails; definitely not in the beginning when your prospects are the most excited about what you have to offer.

Educating Prospects

E-mail will be your best channel to do an educational process, but I'd recommend not relying only on e-mail. Another way you can reinforce communication with your prospect, is to use social media as an educational channel. Facebook allows you to upload collected e-mails, and Facebook will then try to match these mails with the emails within it's system and create a new "custom audience." Now you can target these customers by posting on Facebook. Remember that the more they see you and hear from you the more they'll like you.

Unfortunately this will not be free. These people will probably not be liking your Facebook fan page, so in order to see your post you'll have to promote and pay for this. What you should do here is try to get them into your fan base so that you can communicate with them "for free." Ask them to like your page to get more great information. You might have noticed that I only recommend asking to like the fan page at this stage. The purpose of liking your fan page should only be to get a "cheaper" education source, not to acquire prospects.

The main purpose of using Facebook, is to generate traffic out of Facebook to your website in order to get their e-mail. Now that you have the e-mails, the objective is to nurture them, and Facebook can be a cheaper way to do it. Even if you have them liking your page you will not be able to reach all of your fans for free. Facebook cleverly changed the rules some years ago and the amount of fans on which your post will appear in their News Feed will be between 6 percent and 15 percent. This will depend on the News Feed algorithm·that Facebook uses. It's a kind of engagement algorithm.

Facebook looks at how your fans engage with you by liking, sharing, or clicking on your posts. The more fan likes you have, the greater the likelihood that Facebook will show your post to them. It might sound strange but one of the best tactics to improve this is by regularly posting some very viral articles or videos, even if they are not related to your product or service. It will increase the engagement of your fans. Post viral stuff that people will share or like and then you increase your likelihood to being seen. Then when you post your content the chance that it will appear in their post will be higher.

Some people like to watch videos, others prefer to read or to listen. That's why you should try a variety of media for leveraging education content. Create a YouTube channel and start a podcast and ask them to subscribe to your channel.

Education is a broad topic and on what you "educate" your prospect will highly depend on your product or service. What cannot be stressed enough, is the importance of motivating the prospects to consume your content. If you have a SaaS—software as a service, you might have been given access to a free version of your software or a free trial period. The main objective will be to help and motivate your users to use your free software. The same is true for free apps. People will not buy from you or upgrade to a paid version if they don't feel the need.

A great way to motivate usage is through gamification. The idea is to learn by playing. If you can have people use your software or app combining it with a game aspect you'll definitely have success.

People love to play and share this with others in a type of competition or collaboration. Webinars with live video is a great way to teach and have the full focus of your students. Offline, live seminars offer the best environments to educate your prospects and sell them high-ticket items afterwards. However if you have a big worldwide audience it's not always easy to do and can be quite expensive. Excellent alternatives to live seminars are webinars, where you invite people for a one to two-hour crash course on your topic, to give them nothing else but great value. As a matter of fact, webinars combine various steps of the sales funnel: They can be the first lead magnet, the education, and the sales offer. You have their attention and increase their motivation, and at the end of the webinar, you offer them something to buy from you.

Now that we have educated our prospects and set up the relationship with them, the emotional bank account should be well funded enough that we can start withdrawing some money from it and pitch. But before we start selling our core offer we can apply a technique that few marketers apply or even know.

This is a concept called the "Tripwire," it is meant to transform as many prospects into buyers as possible. The formula is simple: "Make a small sale before asking for your core offer." Psychologists call this the foot in the door.

From Prospect to First-Time Buyer: the foot in the door concept

Up to now, you have identified the niches of your customers, teased them with ads, led them to your website to opt in and offered them value education.

So far, these stops have helped to develop your relationship with your prospects and positioned you or your brand as a credible expert in your field. Now you can motivate these individuals further to take action. You cannot rely on people buying only when they are ready.

You cannot say, "let them go, and when they are ready they will call us." This is what I call "hope marketing" and it is not productive. You have spent a great deal of time and effort to gain their trust. Because you have established goodwill, you are now able to contact them and ask them to take action. But, just because you have built this relationship, people will still see a relative risk in buying and making a prospect a first-time buyer is really crucial.

Therefore, let's have a look at the experiences in the off-line world and try to simulate these online:

In a study conducted by Freedman and Fraser, researchers asked housewives to put a large sign advocating safe driving in their front yard. 15% of them accepted. In another group the researchers first asked either to sign a petition or place a small card in a window in their home or car supporting safe driving. About two weeks later, the same people were asked by a second person to put the large sign in their front yard. The results were amazing. 76% of the people who agreed to the first request now complied with the second, far more intrusive request. The very small commitment leads to the bigger one. And now that you have a trust relationship with a huge emotional bank account this step should be fairly easy. But there is even more behind this commitment.If you are familiar with off-line retail practices, you definitely know what a loss leader is. It is a pricing strategy•where a product is sold at a price below its market cost to stimulate sales of other more profitable goods or services. This product or service is really so cheap you feel you cannot not buy it. Y ou would in fact feel bad if you didn't. This is the bait to bring in customers to your shop, to commit to a small purchase and have them buy more of whatever else you have to offer.

In buying a product there is a chemical process associated with it. Y ou will release some dopamine, which modulates the brain's ability to perceive reward reinforcement. Y ou can compare it to a certain degree as if you were taking drugs like heroin or cocaine. These drugs artificially increase the levels of the naturally occurring neurotransmitter, dopamine.

After that purchase you want to repeat the experience. Haven't you had the experience of resisting eating your favorite kind of cookies, but when your willpower was weak you ate one and after that first one, you did not stop and finished the whole box. It's the same effect of that glucose drip: you want to buy more. You might be shopping for a couple of hours without buying anything, but after you bought the first thing, many other purchases followed quickly. The key was opening the wallet for the first time! This is a big difference from giving away something like you did during the conversion phase. Here there is a "shoppers' hype" taking place. And by selling instead of giving something for free, you also take away the suspicion that there might be a catch. A trial or free product or service does raise some questions. People look for the fine print.

Can we replicate this process online?

Yes you can, and it's even easier because you can do the selling of your core offer immediately after their first purchase.

You propose to your prospects an irresistible offer, something they cannot resist to buy on impulse. The price range should be from $5 to $20, you can ask more if the perceived value is really great. It is important that there is a big difference between the perceived value and the price they'll pay. Ideally this item should be linked to what you sell afterwards. The service or product should have a good intrinsic value but should be "part of something bigger." This will motivate the purchase of that bigger ticket item.

Before the internet, National Geographic sold beautiful books for nearly nothing, but they were part of a collection, and once you bought the first or second item, there was a drive to purchase the rest of the collection. Online you could sell a software piece and sell a course afterwards or do it the other way around and sell a webinar and the software afterwards.

In the past a lot of companies have tried to make money upselling added values. You can try to invert this process and sell these added values ridiculously cheap. In fact you could even sell at cost or even at a loss. If you have a product that is priced substantially lower than what a competitor is charging you should definitely see a big conversion.

But it is crucial to analyze your whole sales funnel and consider this step as part of the acquisition process. If you know how to make money afterwards, you can put more money into the first phases: buying traffic, the bait, and the loss leader, so that you can really outspend your competition. The real purpose is to convert as many qualified prospects into buyers.

The greater the lifetime value of the customer the more you can afford to spend on each one.

Please note, that the "shopping hype effect" will be the strongest right after purchasing the loss leader, and the faster you do your upselling, the more successful you'll be. The effect will indeed decrease with time, but even after one month, the conversions compared to that from non-buyers will be a lot higher.

From First Time Buyer to Customer: Your Core Offer

Now that your prospect has opened his wallet and is a fresh "first-time buyer," it's time to really bring him over the line and convert him or her into a customer. You have to motivate him for the bigger purchase. Realize that the former step is not a conversion to a customer, because a customer should be someone (or some company if you are in B2B) that you make a certain profit on or at least break even. In the "First Time Buyer" step you are still investing in the acquisition of the customer and in most cases will not yet be making a profit, definitely not if you include other costs. Ideally this step should come as quickly as possible after the former step, and should really be the next screen your prospect sees.

This step is really where the rubber meets the road. Most marketers will have this step as the second step in their sales funnel, which is cold-selling. They will directly try to sell to the freshly gathered prospects without any nurturing. There might be a small part of these prospect that are ready to buy, but if you introduce the nurturing and the foot in the door principle your chances will be a lot higher in converting these prospects into customers and clients.

What we have done is nurturing the lead, we have awakened his desire to really want our product. At this point the prospect is really so "hot" that this step should be fairly easy. This is just the "closing" phase. We have placed so much goodwill and value in the emotional bank account that pitching now should not be considered as withdrawing goodwill, but a logical step in the process. In this step you will try to optimize your total revenue, not the total conversion. You have to position your price in the most optimal way: 1,000 conversions at $10 is a lot worse than 300 at $50! Therefore you should test out and see where you can position yourself.

But be careful, because the most important thing you should have is an irresistible offer. Your prospect should really feel bad about not buying it. You brought him to a point that he has the desire to buy, and now you offer him something great. You might think that getting your prospect to buy is inevitable if you have an irresistible offer.

But in most cases people really need to be brought to a state of desire and then be pushed a little bit. This is the case for most things in life. Here is an analogy.

Let's say Susan goes over to a work associate's house. The associate says, "The kitchen is down the hall. Just help yourself to something to eat or drink." Most people will be too shy to do this unless they know the person well. They will not get any food on their own. However, if the associate brings the dish of food over to Susan and says, "Do you want some," the probability is much higher that she will take some. That's why it's important to motivate people to buy.•

This is the key objective in this process: Motivate to Buy. But how do we do this?

In old school marketing, this was the role of direct-marketing pieces or the role of the salesman. That's why many copywriters have this great definition that copywriting is salesmanship in print. The sales copy is meant to be the substitute for the sales rep and scale your sales.

So you should not write prose or literature. In fact the worst thing to do would be to hire a "good writer" for this phase. The key to successful copywriting is following a psychological SEQUENCE. The same as we do in our sales funnel. The words are way less important than having the right sequence.

The following is a solid base for copywriting and summarize some teachings from the big masters to ensure that your copy will work.

You can split the content in many parts, but here's a seven-step formula:

1. Grab the attention with a headline and sub-headline

2. Describe and expand their urgent problem

3. Give them a unique promise or solution

4. Substantiate this with proof that your solution will work

5. Make an irresistible easy and user-friendly proposal

6. Call to action

7. Recap the benefits and proposal

It is crucial to follow this sequence. You cannot skip or switch the steps. Compare it with dating. There is also a sequence. You don't ask to marry someone after the first chat. Some people argue that long sales letters or long pitches do not work. This is completely wrong. Indeed, many prospects will not read your long sales letter or listen to the whole pitch, but those are the people that are not interested in what you have to tell them.

People don't give you their money without giving you their time. That's why webinars or live seminars are so great to sell to people. The more time they spend with you, the more likely they will buy from you. I have personally seen an online marketer sell a $15,000 dollar management service contract live, to an audience of 250 people where 62 people made a deposit and signed the agreement within 10 minutes. Of course it was not 10 minutes, but the whole 2-day seminar before that contributed to this conversion!

So Let's Dive Deeper into These Seven Steps.

1. *Grab the attention with a Headline and Sub-Headline*

The first step is the one you'll also use for your e-mail. In direct mailing it used to be the key element. We have already elaborated on headlines in the educational phase. This is really key if you want to have the chance to pitch to them. So unless you offer your product or service directly after the former step without an e-mail, you better choose a good one. The headline should already include a promise or provoke your prospect in an intriguing way. Curiosity is great and will work, but it's even better to include some great benefit. This will mostly outperform the former.

It's not easy to come up with great headlines and therefore it's good to brainstorm and make at least twenty proposals and then edit and choose the best ones to test them out! Start with a headline that you think will work, the control headline, and compare it to your new creations. One thing you should not forget, is not to see the headline as a separate piece of the puzzle. It should be integrated into the rest of your pitch. You'll tease your prospects and bring them to your landing page, but if the copy or video is completely out of sync with it, they'll be lost! So if your headline is working, you will be driving them to your landing page where you restate your headline and substantiate this with the sub-headline. If you have used a promise in your headline the sub-headline should briefly explain how your product or service will fulfill this promise. Explain the mechanics. But very briefly! Don't make additional promises; just validate what you stated in the headline.

2. *Describe and expand their Urgent Problem*

Once you have them on your landing page and after your headline and sub-headline intro; here you start identifying their problem. You should speak the same vocabulary. Try to explain their problem or desire better than they can themselves.

An issue of needs and wants. There is a big difference between the two, and we have to understand this in marketing. A need is really to fulfill a basic necessity such as water, air, food, shelter, basic clothing, or transportation. The need for food is an important issue in some developing countries, but in developed countries most people will base their decisions on wants. They have a choice. So if we have the choice, it's rather a desire or want than a need. Your goal in this step is to elaborate on the desires, or problems for which the desire might be a solution. You expand on the desire or make the problem worse. You pile the desires up. Try to make the desire more urgent.

Imagine that you sell alarm systems. You might stress that in the last year the number of burglaries in the neighborhood of your prospect has increased significantly. You can support this with some figures and show the big problems that this has caused. If you sell a language course, you might stress on the benefits that knowing an extra language involve: the better jobs, the independence, etc.

3. *Give them a Unique Promise or Solution*

Now you reveal to them your solution. You should not talk about the features but about the benefits. People want to think that we are rational buyers but the reality is different. Except with professional (B2B) buyers, we normally act on emotional triggers and after we have purchased something we try to rationalize our actions. A car might have the following features: 200 horsepower, 6 airbags, 30 miles per gallon. The benefits are faster driving, protection of family, And saving money.

So we have to build on the benefits of our product or service. But don't mention too many benefits; ideally you should concentrate on one. Every benefit you mention, you should substantiate and prove afterwards. If you fail to do it for one of them, you'll lose your credibility and your pitch will be weak.

The human brain will try to find these weak points in your pitch. The best promise should be one unique benefit; the unique selling proposition. The more unique the better, if the benefit is important enough to fulfill the desires of your audience. This uniqueness should contrast with former solutions or solutions of the competition.

An ideal way to describe this benefit is projecting your prospect in the future by saying: "Imagine."

"Imagine what your life would be with this benefit, with this solution. Compare this with where you are now!"

4. *Substantiate this with Proof that your solution will work*

The proof is the most important piece of your sales pitch. Proof alone can sell. It's the strongest part but also the most difficult to find. This requires work but it's what the prospect is looking for. Without proof the distrust remains.

By now you should have created a lot of trust with your prospect, but he or she will still look for this extra piece of proof in order to really purchase from you. You'll have to substantiate this enough in order to convince the prospect that You or your product is the right solution for him.

Here are some of the best ways to deliver proof:

Demonstrate that something works: If your product allows it, show a recorded video where your product is in action. This is one of the most powerful methods.

Testimonials: Social proof is very powerful and should be used as much as possible. Think of all the ratings, likes, and shares. In chapter I'll reveal how you can use your former customers to help you with it.

Endorsement from an authority: If an authority can be linked to your product this is also very powerful. It's better if it's related to your niche, but even if it isn't, it can work. One of the authorities to use is the prospect's friends! We love to ask trusted people for advice. But with the education and great value you have given your prospect so far, by now you should also be a trusted expert. If you or your product have been featured on popular media or the local newspaper you can borrow this too.

Explain the mechanics of your product or service: The proof can be found in how it is built.

A creative guarantee: like a 120 percent money-back guarantee, try it free. Only pay if you get results.

Specialization: If you are "the specialist of a niche" that will also give a lot of credibility.

Research has proven that specialization builds trust among Web users. In a study conducted by Penn State University, researchers randomly assigned a group of students to buy wine on a website. They were helped to make their choices by recommendation agents. There were 2 groups and the conditions were identical. The only difference was that in the first group the recommendation agent was called a "wine agent" and in the second group it was identified as an "e-agent". The participants trusted the "specialized" technology significantly more than the general one. Apparently this is a general rule and the more specialized layers there are, the more trust is perceived. Research explains this as mental shortcuts that help us decide. We see this constantly in life: a statement made by someone with a white uniform is perceived as more credible, a long essay is seen as a strong essay.

Acknowledge disbelief: Your main goal with your sales copy is to tackle all objections a prospect might have. But sometimes the disbelief is so strong that the best and most credible way is to acknowledge them. Admitting shortcomings of your product is very powerful. But these should not be related to the main benefits of your product. The trick here is to *admit less important benefits* while *reinforcing the main benefits.*

The proof is really crucial. If your proof is strong enough, your copy can be weak. But bear in mind not to focus on too many benefits. Every belief you have to suspend, you'll need proof and have to substantiate.

5. *Make an irresistibly Easy and User-Friendly Proposal*

Now you propose your offer. What you will exchange for the money. It's important that your prospect perceives the offer as something easy to use and user-friendly. Be very clear and explain in detail what you have to offer.

Ideally here you can also add some bonuses. Bonuses do not have to strictly relate to your offer. And tell them the price. It is extremely important to justify the price compared to something they know or commonly buy. Bring it back to a daily cost. Justify the price for the time and money invested, such as courses taken, and more important try to juxtaposition your price: "normally it costs x, but today you'll get it for."

Try to split your service or product into value pieces and show the price of every piece. The sum of the pieces should be a lot more than the price of your offer. Some people argue that people buy on price or you might think that your product is too expensive. But look at it from a weighing-scale perspective. The price you ask should be equal or less than the sum of the desires to buy your product. So instead of lowering your price it would be better to try to increase the desires, sharpen or expand the problem, and show the benefits of your solution. This is value-based pricing!

Another aspect that you should take into account when proposing your offer, is the risk perception. People fear every time they have to open their wallet. Every purchase has a risk associated to it. And not only a financial risk; losing the money in case the product is not meeting their expectations, but also they might feel "stupid" for their "irrational purchase" that they cannot rationally justify afterwards. Often the risk the customer is taking is higher for the customer than the seller. At least that will be the customer's perception. Your objective should be to lower the risk for your prospect as much as possible.

For example, let's say I am going to help to build your website. I could propose to do this for $10,000 to cover the design and development of your new site. Take it or leave it: That's it. Whether or not the design works is your problem. I'll do the work and get my money. But you do not know the end result. In this case, I am placing 100 percent of the risk on you. On the other hand, I could say, "I will do your design, and you will pay only if you get the agreed results afterwards. We'll define this for example as x leads per day." In this case I take the whole risk.

This 100 percent risk approach can be quite successful for two reasons:

a). You don't have to convince your prospect by telling them all the benefits. The proof is built in!

b). People are attached to future money. We prefer to use credit cards and pay afterwards.

This approach where the seller assumes 100 percent of the risk is becoming quite common. In fact most of the app business is based on it. Download it for free and pay only when you really need it or want more. In e-commerce free shipping has also become a standard. According to comScore, free shipping is becoming the norm. Particularly around holiday time, as many as 49 percent of e-commerce businesses offer free shipping. Some companies have even gone a step further: They offer free returns. You can order shoes for example: try them on, and have thirty days to return them if they don't fit; all with free shipping and returns. Even though they had 30–40 percent return rates, this practice had the effect of lowering the barrier of buying shoes online drastically.

Now that you have proposed your offer it's time to get your prospect to take action.

6. *Call to Action*

You should not expect that the prospect will take some action if you don't
ask him. As stupid as it might seem, most missed sales are due to the lack of
a detailed description or being too vague about what your prospect has to do.

Detail the steps: "Push on the button below, fill in your name and credit card
details." You should really be talking to a kid or a dummy, but it's proven that
this is the way to do it. These steps should really be like commands, not
requests.

One point you cannot forget is to add some scarcity into the sales process. You
can do this by means of only having the offer for the next twenty-four hours or
next couple of days. A timer will really help with this. If you don't discount
Your product, you may remove the bonuses if they do not take action. Even
though people know that some of these scarcity techniques are made up, we
still fear losing the opportunity.

You might even stress this by adding: "If you don't take action now you won't
have it." The fear of loss is always bigger than the desire to succeed. But be
advised, that you should be honest with your scarcity, otherwise it will not
work in the long run!

7. *Recap the Benefits and Proposal*

The last part of the sales letter is the PS or PPS (postscript or post postscript).
Here is where you should take the opportunity to recap the whole sales pitch,
but in reverse mode: "What will happen if you do not take action now." The
PPS can be used to recap some single benefits and motivate them to read more
of the sales letter.

In fact most people read sales letter as follows: They read the headline and
sub- headline, then they go and look for the price, and if they are motivated to
buy, go back and read either from top to bottom or in reverse order. But they
mainly read in order to find some inconsistencies.

But the sales letter is not the only communication mode you will use.
Online there are multiple options that you can use to do your pitch:

1. A classic (long) sales letter

2. A Video Sales Letter (VSL): This is cutting your sales letter down in
pieces and animate them with a PowerPoint or keynote presentation. But
only using text. As strange as it might seem, this works really well and is one
of the best ways to present your offer.

3. The classic video: a recorded video with more visual content than just text.

4. A webinar or teleseminar: If your product or service is suited for it, this is
definitely the strongest approach. You will have the attention of your
prospects

during an hour to an hour and a half and have the opportunity to bring them to a state where they really are eager to buy. The conversion rates are typically the highest here. In the off-line world the same happens with live seminars. Definitely, if you add some scarcity or extra bonuses for the quick decision takers.

The first three options will be hosted on a landing page, and the most common way to bring your customers to one of these is via e-mail. You can also do a direct upsell after the former step. For those people buying the "loss leader" product, you can bring them directly to your landing page. This should be the most effective way of taking advantage of the psychology behind "consumer hype."

NOTES

NOTES

Chapter 22: Maximize Sales

Your first sales transaction should not be the end objective of a sales funnel, but only a beginning.

Now the real monetization starts. Many businesses do not exploit this enough. If you want to increase your sales you have three options: Get more customers, get them to buy more frequently, or you try to get more sales out of the transaction.

Getting new customers has been the process addressed so far, and you know that it is a lot more expensive to find a new customer than to sell to an existing one. Having the customer come back is indeed easier. But the best way to increase your business is through maximizing the current sales through upselling, cross-selling, or selling a product bundle. This has never been as easy as it is now online. Most of the up or cross-sell is pure profit, and it's crucial to understand that if you are able to improve this step, you will be able to spend a lot more in acquiring customers and beating the competition.

Upselling or cross selling has often had a bad connotation. People are being sold something extra they do not need, and I don't mean you should do this. No one wants to be "upsold" or pushed to buy more. However this practices should be a positive thing. Think about it. When you buy a suit, perhaps you want a complementary tie? When you buy a car, an extended warranty could be something you value, or imagine you are leaving Disney World; wouldn't you like to buy a souvenir to remember the great moment you had with your kids?

Whatever you sell, there is always some complementary product or service you can offer your customer. And ideally, this should be offered right after the main sale. Remember that you have created trust with your customer. The customer knows you, and now you also have a relationship with him. So why not propose it. Your customer is still in the hype of buying and might want something extra. It's important to understand what you can sell in order to maximize this process.

There are five main types of "extra" sales that can be categorized as follows:

1. Upselling

2. Complementary services or products

3. Continuity

4. Similar products

5. More of the same

Upselling

The first maximizing opportunity is offering some extension of the product. People might have a desired end result in mind, and the product or service that you sold them will help them get that result. However, they might want to have it quicker or with less hassle. With every purchase there is some small or bigger learning curve to use the product or service to its full capacity. Therefore you might offer them services that will shorten this and lead to quicker results. Here you might include services like "made for you"; a tool that will help them implement your course or a course to learn how to use your product or service more in-depth. The upsell might be filling in some missing pieces of your service or product. Typically the upsell will be at least as expensive or more than your core product.

You might even offer some consulting or coaching, but because these services are typically more expensive, it is recommend to leave your newly acquired customers on their own for awhile in order that they use your product or service, and after they are happy with it, have been able to use it, then ask them whether they might want some extra help. Ideally you can organize a webinar to give them extra value; again, going back to the education phase; before asking them the magic words "do you want some help."

Complementary Services or Products

You might also offer your customer some added-value services. These include things like warranty extension. It might also be more or new features of your product. The best example is a car. You want to buy a car. You will be offered electronic options, Internet in the car, better audio, extra warranty, leasing options. You might think your product is not suited for that, but if you reduce some standard features you can create some added values: e.g., more bandwidth if you sell some SaaS, extra or better support, more credits or accounts. The big difference with the upsell is that the extra sales will typically be less than the core sales.

Often the term "upselling" is also used for this in business, e.g., you sell a deluxe room instead of a standard room. In this example the "extra sales" is the difference between the standard room and the deluxe room. Unless you are lucky to sell a presidential suite, the difference is less than the core value (the value of the standard room). You must realize there's a distinction between both. It is the tie when you sell the suit! The reason is that you can try to upsell your bigger ticket item, and if your customer does not buy this, offer these complementary services, which in relation to their purchase might have more success.

A strategy that you might apply here is bundling your core offer with some of these complementary services. For the upsell you can also include them as bonuses. This is a great strategy to increase the value perception, definitely if you are competing with a more commoditized product.

Continuity

This might be one of the most lucrative in the long-term. This might be access to a premium subscription or a closed forum to get more out of your purchase. The power here is that you are selling continuous education. They will now pay you to educate them further and you get a continuous revenue flow for this!

Similar Products

"Customers who bought this also bought that." You know this from Amazon.com. This is typically a "cross-sell." You offer a product that is not directly linked to your core sale but is in the sale "market." Typically you should have similar prices not higher. The idea behind these extra sales is that you are leveraging the "buyer's hype," as you did with the "loss leader" in converting the first-time buyer to customer. You should however offer services or products that are relevant to your market and to your niche. Amazon discovered this a decade ago, and today more than 60 percent of their sales are coming from this process. If you bought or are buying a book on pet training, why not buy another one on how to better feed your pet?

More of The Same

Some products can be sold in quantities, so why not offer this also online. You might not sell two courses to the same person but what about selling "packs" of three body lotions or five pairs of socks. Nearly all consumables can be sold in multiples. Even items that you would not think of, such as books are good candidates. Just propose to buy two or three of the same book to offer to friends. You can also be more creative and offer to buy some items in advance at a lower per item rate but only deliver them when they need it.

Audible.com, a subsidiary of Amazon does a great job on that. You prepay on a yearly basis and every month you get a new credit that you can use to download an audiobook. What you have to do here is put the multiple prices in perspective to the individual price, e.g., they just bought one lotion at $30. If you buy two more you get them for $15 each. You can really decrease your price a lot because you do not have to include your acquisition cost, so every bit on top of the marginal cost of each extra item is pure bottom-line profit!

These are the main possibilities you can offer your customers. Once you have decided what to offer, you need to design a flow of how and when to offer this.

It is crucial to incorporate this phase automatically in your sales funnel, and based on some actions, offer different options. You might even include an upsell in different payments if they do not buy directly. The power here is that you can really personalize your actions. Every customer can be sold differently based on their actions. This was really tricky to do before in the off-line world. Today however customer relationship management software tools make this very easy.

NOTES

NOTES

Chapter 23: Value Customer Relationships

When traveling, you can often become frustrated about the quality of the service and food at many restaurants.

The reason for these bad experiences is that they see the customer as a one-time transaction and believe that 90 percent or more of travelers will not come back. So why bother to give these tourists a Wow effect or decent experience. The quicker they can get rid of the customer the quicker they can place a new one at a table. This practice might have worked in the past but in this new era with all the social media review sites there is a greater transparency and in the end they will suffer. The good will be better and the bad will be worse.

Don't fall into the trap of the typical tourist restaurant where the end goal is only to make more transactions. You don't want to see them only as a once-in-a-lifetime customer rather than using the transaction as the beginning of a lifelong relationship. Leverage the great opportunity that social media offers!

You should consider the Life Time Value of each customer: What is the expected value that an average customer will spend until he stops using your services or products, or until he switches to the competition. We can evaluate the process in which we created our customer as the cost and effort, but now we enter in a return on relationship (ROR). This process should be a lot easier and will get better results, but in many cases, a lot of companies do not take the time to invest in it. You might have heard many times that it is easier to sell to existing customers than it is to acquire new ones.

Today this statement is even more relevant for various reasons:

a). The customer knows you well. If you have done proper work in your sales funnel, the new customer already knows you, he trusts you, and you have had your first relationship with him. You are not a foreigner to him, but he should see you as the "expert." He bought from you. This is indeed a big step. If he likes your services or product; and you should always try to deliver the best you can; it should be easy to have his attention for further communication. You shouldn't spend a lot to get through the noise, and you don't have to do all the initial nurturing.

b). You know the customer. You should have more information about him. At least you have some interaction and transactional data. What did he buy, what did he download, or click on. How long did the process last? Perhaps you have asked some pertinent questions along the way in order to be able to segment him better and try to have a one-on-one communication with him.

Your task now is to maintain the relationship and improve it even further.

The first thing you should do right after the first transaction is to create a Wow effect. It's true that in today's world it is increasingly more difficult to surprise people and give them experiences beyond their expectations. We are used to instant gratification. Next-day delivery is not enough anymore.

We don't have patience. We are easily distracted. We have all the info at our fingertips. Even going on a trip where you haven't been before is not a big novelty anymore. We look at Google Earth, see some videos or have a virtual tour of the hotel where we are going to stay.

So how can we create a Wow effect in this environment? You could even argue that the expectations of our customers are so high that when we deliver our product or service, it can create a negative effect because our customer expected more. But there are still opportunities.

In business environments there is a huge opportunity because most companies stop the sales process right after the transaction. They've received the money so let's go hunting for a new customer. You see it over and over again. It's amazing that when you buy a car, even very expensive cars you have to wait months; sometimes as long as nine months to have your car delivered; you don't hear or see anything until the car is there. No e-mail, no communication at all.

Don't speak about a Wow effect. The day of delivery you might receive a call that you can come and pick up your car. What a waste of opportunity. People really desire their new car, like a kid waiting for his Christmas presents. Why not communicate how the process goes, or what you can do with your new car. Give some pre-education. Show some testimonials. This is so easy and your customers will talk about it. They will share your message with their friends and relatives.

But there is more than this of course. The relationship with your client has various objectives:

a). Extend this in time as long as possible. Have the customer return to you as often as possible.

b). Make him or her an indirect promoter of your business through rating and commenting on his experience.

c). Find the ambassadors that will be direct promoters of your business though referrals and affiliation.

This is the process of relationship with your clients: R^3 (Return - Rate - Refer). Let's take a look at each of these objectives, so that you will have a good understanding what you have to do.

R e t u r n

We have acquired a new customer, so what do we have to do to transform him into a lifetime client and have him return and buy again from you? It's important that you segment your clients as well as you can. Each of them will have different needs and a different time-frame, but you can identify three phases that you should tackle differently:

1. The Delivery Phase
2. The Nursing Phase
3. The After Phase

The length will differ from product to product, but most services and products
will have these cycles.

As mentioned above you have to find ways to impress your customer. Think
what a customer will need or do just before, during, or after the purchase. Who
will he relate with? What will he do? What might he need? And try to leverage
this. That is where you can surprise him and even obtain a Wow effect. Take for
example the purchase of a car, house, or even a new iPhone; something that
increases someone's status. After the purchase or before delivery your client
will definitely want to share it with his friends and relatives.

You can find ways to improve this "delivery" phase. But don't over complicate
it. Even a simple thank-you postcard can create the desired effect. A good place
to find examples is in top hotels. They have to look continuously for new ways
to deliver a dream-come-true experience. If you use this in other businesses you
might get incredible results. This will then be the start of a long relationship with
your client.

After impressing your client you will make sure that he uses your product or
service. This is a basic requisite if you want to have a further business relation
with your client. He bought it with an end goal in mind. You should now help
him to achieve the end goal in the best way possible. To do this I recommend
a "nursing" phase. Like a newborn child, your client needs help to use the
product or service. Tutorials are great for this. But don't think the customer
will find his way easily to your website where you posted the tutorials. You
will have to e-mail him with the appropriate links.

This is like the education phase, but now more technical. Depending on your
product your clients can have different end goals and different agendas. Therefore
segmenting your customer base is crucial. This is another advantage of an online
strategy.

You should know you customer by now; you might have asked him more
detailed questions about his business or personal life. You should have recorded
not only his transaction, but also all the interactions with you. Did he click on
some links? Did he watch certain videos? Did he download some papers? All
this information should have been tagged and should now allow you to do a
proper segmentation job. Even if you have, but certainly if you haven't you can
also ask more information through a survey (surveymonkey.com or
fluidsurveys.com). The extra advantage you get from surveys is that you can
also adapt and improve your product with the input provided. You can have a
real two-way communication. But don't limit the communication to simple e-
mails. You can send also some postcards or set up a Closed Facebook Group for
your clients only, where they can help each other.

Once the nursing phase is over you should stay in contact with your client on a
frequent basis. It's really crucial and most businesses fail here. You know the
saying: "Out of sight, out of mind." I suggest you should really plan this in
advance. Identify the key phases in your product lifecycle and try to send some

communication on those key moments. Also calendar the important events whereyou can contact your customers, like their relatives' birthdays, Christmas, Valentine's, Easter, Thanksgiving, start of school, holidays or New Year. Try to fully automate this process, so that no one will be forgotten.

Often companies rely on CRM tools to place as much information as they can and have of the customer in a tool. CRM has been a big buzzword for more than two decades. Companies have paid millions for tailor-made CRM tools. But rarely have I seen good usage of these tools, except perhaps in managing the sales force, but definitely not for improving the communication with the customer, mainly because most CRM tools know a lot about the customers' DNA, like gender, age, address, marital status in case of an individual or company size, turnover, contacts for a business, and combine this with transactional data. But very few if any information is captured of the interaction of the customer, let alone the online behavior. And it is just this behavioral data that is key to improve your communication and delivering the right message at the right time through the right channel. Focus the communication in delivering great value to increase your perception with the client. This will improve the goodwill and you'll be able to do more business with them.

You can improve the value of your clients by either having repeat purchases of the same product or offering higher-end products, like coaching or consulting. But you can also start selling related products: a line extension. You are now a trusted partner and you can start selling related products in your niche to improve the value you get out of a client.

Another way of increasing the frequency of usage is through continuity programs. This is like having a monthly or yearly fee and having limitless (or more) access to your service. Good examples are fitness centers or carwashes. You offer unlimited access for a monthly fee. People will use it more often and you are securing monthly income. Even if you don't have a service you can create a monthly continuity program, create a course, or give some technical support.

Rating and Commenting

When you are uncertain often you decide based on the opinions of others. Think of the last time you wanted to book a hotel, or chose a restaurant when you were traveling. You go to sites such as www.booking.com or www.tripadvisor.com and look at the ratings or comments of others. Also when you buy something, don't you look at the comments on Amazon? Even when there are no ratings or comments online, we ask our friends on Facebook, or look at some forums. We are so used to it. It's like a They (the seller) versus Us (the buyer). And we believe "the weakest" site; the buyer's opinion.
Social proof is so important today and people love to comment, like, or share stuff I cannot stress enough how important these rankings are for your online strategy. Whether you try to attract, convert, educate, or want to sell, social proof is a key element. And now that you have a created a relationship and trust, you have to leverage this! And if you can get testimonials from your clients it's even better

So, what can you do to get this higher ranking? Enhance and motivate people to rate or comment on your product or service. You have to ask it. Build an automatic e-mail to ask for comments, how they rate your service or product and ask about their experience. Make it easy for them, but beware that people are seven to ten times more likely to leave a bad review than a positive one. The negatives will come automatically but the positives you have to stimulate.

Be sure that you only ask proactively people that have used your product or service; those that really have experienced it. In an app for instance you can build this in and start asking only those people that have used your app at least five times to rate your app. The probability of them ranking your app will be higher. Asking people is also a way of keeping in touch with your customers.

Even so, your clients will give some negative comments. These comments should allow you to improve your product. It's crucial to have a two-way conversation and answer these comments. Never blame a customer or get into a discussion even if you don't think he is right or didn't use your service or product in a proper way. Acknowledge his comment, apologize, and try to give value and do this publicly!

Beware about trying to beat the system by placing false reviews. Google has penalized sites for doing this. Companies trying to play with algorithms have become a big problem. Sellers can go to a site such as www.fiverr.com and have people download their app in return for a five-star rating. With higher-priced services, such as a hotel, the person needs to have actually stayed there to write a review. But, with lower-ticket items, sellers can ask people to buy it and rate it. So, a lot of cheating goes on. Just make sure that they are the real thing. After someone makes a purchase, motivate that person to write a review.

Referrals and Affiliation

The ultimate desire for a company is that your product or service spreads virally. Unfortunately this is the case only in rare occasions. Sometimes you'll hear about marketers wanting to design a strategy to make the product viral. Personally I think this is like hoping that it rains in the desert during summer. If you understand some of the basics of why some things go viral and others do not, you can increase the likelihood that you'll get some free advertising.

One of the key ingredients is social currency. To get a better understanding look at young children. What do they do after drawing a picture? They all do the same thing and show it to their parents. This sharing continues through our life. We want to show the car, the house, and the clothes we bought. We want to share our holidays, our achievements. They say that people who climb Mount Everest feel more happiness in sharing it afterwards in base camp than the moment they reached the top.

But it's not only about purchases, experiences, but also about our opinions and what we like. This is also the main reason that social media has grown so quickly. It created the perfect platform to share even more. But we don't share everything.

We prefer to share things that we like or things that may make us look good. Every "share" is like a social currency. We want to be associated with what we share. This can even lead to people who are not real experts on a topic but curate information and share the best things about it to be seen as experts. But it also means that people will normally be selective in sharing, because of this social currency. And you should therefore, only motivate your clients that are really raving fans of your product. They have to feel associated.

An often question asked, is if it would be a good idea to do a member-get-member action (MGM). Personally I don't think it is a good idea. You cannot buy referrals. People will do it intrinsically. Not because they want to help you or be paid, but because they want to do it for themselves.

Let me give you an example. Imagine you ask me for a good restaurant in a given city, and I give you the name of say, Le Chalet de la Forêt. Even if you go there and you liked the food, but afterwards hear that I'm getting paid for every person I send to the restaurant, my credibility or social status will decrease in your eyes.

Just understand, that when you select a target you should get very focused and narrow down your niche. The same is true for finding the clients or partners that will bring you leads. Those are your good customers that know and trust, but above all, like or love your product or service and have a good following on social media.

Most referrals happen when we are in a conversation with someone about a topic and relate our own experience with it. Let's say you are talking about lower back pain with your friend and remember you had a great experience with a chiropractor. You directly recommend it to him. Notice that this recommendation s free, (1) you don't get compensated for it, (2) you have used his services and (3) had a great experience with him. Another example is if a headhunter asks you if you know a good candidate for a certain job. Most likely you'll only pass him candidates that you have worked with or know very well and had a great experience with. You don't want to lower your "social status".

If we translate this into our business, we have to identify clients that will recommend by using two main parameters: They have to be on one hand, happy clients that believe in your product and on the other hand, influencers with a good network.

They have to be confident clients that believe in your product, which means that they have bought it, used it, and got their desired end result. And you should be the reference for them in that product or service category. An effective way to segment these is through the RFM method. Where R stands for Recency, F stands for Frequency, and M stands for Monetary Value.

We identify the most recent purchasers that have bought often, with the highest total purchase value. In most businesses, twenty percent of the customers make up eighty percent of the business. If you dig deeper: twenty percent of those twenty percent, or four percent, make up 64% of total business. This is true in most industries. Your task is now to nurture them and build a splendid relationship. Hence the constant communication!

Besides being a good client and friend. you should also find out if they have a good following on social media; do they have many friends on Facebook? Are they actively posting and sharing? Do they have a blog? You should identify them. This parameter is even more important than the first. Many tools exist today that will help you identifying these influencers so that you can transform them into your marketing ambassadors.

Once you have identified your fans, the objective should be to motivate them to bring you leads. And remember, they will not do this to do you a favor, except perhaps if they are relatives or good friends. They will do it because they want to raise their status with their friends. How do you motivate them without paying for this?

Referrals happen in a conversation about a topic:

1. Your fan should notice that the topic is related to your service or product.
2. They should think of you as the reference.
3. They should introduce you.

The best way to increase the likelihood that these three steps happen, is to continuously communicate with your clients and give extra value to improve your relationship and expert status (they think of you as the reference). Trigger their minds with questions such as, "If you know someone who might be interested in," so that they actually will look for situations where they can help people (they have to notice that the conversation is about that topic). And finally give them tools to increase the likelihood of introducing you. These can be discounts, special VIP treatment, and extra bonuses, not for them but to give to their friends so they raise their social status!

Besides the free referral model, there is indeed a paid one that you should not neglect: affiliate or JV partners. But this is totally different and here you really pay people a commission to sell your products. But they'll do it as professionals. They will act as an external sales and marketing division and have to inform their customers that they get compensated for every sale. It is crucial to recruit these partners. They will help you gain the speed that is needed to grow your business before someone else copies it, and overtakes you.

online. It has become part of our life. The average number of daily likes on Facebook alone are in the billions! Look at the success of rating sites like www.yelp.com that get over 100 million visitors per day! It shouldn't be a surprise that the big companies use the ratings and number of comments as a key parameter for their ranking algorithms: Google for the search results, Amazon to rank the products; Facebook to show post and Apple to rank the Apps.

NOTES

NOTES

<u>NOTES</u>

Chapter 24: Automate Your Business

Many businesses often face plateaus of growth.

This growth usually depends on available resources and time. These resources can be spent either to operate or to contact more customers. The business then has to decide to employ more people or more sales reps with the risk that they might not grow the bottom line. In the past, one solution was to spend more on below the line marketing like direct mailings. It was indeed a way to scale in a cheaper way. Then came the Internet and now online marketing is even cheaper. Online marketing is not only setting up a website or mass mailing to all of your prospects, there is a lot more. You should now have a fair understanding of what to do.

The complexity however is that each prospect has a different nurturing need and different time frame. And most of the follow up we wish to do often, keeps staying on the wish list. There needs to be an automated process behind it. A system that follows up with each customer or prospect based on his or her needs and at the desired speed. A system that not only allows doing this automatically without increasing the sales force or marketing department but also helps the sales reps to be more efficient and effective by flagging the "hot leads" that are already educated and prepared for a visit. In some cases it even allows to completely bypass physical sales reps and automate the entire funnel from finding the prospects converting him, upselling him and keeping him in a systematic way.

Marketing Automation is the integration of all the bits and pieces that might exist in the sales and marketing department, into one holistic automated software. It allows looking at a list of potential customers and prioritizing them based on the likelihood to buy. The great mistake that many companies make is that they concentrate all efforts on choosing technology, and then automate their existing process. But this is not the way you should automate your business.

Automation also does not end once someone becomes a customer. Often the real value creation comes from the retention of your clients and improving that customer relationship over time. This means more than sending a monthly newsletter, but personalized content based on their behavior, just like a real friend relationship. We are not used to automatic and instant communication. We have been used to making sales happen. You called the prospects or visited more customers when you needed more sales. The automation will replace the individual events and make it evergreen. We will only broadcast to a segment when it's relevant information for all of them. Mostly this will happen when the information is linked to a certain period of the year. For example you might want to do a back to school promotion or a Mother's Day communication.

Once you have designed the roadmap, you need to feed it with content. This is often the biggest challenge. So much content is being produced every day that prospects and customers are filtering all this information and only read the information that really interests them.

Content where we brag about how good we are or in which we try to only sell stuff in it will definitely not pass the gateway.

So we have to do a very good job in giving the customer or prospect what he wants; answering his main problems and helping him in his buying process. This is a new way of thinking about Marketing, where content is king. The content should not be created from scratch and most companies already have a lot of content that just needs to be repurposed or repackaged. You can use speeches, videos, photos, and even former newsletters. And if you still need more, just curate existing topics. Good content is perhaps the most important piece and something that you cannot really automate. It's the fuel to make the whole machine work.

As an advocate for WordPress as an easily managed online platform, there are great plugins that automate website posts to your social media accounts, as well as, automating management of contacts, sales and on-site website advertising.

However, the most used plugins, are the ones that automate website posting of content, from either scheduled posts, or automatically pulling content from other sites such as YouTube and posting that content to your own site.

Here's a Great Resource for Paid WordPress plugins:

https://ThemeForest.net/category/wordpress

If you put all the pieces together: a clear roadmap with great content along the way integrated in a marketing automation tool you will see spectacular results with less resources. On top of that it will give you the extra insights and metrics in order to improve even further your machine.

<u>NOTES</u>

Part VI: Talk is Not Cheap

In every business, there's the additional cost of advertising... and it is no different if we want to Build a New Black Wall Street.

Take for example, #BlackLivesMatter. All of those signs and banners were not free, and because of that promotional material, #BlackLivesMatter got the attention of the public at large, not just within the black community.

There are over 900 million facebook users, 350 million Americans, 40 million African Americans, and an average community has a population of 30,000 people. To reach even a small percentage of these people, your business plan must include advertising costs.

And at the end of the day... Black Power Groups talk the talk, but they're not starting any legitimate businesses to make money for creating job opportunities for our unemployed youth. This must Change!

Chapter 25: Social Media

To get someone's attention today, all you need is understanding of your target niche audience and attract them with value.

To understand your target audience very well, you have to narrow your niche, know what these people want, where you can find them, and be laser-focused when contacting them, rather than using broad and expensive media.

By narrowing down your niche, you can better understand these people and know where they hang out, what they read, and what they actively search for! It's not about shouting loud through big media campaigns or by sending out hard-sell advertisements. Instead, it is being clever and teasing your niche with great value in the places where you can find them.

You don't have to spend thousands of dollars and kill an ant with an atomic bomb!

You have to know how to leverage the online superhighways. Take Google, for instance. What are all the keywords that people search for in Google? You have to analyze people's searching patterns and what they specifically are looking for, and offer value and a solution for free to those searchers. Another way might be by creating a Kindle book on Amazon, or via an app on iTunes, or being in front of them in Facebook's News Feed.

These are the highways where you can cherry-pick the people in your niche. It will cost you some money, but nothing compared to the mass media budgets and will quickly bring positive returns. The key then is to track and improve your campaigns and follow up with your lead.

Using these highways is as if you have an off-line shop, deciding whether to put your store in a commercial mall that is well advertised and gets thousands of customers every day or in a small town where you will have to slowly grow the business until people come to you.

You have to really understand the way to target people on those highways. Google is like the Yellow Pages of the past. When consumers were looking for something in particular, they would use this big yellow book and search for a solution. Being listed was crucial for any business. Today a listing in the phone book has been replaced by Google searches. These searches might only represent

5 or 10 percent of the total potential customers. But the ones that are searching on Google are the best prospects because they are already proactively looking for a solution that you are offering.

Facebook, on the other hand, is more like the off-line coffee shop where people are sitting around and talking to one another. If your product can be found in the conversations going on in the coffee shop, you might consider it an ideal place to interrupt anyone interested in your topic.

People read Facebook as a personalized newspaper today. And for you as an advertiser, this is one of the best places to where you can buy laser-focused cheap traffic, certainly if your product is related to hobbies, music, media, or fashion or entertainment.

Chapter 26: Open The Door to Your Customers

So, how do you attract your potential customers in a world of clutter and so much distraction?

In Internet marketing terms we need to create traffic. For this, we will not use the classic "branding" methods or "broadcasting," that has been so misused by corporate companies. Instead we'll use direct-response marketing (DRM).

DRM evokes an immediate response and entices individuals to act upon our ads or teasers. DRM has immediate cause-and-effect results that you can track. You can test, optimize, and scale. You set up a sales funnel, and always split test with two options. When you have enough statistically significant data, you pick the best one and create a new piece that you split test against the "winner." This way you'll always improve your results!

So let's go back to creating a way through the clutter. Some studies say that we are exposed to some five thousand ads each day, of which we remember nearly none. So how will you win the battle and get someone's attention?

What you have to do is look at advertisements from another point of view. You know by now what the questions are in your prospect's mind. You have to give them a piece of the answer. It has to be tailor-made to their needs and related to the outcome you are going to sell him in a later stage.

You need to make "educational ads." Today we call them native ads. What this means is that the ads are not seen as sales pitches, but as valuable information. In the newspaper and magazine worlds this has been called an infomercial. You want to show your prospects only "the cheese" and not the "whiskers." Therefore it is important that you don't stuff your ads with logos or promises that seem unrealistic. No branded ads or logos that trigger filters. Instead, the buyers are looking for "cheese," or information that can be considered of value. In the off-line world it is very similar with direct mailings. If the envelope looks like a commercial letter, it will go in the pile for the trash can.

The ad should be something they are really interested in, something really compelling. It's compelling, because you cannot, not pay attention. For example when you're driving by an car accident, and all the people in front of you are slowing down and people are screaming, "Idiots! Morons!" They have to gawk at the car accident, to see if anyone's hurt, dead, maimed, whatever. And it's kind of a morbid curiosity, and people get angry because there's a big, huge line. Then, the moment you drive by it, you slow down, and you become one of those same people that you're complaining about!

The big mistake that businesses often make is they think that compelling prospects to call you means getting your name out there, getting people to know who your business is. And that's not it at all. The very best thing you can do is put your own ego aside and focus only on what your prospects really want, without even any mention of you or your business up front. Once you understand your target market, you're not going to try and convince them to do something; you're going to get their attention by showing them how to do something that's already on their mind. They're already thinking about how to do this. This is not new science, however in this world of clutter and overly distracted people and online, where everything is anonymous, it's only more relevant than it was in the past.

With this basic principle in mind, let's look at the various channels that you can use and how to use them.

Consider this marketing myth, you don't have to build traffic from scratch. This is one of the main errors people make. They want to build their traffic completely themselves. This takes lots of effort and is time-consuming. It's like wanting to build your own railway infrastructure while high-speed trains pass by. This infrastructure is already is there for you.

The five main high-speed online channels are Google, Amazon, iTunes, YouTube, and Facebook. Of course there are other smaller ones out there, but let's concentrate on the big five.

What you now have to do is understand "how to use them properly."

It's important to view traffic from the "prospect's point of view," and understand the prospect's mindset when he is consuming information through the channel.

When you have a burning problem you will look for a solution as soon as possible. In the past you might have used the Yellow Pages, but today most likely you'll type your search into Google. This is a completely different way of consuming information, than if you are reading some posts on Facebook.

When you are querying Google you are "proactively" looking for something at that exact moment, and for an advertiser, the task is to compel that person more than the others. Your prospect is looking for a solution. Compare that with getting the attention of someone reading something that has nothing to do with your service or offer. In the second case you have to disrupt the train of thought and be very clever to get their attention. Here you are targeting a potential prospect that is thinking or doing something else!

Here are five main categories to help choose and better understand the different types of traffic:

1) Search:•Here the prospect is actively looking for something matching "your" solution.

2) Interrupt:•Here the prospect is not looking for your solution, but you've targeted the ones that might be interested and you are trying to interrupt them with your message.

3) Informational:•The prospect is reading related information to your offer. This can be in online press releases or specialized press.

4) Direct Contact:•Here you are directly contacting your prospects, they might be interested or not at this stage.

5) Indirect Contact: Partners and affiliates: A third party that already has interaction with them is contacting your ideal prospects.

The order in which these are listed is important. Because it is a guideline on how you should progress. Search is a smaller group, but definitely the most sophisticated or proactive prospects, and they are more likely to convert into buyers. They are already looking for a solution. They represent only a fraction of the total addressable market. The "fishing pond" of prospects is a lot bigger. Most of them "might be interested" but do not have an urgent need yet to buy your product. They also might have a longer decision-making process. Therefore it's important to first learn how to attract and convert the proactive prospects before starting with the others. We are interrupting them in a state that might not be very optimal.

The last category, the partners, is often forgotten but of extreme importance. It should definitely be leveraged only when you have tested and optimized the other channels. Your whole sales funnel should be well in place, so that you can show your partners some results before they start contacting their customers. That will increase the likelihood that they actively promote your products or services.

Let's take an in depth look at these various traffic modes.

1. Search

When someone types a keyword in Google, it means that person is actively looking for an answer to a question. Search terms can be more or less detailed. You can just look for a general term, such as "water," or be more specific, such as "bottle of water" or even more exact such as, "where can I buy a bottle of water?" Today, more and more people are putting complete questions into the search engine. A general word can be anything from "shortage of water" to "purified water." For example, "I want to buy a bottle of water. Where can I find it?" is a very long search and only a few people will ask such a long question. Yet this person is much better qualified, because he or she is looking for something specific. The same is true for specific brands: When people put in more detail for search terms, they are already thinking about specific needs. This is very important to understand, because you will have to design your ad copy and landing page—the page they will land on after clicking on your ad—accordingly.

Search can be divided into two main categories: paid search and free or organic, search. It's important to clarify some terminology. SEA: Search Engine Advertising, is the function of paying for certain keywords and being ranked for those in the "paid section" of the search results and SEO: Search Engine Optimization, is a means of improving your organic search ranking.

A lot of myths exist about organic search and SEO. Most of the searches happen on Google. You type a keyword and get a search result. The results that are not located on the top or on the right side of the page are the highest organic search results. Google ranks these results based on a "secret" algorithm, which is changed quite often and always remains a black box. Google does this to counter those who know how to manipulate these results. This has happened a lot in the past. Some tried to spin content with a lot of keywords to rank artificially higher. If Google allowed this, the search results would not be optimal and people might leave Google for other search engines. That's why Google tries to deliver the best result it can, both on the free (organic) as on the paid results for any given query. In the last few years Google has made major changes in its search algorithm to penalize these websites that were trying to game the rankings.

The first update was Panda, which looked at a whole website for quality, statistics elements, and user experience. The second was the Penguin update: Google looked at all those cheating links that were received through content farms•and linking to sites. Now, Google started giving negative points for this. All links from these pirate sites decreased a website's total score and ranking on keyword results.

Take a look at the two types of traffic building techniques through search: paid and organic

a). Paid

The concept of paid search or SEA is simple: it's a bidding system where you pay to get your ad in the search results for a certain keyword and only pay when someone clicks on your ad. Based on your daily budget your ad will appear till the budget is depleted. The system is a little bit more complex than just the highest bidder gets the best rankings. It's based on a Google algorithm. When someone clicks on your ad you pay, also known as PPC, (pay per click). Your CPC (cost per click) will again depend on Google's algorithm. A good ratio is a 2 percent CTR (click-through rate) on your ads. This means that for every fifty times your ad is shown someone clicks on your ad.

Another system, that is less used is CPM (cost per mile). Here Google charges you an amount that you bid to show your ad a thousand times. I would not recommend starting with this. This can be used to lower your costs once you have a very high CTR.

So how does the Google algorithm work? To understand this, look at the example below. Four advertisers are bidding on the same keyword. Let's say it's "internet marketing." Look at the table below to see the various bids for each advertiser. So Advertiser 1 bids $10, Advertiser 2 bids $6, Advertiser 3 bids $4, and Advertiser 4 bids $2. Intuitively you should think that Advertiser 1 will always show up on the first place because they are bidding the most.

This however is NOT how the system works. Google has created a Quality Score in order to improve the relevance and optimize its ad income.

Imagine that Advertiser 1, who bids $10 gets only 1 percent clicks, and Advertiser 2, who bids $6, gets 8 percent clicks when the ad is shown; Google will make $10 for Advertiser 1 and $48 for Advertiser 2 on every 100 times they are shown. Therefore Google will rank Advertiser 2 higher than Advertiser 1, even if Advertiser 1 is bidding more. Google has all interest to place Advertiser 2 above Advertiser 1 in the search results. Google will not only use the CTR to rank the different advertisers, but also includes some relevancy parameters in its algorithm. The main parameter that will be included with the bid price is called the Quality Score. Google will multiply the Quality Score and get an Ad Rank that will define the final position. (Ad Rank = max bid * Quality Score) .

You see that for this example even if Advertiser 1 is bidding the most; five times what Advertiser 4 is bidding, his ads might not even appear.

Important to note is that often the actual cost per click and the max bid per click will not be the same. You may in fact bid $6 but usually in the end pay less. Google will discount your CPC down just to appear above your competitor with $0.01 more. The actual formula to determine this is: actual CPC = Ad Rank to Beat / (your quality score +$0.01)

For Advertiser 2 this is: 20 / (8 + 0.01) = $2.5

For Advertiser 3 this is: 10 / (3 + 0.01) = $3.3

In our example you see that Advertiser 2 is paying less than Advertiser 3 and has 2 positions higher even though he is bidding $6 compared to $4 for Advertiser 3.

It might seem a bit complicated, but the point stressed here, is the importance of the Quality Score, hence the CTR. Because improving your CTR you'll end up paying less, while getting more clicks!

How do you achieve this?

Two key factors are crucial: 1) Thorough keyword analysis. 2) Compelling ad copy based on the keywords

Many companies; even SEO managers limit themselves to too few keywords, mostly "broad" terms. They should also focus on phrase match and exact match as explained here below:

Broad match:

Broad match means anytime someone types in a keyword phrase that includes that keyword. If your keyword is more than one word, it will be independent of the other. For example, if you bid for the keyword: dog training, you will always be bidding whenever someone uses a phrase that includes both words "dog" and "training" no matter how it is used. If someone keys in "best training for a dog" you will be bidding for that phrase.

Phrase match:

With phrase match, you will be bidding whenever some types in a keyword phrase that contains all your keywords, but they'll have to be in the right order. In our example "dog training," the keyword phrase has to include dog training in that order and not separated. So it would not work for: "best training for a dog" but it would work for "best dog training."

Exact match:

Exact match is when your keywords match exactly with the keyword phrase being searched. In our example only when [dog training] is typed in exactly will your ad show up. Finally you also have to define the words you absolutely want to exclude. For example, if you are giving a course on dog training, you may want to exclude the searches for "free courses". Therefore you should exclude the word "free" from all the searches. You need to understand there are many keywords and it is suggested that most companies come up with a thousand keywords! Start with the ones that you think are really linked to your product or service and exclude the ones that are not.

After you have identified a hundred or more good keywords the next part is to create compelling ad copy that will improve your CTR. Your Ad copy will directly impact your click rate and conversion. Best advice is to arrange similar keywords into ad groups. Ad groups will group all the keywords that will have the same ad copy. Now you can test different copy on all those keywords in the ad group.

Testing is all-too-important. The best framework for ads is a headline followed by three lines, with the last line being your URL. The headline must have your keyword, because it relates to the person's search. The second line should always give some benefit, and the third line should give some feature or offer that motivates people to click on the link. This is the first step toward conversion.

What do you do when you have thousands of keywords with different copy? One method is the "peel-and-stick." You have all those keywords separated into ad groups. When one keyword is doing very well in an ad group, take that keyword from that ad and create a new ad group with this word in the headline. Typically what you will see is that your click-through rate on this newly created ad will increase

Two last notes on SEA:

Your results might not be optimal when you start and this might be because Google puts up artificial barriers for new advertisers. But if you do your work properly you'll see the benefits.

And don't be obsessed with your ranking. It's not always the best to have the number one position. You might get the most clicks, including many impulse clicks with low conversion.

b). Organic Search

Once you have your initial paid search results and know which keywords are the most valuable and convert into paying customers you can selectively choose keywords to optimize organically.

Sometimes it is possible that some keywords are so expensive due to the high competition and that you are not getting a positive return on investment (ROI) out of them; so then, you'll have to invest in getting the intelligence to optimize your funnel and then start concentrating on SEO traffic to make this a winner.

How does Google work and what can you do to get some positive results for SEO?

The Google algorithm is a black box that changes continuously and it might seem mysterious how Google ranks one or another webpage. However it can be boiled down to two parameters that are:

1). On-site optimization: everything you can do on your site

2). Off-site optimization: all activities outside your site

One site is making sure that your website is properly designed and that it is easy for search engines to find and index you, making proper use of the most important keywords; the ones your customers are using when searching for your product or service.

Use the Google Webmaster Tools to make sure that your pages are indexed: www.google.com/webmasters/tools. The hard truth however is that having a search engine friendly site will not increase your rankings, it will only avoid being degraded.

Make sure your content is well designed around your major keywords. These will tell the search engines what your site is about. You should have found these keywords during your SEA activities. These keywords should appear in your titles, subtitles, and content.

But the single most effective approach is off-site optimization: the links that your website receives from other sites. But not all links are equal. Google rates those links based on the importance of the other sites "page rank." You can see it as a voting system where the higher the ranking of the page that links into your website, the more "points" or "link juice" you receive. This ranking is known as PageRank (PR). This goes from 0 to 10. These rankings change, but normally PR 10 (example, Google itself or usa.gov) is for only a dozen sites and PR 9 (example, W3.org, youtube.com, bbc.com) around 144 sites. The higher the PR of an inbound link the more it will count for Google.

The link itself is not the only important piece; the "visible keyword" in the link that is called the "anchor text" is of crucial importance. This is what Google will take into account. If you have a site about salmon fishing it is not enough that some other websites link into you, you need them to have your "keyword", here "salmon fishing" in the link. Now Google will give you points on that specific keyword, because it now knows that your page is specifically about salmon fishing. The best way to improve these rankings is deciding what keywords you want to rank for. Then you start creating content around these topics. You can do this yourself or be a content curator, meaning that you act like a museum: You don't have to be the painter, but you bring all nice paintings under one roof, or on a page. It's important but time-consuming work, that in the long run will give results.

Do not improve your SEO only for Google; the second biggest search engine, YouTube is easier to use for ranking.

Even if the number of videos produced and posted on YouTube every day is skyrocketing, comparatively they are still very small compared to all other content produced, and the interesting part is that it is still possible; depending on your keywords, to rank quickly in the top positions for YouTube. On top of that is a side benefit to it. Google owns YouTube and loves videos if your "topic" is appropriate for it. Therefore you'll often see a number of videos in its top ten search results. For example, if you type in "how to fish salmon" a number of the top ten results are videos. The good, or bad thing, is that YouTube still cannot identify what your video is about, so you'll have to tell them. This is done in your title, tag's description. Place as many keywords as you can, but do some research before!

Bear in mind SEO takes time and that you'll not see results quickly. You cannot create content and build links hoping that in six months you will rank high on the search for keywords. I'm not saying that you shouldn't work on this, but it is time-consuming; meaning it will also cost money, and you are not sure how Google might update its algorithm. However, in the education phase of a sales funnel, you'll have to create content, so why not use it for SEO purposes! Try to balance organic traffic with SEA. Paid traffic will give you the speed!

c). The other "search engines"

Marketers often forget that there are other search engines that they can use in addition to Google. And I don't mean Bing or Yahoo! These you can target from your AdWords account. There are other platforms where millions of people are searching every day. Heard of the App Store of Apple, Google Play, or Amazon?

More than five hundred million people are registered, most with their credit cards on the App Store and more than two hundred million are buying on Amazon! Not bad if you can tap into those channels?

Do you know that anyone can sell products on Amazon? Amazon has created an amazing platform that not only allows you to market your product but even will collect the money and even has logistic services, to do the picking, and shipping to your customer.

Same with the App Store or Google Play. Make an app and sell it on their platform. I've personally built a living selling apps on the App Store.

But there are other ways to use these engines and leverage their traffic power:On Amazon you can write an e-book for Kindle on your topic (keyword). When people are looking for your keyword you are in the ranking. You can either sell at a low price or give your book away and use it as a platform. Inside your e-book you can now send the readers to your website and enter your sales funnel! Great lead generation!

With the App Store you can do the same with a free app. Then motivate your users to register for some extra tools or information. You get the users' e-mail and have them entering your sales funnel!

The advantage of apps is that you can even do push notification, which is the ability to communicate without knowing their e-mail. If the user allows you to send messages out of your app; you can then send them messages based on some behavior, on some specific moments or you can broadcast some messages, just as if you would send an email.

Podcasting is another easy way to get on the search engines. You can put a podcast inside iTunes, so people can find you with the right keyword and this can be a source of your growing traffic. The same thing happens with Apple Newsstand. You can create a free magazine that can be the first platform for your sales funnel. These are all great opportunities that very few companies use.

Search engines are the best way to start your traffic and set up your sales funnel, but search will only give you a fraction of the potential customers: only those that are already proactively looking for a solution to their problem. To tap into the bigger pond of those that are not actively searching you have to interrupt them.

2. Interrupt

Search traffic is a fantastic way to get new prospects into your sales funnel. People are searching for a solution and you can put yourself in front of them with your solution. On top of that, it is very constant. If you design it well, you guarantee a continuous stable flow of traffic. That's why it's the best traffic you can start with. The caveat with Search traffic is that it is limited. If only 50 people are searching for your keyword per day, your maximal potential is 50 new prospects a day, assuming they all are new.

Generally speaking, search only accounts for between 5 and 30 percent of the total potential. So how can you leverage and tap into those people that are not actively searching but may be interested. You'll have to get their attention! Be aware that this is more difficult, because you are going to disrupt their train of thought and really interrupt them. Interrupting is a big word. There are different levels of interruption.

The likelihood of getting people's attention will increase if: a) your prospect is open for some interruption, and b) if the teaser you use is compelling.

It is crucial to acknowledge this. So when are people "relaxed" and open to new suggestions? In the off-line world when people are rushing to arrive on time at their work your chances are very small. Think of the ads you remember after your last journey. But if you are at the movies, watching television or reading your newspaper at a Starbucks your state of thoughts is completely different, and you will more likely be in a relaxed state and open for novelty, if the interruption is appealing or something that interests you.

In the online world there is a kind of Starbucks where people are "hanging out," passing their time when bored: Facebook. And what about YouTube: the new television. These places are ideal to interrupt because people are in a relaxed state of mind when they are consuming content. In fact they are looking for interesting stuff. Facebook is their newspaper and YouTube is their television on demand.

The interrupted people might not be proactively searching for your solution, but it's up to you to choose whom to interrupt. You can and should target them based on their interests and sociodemographics, as well as, on topics they are looking for. Blogs are the new specialized magazines, so if your topic is related to the blog's topic, chances are they might be interested. What about someone reading a blog on black-and-white photography, wouldn't they likely be interested in the new gear that Nikon or Canon is launching?

The first rule is to target the right people and the second rule is that you have to attract your prospects in a compelling way!

In this "new" connected world of easy distraction, people are very difficult to attract because of their "ads" filters. Some innate filters will try to block everything that seems like an ad. This is even more important than with AdWords, but so many companies overlook this. So, to catch a mouse, we use cheese!

In a disruptive advertising model there are three channels:

1). Social media
2). Blogs and specialized websites
3). Apps

SOCIAL MEDIA:

Social media is the best of the three because of the reach and the targeting possibilities. The objective is definitely "not" to get shares or likes, these will be byproducts. The objective is to "find" the right people and compel them to get "out" of the social media context and enter your landing page and your sales funnel. You put $1 into advertising and get a multiple out of it! Likes and tweets have no real monetary value, your sales funnel does!

You have various options to choose from in social media but concentrate on Facebook and YouTube, and if your market is B2B, LinkedIn might also be a good option. Facebook has more than 1.3 billion users and 1 billion connecting on their mobiles. Nearly 2/3rds of the online population is on Facebook. In developed countries you might even say that 75 percent is on Facebook.

Here some other interesting figures about Facebook:

* 76 percent of the total user base looks at Facebook once a day
* Average time per visit is twenty minutes.
* Average daily likes are 4.5 billion: This is four times a day per person.
* 50 million fan book pages.

Advertising on Facebook has even become better. In the past you could only advertise on the right side of Facebook News Feeds. But the click through was relatively low, less than 1 percent and sometimes closer to 0.1 percent. Then they allowed you to be placed inside the news feeds, like "infomercials" in between all the posts of your "trusted" friends. This is a subliminal way to advertise, if your ad is not perceived as an ad but as content, hence the native ad name. Now, you are enticing readers with cheese. The rate on these News Feeds is twenty to forty times higher than the traditional ads on the right-hand side. This is amazing, especially since you can laser target.

Some parameters you can use to target your niche include:

a) Country, age range, and gender of the target audience
b) Precise interest categories
c) People with children of different ages.
d) People on different types of devices, such as only those using Android or Apple's iOS.[28]
e) Users who are already connected to your friends
f) Those who are interested in a certain page(s) or those who are fans of your competitors. This is really huge and can be a treasure.
g) By education, language, relationship status, and workplace

But there is even more power if you use Facebook's own "Power Editor" tool. Here you can even create custom audiences. You can upload a list of prospects; these can be a list that you bought, your own lost customers, or old prospects. If Facebook matches the e-mails or phone numbers, you can target them with your ads! This can even be used as another way of communicating with your customers. Besides sending them e-mails, you can now also appear in the news feeds of your customers.

But there is even more gold inside Facebook. You can now also create an audience with similar profiles to your uploaded list:

1. Upload your customers into the Power Editor.

2. Facebook looks for matching phone numbers or e-mails and creates a customer audience.

3. You now ask to create an "alike" audience.

Besides getting prospects into your sales funnel, there are other additional benefits with these ads, FaceBook calls them promoted News Feeds. Some people will also "like" or "share" your post and this will be visible on their friends' pages as trusted news.

The cost per clicks will depend on the country you are targeting and can be very different. In developing countries, South America and some Asian countries, or the Middle East the cost per click may be as low as two cents per click. Europe will vary between ten going to fifty cents. Scandinavian countries are relatively expensive. Same for the United States, United Kingdom, and Australia, where clicks may be between $0.50 and over $1. You will have to set up your sales funnel to test and see what you can afford. Remember the better you can monetize your prospects afterwards, the more you can spend on advertising and outspend the competition.

The second form of media buying is through an intermediate player. There are many out there, but the easiest to start with is the GDN (Google Display Network).

Google has created a network of thousands of websites where you can place your ads. You can set this up very easily on your AdWords account.

The GDN also works on a bidding mechanism. Simplified, it works as follows: You bid a certain amount per click. Google takes the available ad spaces for a certain keyword, topic or interest, which goes to the highest bidder first and places that ad till the daily budget is depleted. Then it goes to the next highest bidder. Here too there are many options to rotate your ads, to show them only on certain times of the day or days of the week.

More important is the targeting of your ads. This is slightly different and essential to understand. You can either target websites that match some criteria like topic or keyword, or you can target all the websites certain types of people that you target visit. To which, it is not recommended to use the last one.

Media buying can be the best way to increase your business rapidly, but be careful because you can burn through money very quickly. You should bid on a pay per click basis and typically 25 percent of what you bid in AdWords. These leads are not so qualified! Start with a low budget to learn and optimize on a daily basis. You'll have to pay for this learning curve, but it will be worth it in the end.

The same is true for the third way of buying media, which is RTB (real-time buying). Here you are also placing your ads where they are not filled yet, but at a lower price. SiteScout is an ideal place to start with RTB to manage your campaign. You can start with $500 and have a good control on where your ads appear.

When you start with banners always split test various designs. If the CTR of a banner starts dropping, you might consider changing it. In Online terms this is called banner blindness, which means people will not look at your banner anymore, and then you know it's time to change the ads.

As a newbie, try social media first and later go into media buying when your sales funnel is well defined.

APPS:

People on the go are not in a "relaxed" state of mind. Nevertheless, apps can become a game changer when the app itself becomes the content, allowing access to the mobile crowd. Apps can be designed as mini-eBooks, or even repurposed games that push prospect directly to your landing page.

As people are increasingly using their smartphones for various purposes this medium will also be used to promote other products and services. As people are behaving differently on the move than when they sit in front of their desktop you have to really evaluate this thoroughly. Location based advertising with promotions and calls to actions have a great opportunity here.

In the future, mobile will be more important in terms of advertisements.

3. Informational: Press and News Releases

The business of "newspapers" has completely changed; some even discontinued their print editions. But in fact the main impact is not this transition from off-line to online. Many newspapers still charge for the more in-depth online content. The dramatic change lies in what could be called the "shelf space model."

In the past a printed version of a newspaper had a limited number of pages and much news content competing to be in the printed edition. Today there is an abundance of space and the content is limitless. This means that newspapers face another challenge: to get as much content and not to cherry-pick anymore between a finite number of content pieces. Of course the articles have to be "newsworthy" but newspapers are now more than ever looking for new content. So your task is to make their life easier and to provide them with as much content as possible.

Don't mix up content with advertising, however. Your content should be noteworthy and educational, teasing the reader to come to your site. If they pick up your content this will be free traffic! A news article is hot on the day of release, but it does not last forever. The free traffic you'll get from it will only last a couple of days or weeks. Therefore it is important to create press releases on a regular basis.

Make a list of the most important news sites in your geographic or topic area and find the main reporters that you'll send your content to. But there are also some companies such as vocus.com or www.prnewswire.com that will automatically send out your releases to the best online news sites.

Remember how you identified keywords and related key topics? Another way of getting coverage is to actually contact the specialized press, such as website blogs that are writing about your topic or related subjects. You will target all those specialized sites that are targeting your niche. And, you can give them information about your topic. You don't even have to write it yourself. Find some influential blogger, someone with a lot of followers and ask them to write you an article. You pay him, but let him also refer to the article on his blog with a link to your site! This will multiply your traffic!

4. Direct Contact

A classic way to contact people is directly through a letter in the off-line world and through e-mail in the online world. You buy or rent a list of e-mail addresses and send them your e-mail. You can get qualified list from various companies for B2C (Business to Customer) or B2B (Business to Business). For B2B, another way is to create a database of people through scraping the e-mails of contacts on your prospect's websites. You might for instance want to target all architects or plumbers in your local area. You could look at the yellow page or some directory sites and collect all names and e-mails of your target group. This is all very easy but be aware that the results might not be very good, and it can be dangerous, too!

Consider that this way of contacting is the same as cold-calling. You contact someone that does not know you and try to tease him or her on a moment that you do not know is convenient. The prospect might be reading his mail during a meeting, in a restaurant, or even in his car, and might not be in a state of mind to listen to your message. So don't be surprised if your results are not higher than a 20 to 30 percent open rate. Remember that these people who you are sending e- mails to, are people who have not opted in to receive messages from you.

You might not see this as a problem, but depending on the country there are strong rules and laws. The CAN-SPAM law in the United States, prohibits this cold-e-mailing and considers this spamming, even if you have bought or hired the list you are mailing to. Worse is that you might be caught by Google, and banned so that your URL can be cancelled. In Canada the new law even foresees severe fines for spammers. If you decide to use this approach, be very cautious. If you still want to do it, the best advice is to send e-mails in small batches and to put as many contact details in your e-mail, such as your company, contact e-mail, physical address, and have an unsubscribe possibility. This is even a requirement by some laws and advertising associations as a credibility device for not being seen as a spammer.

5. Partners

Initially, it was stressed that you should not start by building your own traffic infrastructure but rather use the existing mega channels such as Google or Facebook. But there are other channels that are great opportunities you can use as leverage: JV partners, Affiliates and your customers.

a) JV partners or joint venture partners, are companies or individuals that already have a list of customers that match your niche. They might be selling complementary or even similar services or products or just targeting the same niche. So why not ask them to contact their list and help you out? They will contact their list of customers who they have a relationship with and have opted-in on their list and offer your product. If you sell toys for kids between three and six, why not contact an e-commerce seller of kids' clothes? Or if you sell courses on running your first marathon, why not contact fitness related sites.

The JV will normally be paid when people buy your product or service. Depending on your type of product or margin, commission payouts vary between 30 and 50 percent. Sometimes even over 100 percent! Yes, you might give your full revenue completely away. This might come as a surprise to you, but if you have your sales funnel well designed, you get a new customer, who is top quality and to whom you are able to upsell other products! Before you contact JV partners do your homework.

Only start with affiliates when you have done the previous steps and optimized your sales funnel. You don't want them to be your guinea pigs. You have to show

146

them your conversion and sales numbers. They should be motivated to sell your product. They don't want to burn their list with "poor" products or services that are not converting.

b) Affiliates, are the second form of partnerships. The names of JVs and affiliates are often mixed. But you should consider an affiliate as a sales representative who doesn't really have a list, but will invest in creating traffic for you. This has been a very lucrative business for many years. Affiliates have typically promoted products through networks such as Commission Junction or ClickBank. These are affiliate networks that offer all kinds of products and service, that you can sell and get paid a commission.

c) Your customers. They might be great partners and generate a lot of traffic for you, so don't forget them. Do this only when they are customers. Give them the possibility to share your message whenever you contact them. Perhaps you Can give them some bonuses if they give you e-mail addresses of potential customers or you might even pay them. What is it worth for you to have your customers bring back leads? Let's say that you pay $1 for every prospect, why not give it away to your customer? He might be your best affiliate or partner.

There are some great software products that automate this process and can be a great way to create a lot of new prospects in a short period of time. Wordpress has great plugins for setting up an affiliate system.

<u>NOTES</u>

<u>NOTES</u>

Chapter 27: Customer Emails Still Have Value

At this point in the game, you've gotten through the filters of the prospects in your niche and you've created enough interest for them have clicked on your ad or link.

Now they are entering your world. They are your visitors! You want your visitors to "arrive" on your landing page. This can be part of a website or a stand-alone page.

Your objective now is to get their e-mails.

The time when people gave their e-mail away for nothing has gone. Internet users are providing their e-mail less and less, because they do not want to be spammed later. It is part of someone's privacy and they will only give it in exchange for something of real value for him or her. Actually, you're buying that e-mail.

Your task is to give that value in exchange for the e-mail. Unless you have something to offer you'll not get it. This e-mail will be the basis of further education of the customer, but you'll have to build trust before you can go to the next step. Don't neglect this. You have done your work and paid for the clicks in order to get your visitor. Don't throw that money away. You have to convert as many visitors into your funnel, or in other simpler words: Get their e-mail! The key metric here will be your conversion rate. Measured by dividing the e-mails you get (the conversion) by the total unique visitors.

So how do you do that? How do you get the highest conversion rate?

Some studies have showed that in fifteen milliseconds people get an impression of the webpage and decide to stay further or leave directly. It is therefore very important to have coherence with the ad that brought them to your site, both in style and in offer. The "bait" or "lead magnet" has to be there. And the visitor should not have to look for it.

Psychologically, the process you have to lead your visitor through is the classic AIDA concept:
*   Attention
*   Interest
*   Decision
*   Action

You have to get your visitors' attention, wake their interest and then desire to finally take action and give you their e-mail.

As important as coherence with the teaser that brought them to your page, you have to have a clear page where you "lead" the visitor. The main problem of most landing pages and websites is the massive clutter. Marketers typically want to put as much on the website and want to highlight as many benefits as possible. But the more you highlight the more this fades out.

Leading people is offering them as few options as possible. Great restaurants don't have a ten-page menu. This is one of the main paradoxes. The more options of choice the less people decide. The same is true for your website. What you have to do is remove all the visual clutter. Try to be like a sculptor, remove the unnecessary wood around the trunk to get that great sculpture. You have to remove everything that is irrelevant. Don't distract the visitor. Show him what you promised and tell him what to do to get that. In a later stage you can educate him more.

The first thing that you want from your visitor is his attention. Be careful with images and videos. They absorb most of the attention and if this is not in line with what the visitor is coming for, remove them. Don't put too much text on the page. Your website should be minimalistic. Forget navigation: You don't want your visitor to escape.

The next stage you have to bring him to, is to get his interest. If you have done your work properly you have already identified the best bait for your niche. That is also the reason why your visitor clicked on the ad and arrived on your landing page. So your task is to keep his interest and increase the desire to get it (action). Is your bait clearly placed on your site? If your visitor cannot find something easily it does not exist. Lead him to the bait. And present it in the most desirable way that they decide they want it. In a face-to-face conversation you have body language that you can identify and adapt to increase trust and credibility. The visitor should clearly see what they would get and feel safe to give their e-mail. They want to be in control. Finally tell them clearly what they have to do to get that "lead magnet." Give instructions as if you were talking to a child, taking your visitor by the hand.

Don't surprise the visitor. Don't show your whiskers! Bear in mind, that this is the first real impression that your prospect will have of you and as the saying goes: "You don't have a second chance to make a first impression." Consider this webpage as the book cover or trailer of a movie. Consider using some testimonials or well-known brands that have used your product or services to borrow extra trust. Also add a privacy policy, in which you state how you will handle the data of your prospects. This is often forgotten but very important.

At this point you might have various opinions on what has to be left out or included on the site, which photo to use, and deciding which one to choose might be very subjective. At this point, in many companies it is the HIPPO, the "highest-paid person's opinion," who will decide this.

But this is wrong. What you should do is create the webpage and test various versions and optimize the best one. To be able to test your pages don't forget to place analytics tools on them. Use Google Analytics to view for example the sources where your traffic is coming from, the time they stay on a certain page, the actions they take and who they are . A key metric you should look at is the bounce rate: This is the percentage of visitors who leave your page directly, without taking action or going to another page. In Google Analytics you can also analyze segments and how they behave. For example you can take all visitors coming from a certain source, the new visitors, the visitors that remain longer than a certain amount of seconds.

To help you with a better design you can use tools as www.clicktale.com or visual web optimizer (vmo. com) With these tools you can view the mouseovers and clicks of your visitors or simulate it. Apparently there is an 80 percent correlation of eye movement and mouseover. Therefore this analysis gives you a good basis for how to improve your webpages.

But even if you have optimized your fantastic landing page, the reality is that not all your visitors will convert and give their e-mail. Conversion rates are generally between 1 and 2 percent for pages doing "cold-selling". Compare this with the 3 to 5 percent in the old-time direct mail rates. It might be between 10 and 30 percent if you are offering something for free. But even if you have a fantastic offer and landing page it's rarely over 50 percent. Your visitor might be interested, but was distracted or not ready yet to consume your lead magnet.

So, will you leave all these potential future customers and never contact them again?

No, you shouldn't. And there is a great technique to do this. It's called retargeting. Retargeting is a second chance to get back in front of those visitors who did not convert. So even if they did not opt in, even if you don't have their e-mail you can get back in touch. Retargeting works as follows: You place a simple script, called a tag, on your page, and when someone visits your page it places an anonymous cookie on the visitor's browser. When that person visits informational sites (news or blogs) that allow advertising or Facebook you can get in front of them via banners or text ads and tease them back into your funnel.

Retargeting will only work if you have minimal traffic to your site, due to privacy reasons.•Most providers of retargeting require a minimum of five hundred or a thousand visits before you can start. And more important, you have to have your full funnel in place before you spend money on retargeting. With retargeting you can now show your ads only to people who already showed some interest. You can do this during a period of 30 to 90 days. However be careful with it so as not to stalk people with your ads. Therefore set some limits on the frequency they might see it and stop when they finally convert. Also do not forget to inform your visitors that you are applying retargeting. You can do this by mentioning it in your privacy policy on your webpage.

The most common retargeting platforms are:

* Google

* AdRoll

* Perfect Audience

* SiteScout

Each of them has advantages and disadvantages.

I would recommend to start with Google as it is the easiest and most flexible, and you will not burn through your money, as could be the case with CPM, where you could potentially have no clicks.

Ideally you should also create different landing pages or offers if you see that your returning visitors do not convert. They did not take action twice!

Retargeting can also be used to get in front of your existing customers and do some upsell, cross-sell, or down-sell. This is when you have specific landing pages for your customers, as for example upsell pages after they purchased from you.

In this conversion phase the objective was to trade great information or value in order to get an e-mail. Now that you have that e-mail you will need to do something with it. In some cases we might do an immediate offer, and certainly if what we offer is a low value item. In most cases however we will need to build trust and nurture the customer before pitching high-value offers.

<u>NOTES</u>

Part VII: Structured Manufacturing

Structured manufacturing is the art of creating value. Within the black community we have to look at our talent pool and develop business opportunity that gives our local youth commercial value. And remember, youth includes school age children and college graduates.

Consider this. Every new business needs signs and promotional material. Then there is the management of revenue, which requires Accounting services. To protect your ideas or designs, we need the legal services of an Attorney.

However, if the black owned business community works as a network of corporations, a new sign company will support new business startups, which then has multiple revenue streams to hire local artistic youth. These networks of corporations also contract with a new accounting company that hires local youth for accounting jobs and FTC license training. Creating in-house legal departments creates value for black lawyers to improve their craft in contract law, as well as, opportunity for these attorneys to start law offices that support black owned businesses.

Structured manufacturing is a means to create value across the black community.

Whenever, wherever, you find or hear about a black owned business, try to identify ways to develop commercial relationships with these businesses. These relationships should only include expansion opportunities through the licensing of products, brand name, or even developing a franchise or chain store enterprise from a single location.

Chapter 28: Product Market Growth

To build a New Black Wall Street, what is the business growth strategy in relation to new or existing markets and products?

Applied mathematician Igor Ansoff is often credited with being the father of strategic management, as he was a pioneer of analysing and prescribing how strategy can contribute to corporate performance. Ansoff's product/market growth matrix suggests that a business's growth attempts depend on whether it markets new or existing products in new or existing markets.

The model identifies four routes to growth:

1. Market penetration: Pushing existing products in their current market segments;
2. Market development: Developing new markets for the existing products;
3. Product development: Developing new products for the existing markets;
4. Diversification: Developing new products for new markets.

HOW TO USE THE MODEL:

A long time before the resource-based view of strategy became popular, Ansoff argued that a company should identify and nurture a core capability. To build on this goal, Ansoff identified four components of strategy, of which the growth matrix is one. The other three are:

1. Have a clear idea of the combination of products and markets
2. Develop competitive advantage
3. Create synergy in Ansoff's terms: 2﹢2=5.

The first step in using the growth matrix is to plot the approaches you are considering and think about how you may classify them. The second step is to manage the risks of these approaches appropriately. For example, if you're switching from one quadrant to another, make sure that you:

* Research the move carefully;
* Build the capabilities needed to succeed in the new quadrant;
* Realize plenty of resources to cover a possible lean period while you're learning how to sell the new product, and are learning what makes the new market 'tick';
* Ensure there is a fallback option.

When a strategy for growth shifts from current products and markets towards new products and markets, organizational risk will increase. A new market should be explored, and it takes time before new target groups are familiar with the products of a new supplier.

The output from the Ansoff product/market growth matrix is a series of suggested growth strategies which set the direction for the business strategy, based upon entering a new or an existing market with a new or an existing product in combination with the risks that are involved.

As diversification in Ansoff's model concerns new products and new markets, the matrix is also used to support strategies for innovation. This model defined strategy formulation as an analytical, formal process, consisting of distinct steps supported by checklists and other control techniques.

The growth matrix is helpful as a tool to distinguish and classify different scenarios for growth.

Until Ansoff's publications, companies had little guidance on how to plan for their future. Planning was commonly based on an extended budgeting system, which basically extended the annual budget. Little or no attention was paid to strategic analysis and decision-making. As competition intensified in the global economy, the need for strategic decision-making increased.

<u>NOTES</u>

NOTES

Chapter 29: Distribution for Black Farmers

Black Farmers need distribution networks and food processing plants.

If you think getting distribution for your product or service is easy, you're living in an enormous bubble, my friend. Distribution is critical for any venture and it's not easy to secure.

If you have capital, getting distribution is easier, but you need to know what you're doing, or you will get your ass kicked by the distributors and spend all your money before you get onto the retail shelf.

Distributors are like pimps. They'll represent anyone for money. Getting distribution is difficult in most industries unless you bring a substantial amount of dollars for consumer advertising, along with market development funds (MDF) for the distribution and retail channel. You could get lucky and obtain wide distribution without a substantial amount of MDF, but this depends on the sector and the marketing power of your brand.

Do you have any idea what it takes to sell to Walmart, Sam's or Best Buy? When you are seeking distribution of your product, consider every alternative. Even existing companies have to worry about getting their product on the retail shelf. Look at Procter and Gamble, the large consumer products company. They have a huge division in Bentonville, Arkansas, put there just for catering and kissing Walmart's ass. They want to make sure all their products are marketed and represented well on their retail shelves.

Let's say you have a software entertainment game you developed and you need distribution. Consider the software company, Berkeley Software Design Systems, which produced a very cool computer game. Despite the software company having access to distribution with their other products in retail outlets across the country such as Sam's, Walmart, Best Buy, EB Games, Target, and CompUSA, getting their first entertainment title into the channel was a nightmare.

Entertainment was not Berkeley's forte. They made money selling computer utilities such as the After Dark screensaver, but the new management team knew nothing about the realities of distributing software in the entertainment sector. It couldn't be any harder than selling utilities, so they thought. The company wanted to expand their product line, and entertainment was a hot category then, as well as today. Their business strategy of entering the entertainment sector was right on. Their execution was horrible.

The marketing department produced the packaging, pricing and promotion without input from sales, distribution or retail buyers. The marketing people had a bunch of MBA degrees. They thought they knew it all and refused to listen to any salesperson's feedback. And Berkeley had some experienced and smart salespeople representing them to tens of thousands of retail stores across the country.

The retail and distribution channel hated the packaging and the price point. Entertainment products at the time sold for around $40, and our marketing wizards decided to price the video game at $30. Nobody in the marketing department asked the retail buyers whether they wanted to buy the software and sell it at that price. From a product standpoint, marketing built "a better mousetrap" and expected the retail buyers to run to the door.

What made it worse is that Berkeley's founder brought a new CEO into the company after he received venture funding. After the VCs got into bed with the founder, the pressure escalated to meet new financial numbers and expectations. The sales projections for the game software were unrealistic.

Berkeley's video game was good enough to generate a lot of press, but that didn't matter to distribution and retail buyers. They were already maxed out on their shelf space in the entertainment category. Plus, they were making better margins from other hot games. Even throwing in market development funds wasn't enough. Why? Because every other entertainment company was doing the same, and those companies were throwing even more money behind their products. Some of them were putting millions of dollars into marketing their product during the Christmas season. Berkeley was outgunned by the competition.

What made it more difficult were the expectations of the upper management team to load up the channel shelves with tens of thousands of units during the holidays when every other game software wanted to do the same thing. It was a classic case of a company wanting wide distribution, deep distribution, but not listening to their customer, which in this case, where the retailers.

The retailers can make you or break you.

You live or die during the holidays in the entertainment sector. Retail is a tricky and tough business because if you don't put enough product on the shelf, you could be shit out of luck, when the customer goes to the store and the shelves are empty.

Berkeley's management team started to panic. Without good representation on the retail shelves of the largest retail player in the entertainment software business, you're kind of fucked. What made it worse is that the second largest retail player in the business also hated the packaging. So things got worse, and the likelihood of having wide product distribution was looking grim.

This is a simple example of how difficult it can be to obtain retail distribution. The Berkeley video game did get on the retail shelf with decent exposure, but it was by chance.

A few weeks after the meeting, the salesman ran into the buyer at the airport. They happened to be on the same flight headed to Las Vegas for a computer trade show. On the plane, they bullshitted about everything but business.

After landing in Las Vegas, the buyer invited the salesman to a Cirque du Soleil show with her and her brother. They had a good time, and not once did the salesman mention the product or pitch her on putting more of the Berkeley video game on the shelves. After the show, she did question the salesman about the company and the product. The salesman was brutally honest about the hated packaging and pricing too.

At the end of the Las Vegas convention, out of the blue, she informs the salesman that she would increase the order.

The moral of the story is that you need to have good relationships in distribution in order to successfully launch new products in the retail sector. Yes, you must have MDFs to launch the product in the retail store, but that isn't everything. In the distribution and retail channel, it's not what you know, it's who you know. Otherwise, you don't know•jack•shit.

Another thing to consider, when looking to invest into a company, pay close attention to the distribution penetration of the product or service. And ask some of the following basic questions:

How widely is the product distributed? Is the channel happy with the product?

What are its returns from the channel if it's already on the shelf? What are the marketing dollars for the channel?

What is the MDF ratio compared to its gross margin? Which channels are more profitable than others?

What is the return risk? Does the venture have enough marketing dollars to create consumer demand and get it off the shelves?

Distribution is a pimp and retail is the go-go bar. Respect it. Pay attention to it or you will get fucked.

<u>NOTES</u>

Chapter 30: Long Term Strategy

To build a New Black Wall Street, how can we create a long-term plan for sustained competitive advantage by focusing on new markets, without focusing on competition?

Kim and Mauborgne developed their Blue Ocean Strategy in 2005, building on earlier publications that also explored the insight that an organization should create new demand in an uncontested marketspace, or a 'blue ocean', where the competition is irrelevant.

In blue oceans, organizations invent and capture new demand, and offer customers a leap in value while also streamlining costs. The central idea is to stop competing in overcrowded industries, so-called 'red oceans', where companies try to outperform rivals to grab bigger slices of existing demand. As the space gets increasingly crowded, profit and growth prospects shrink because products become commoditized. Ever more intense competition turns the water bloody. Blue Ocean Strategies result in better profits, speedier growth and brand equity that lasts for decades while rivals scramble to catch up.

HOW TO USE THE MODEL:

1. Eliminate factors in your industry that no longer have value;
2. Reduce factors that over-serve customers and increase cost structure for no gain;
3. Raise factors that remove compromises buyers must make;
4. Create factors that add new sources of value.

Authors, W. Chan Kim and Renée Mauborgne list a number of practical tools, methodologies and frameworks for formulating and executing Blue Ocean Strategies; in attempting to make the creation of blue oceans a systematic and repeatable process. In their 2009 article 'How Strategy Shapes Structure', Kim and Mauborgne stress the importance of alignment across the value, profit and people propositions, regardless of whether one takes the structuralist (traditional competitive, Porter-like) or the reconstructionist (blue ocean) approach to strategy.

Blue Ocean Strategy should result in making the competition irrelevant. Therefore, organizations need to avoid using the existing competition as a benchmark. Instead, make the competition irrelevant by creating a leap in value for both your organization and your customers.

Another result should be the reduction of your costs while also offering customers more value. For example, Cirque du Soleil omitted costly elements of traditional circuses, such as animal acts and aisle concessions. Its reduced cost structure enabled it to provide sophisticated elements from theatre that appealed to adult audiences; such as themes, original scores and enchanting sets, all of which change from year to year.

The logic behind Blue Ocean Strategy is counter-intuitive, since blue oceans seldom result from technological innovation. Often, the underlying technology already exists and blue ocean creators link it to what buyers value.

Furthermore, organizations don't have to venture into distant waters to create blue oceans. Most blue oceans are created from within, not beyond, the red oceans of existing industries. Incumbents often create blue oceans within their core businesses. Blue Ocean Strategy is an inspiring way to look afresh at familiar environments with a view to finding a competitive edge. Unfortunately, most companies have marketing and strategy departments that look for benchmarks to be inspired by and copy rather than trying to be different.

<u>NOTES</u>

NOTES

Chapter 31: Business Plans

What is a Business Plan?

A business plan is any plan that works for a business to look ahead, allocate resources, focus on key points, and prepare for problems and opportunities. Realize that business existed long before computers, spreadsheets, and detailed projections. So did the business plan.

The main problem is that most people think of business plans for starting a new business or applying for business financing. Business plans are also vital for running a business, whether or not it needs financing or seeking investors. Businesses need plans to optimize growth and development according to plans and priorities.

A normal business plan follows the advice of business experts and includes a standard set of elements. A plans format and outline varies, but generally include: description of the company, product or service, market forecasts, management team and financial analysis. However, plans developed for internal needs don't require background details that are already known. But for investors, a clear description of the management team is very important, compared to financial history being most important to banks. Just make sure that your plan match its business purpose.

Nevertheless, at the heart of every business plan is cash flow, which is vital to every company, but hard to follow. Cash is usually misunderstood as profits, and is entirely different. Profit does not guarantee cash in the bank. Second to cash flow, are implementation details. Without understanding what makes things happen, your strategy and formatted documents are just theory until you assign responsibilities, with dates and budges, and lost of follow up with the tracking of results. The business plan is actually about improving your company.

In Building a New Black Wall Street, keep in mind that there are standards that should be followed when developing your business plan. An executive summary normally starts a business plan, which should be short and interesting. Thereafter, include information on the company, the market, the product, the management team, strategy, implementation and financial analysis.

There are plenty of resources to assist in developing a business plan, but here is a brief overview for the presentation of the main components in a suggest order to follow:

1. Executive Summary: Write this last, otherwise it'll be premature.

2. Company Description: Legal establishment, history, startup plans, etc.

3. Product or Service: Describe what it is and focus on customer benefits.

4.	Market Analysis: You need to know your market, customer needs, where they are and how to reach them.

5.	Strategy and Implementation: Be specific. Include management responsibilities with dates and budgets. Show that you can track results.

6.	Management Team: Describe the organization and the key management Team members.

7.	Financial Analysis: Make sure to include at the very least your projected profit and loss, and cash flow tables.

A business plan becomes a real plan after specific and measurable activity, instead of being just a document. Each activity is called a milestone, and give it as many milestones as you can think of to make it more concrete. Give each milestone a name, a person responsible a milestone date and a budget. Make sure that your team understands the plan will be followed and tracked for actual results. If you don't follow up, your plan has no way to verify that it's been implemented.

Furthermore, understand that a business plan is a living document. Meaning that, as you review implementation results with the team members, you will often find the need to set new goals and make course corrections. Keep track of the original plan and manage changes carefully. Even though changes should be made with good reason, don't be afraid to update your plan to reflect any changes.

NOTES

Part VIII: Loss Leaders

In building a New Black Wall Street, the black community must change our mindsets.

If we are to speak of "Black Money Matters," let's leverage our money with practical solutions that will have an impact on our youth and our communities nationwide.

Over the past decade "Freemium" a combination of "Free" and "Premium" has become the dominant business model among internet start-ups and smartphone app developers. Users get basic features at no cost and can access richer
functionality for a subscription fee. If you're networked on LinkedIn, sharedfiles through Dropbox, watched TV shows through Hulu, or searched for a mate on Match, you've experienced the model firsthand. It works for B2B companies as well - examples include Box, Splunk, and Yammer.

These online models work offline in the real world as well, but to build a New Black Wall Street, we have to take this model to another level. The key to our success, is to focus on implementing activity that motivate our youth and by not comparing ourselves to other groups. We are a Great People, and Our Children should live that Fact.

Our youth should have Freedom of Choice within the Black Community for an employment opportunity. "On the Job Training" (OJT) is the Freemium Model, where an improved skillset allows our youth to move up to more fulfilling labor choices, that a New Black Wall Street has to offer through new businesses and as new enterprises develop.

Chapter 32: 100,000 Jobs Overnight

Job opportunities for unemployed black youth are right in front of our faces, if we create them.

Consider the fact that 4 million African Americans have a net income of more than $150,000 per year. Which means that these people are capable of sponsoring a $30,000 per year job for a local employed youth.

These jobs can be initiated with local black owned businesses, or created by the sponsor as a daily activity: cleaning a neighborhood, painting and repairing homes for local seniors, or for whatever the needs are within a local black community. Where there are communities without black owned business, negotiate paid internships with local hospitals, nursing homes, law firms, insurance agencies and fortune 500 companies.

Even if only 3% of that 4 million group participated in a job sponsoring initiative, that would create 120,000 jobs overnight. And realize that a youth is a skilled or unskilled teen or College graduate, between the ages of 16 to 25 years of age.

For sponsors that don't want to be involved in the administration of such endeavors, network with other interested parties and form a corporation that will manage job sponsoring as an enterprise.

Who we are is what we do!

This initiative is an opportunity to change the dynamics of leadership within the black community, and let's our youth know that we support them 100% right or wrong. Such leadership is what we need to Build a New Black Wall Street.

Leaders create jobs!

Please feel free to contact us for Assistance, if you or your group requires help starting a job sponsoring initiative at the following website: www.TheBankOfTheWorld.com

Chapter 33: Black Book Publishers

Black Book Publishers, stop losing out on sale growth opportunity for your books.

Consider this: Purchase (100+) one hundred plus books at cost, to distribute minimum quantities of (10) ten, free of charge to Bookstores, Childcare Centers and Summer Camp Programs, etc..

The cost of a free book distribution promotion, outweighs the costs of travel expenses for live book promotions.

For Black Authors, children's book publishing is a great opportunity to influence the minds of our youth, as well as, having the ability to generate wealth as a publisher.

The Cooperative Children's Book Center in Wisconsin, has been maintaining interesting statistics regarding African American authors since 1985. Nevertheless, recent numbers are what's important here. In 2013, there were (93) ninety-three children's books created by only (68) sixty-eight African American authors. By 2015, that number increased to (269) two-hundred sixty-nine children's books by (106) one hundred and six African American authors.

Your goal as an author is to generate a minimum of 10,000 sales of your book, from a population of 40 million African Americans. 10,000 book sales equals less than (10%) ten percent of (1%) one percent of the African American population.

Chapter 34: Concepts That Work

Several factors contribute to the appeal of the loss leader: Free + Premium = Freemium strategy.

Because free features are a potent marketing tool, the model allows a new venture to scale up and attract a user base without expending resources on costly ad campaigns or a traditional sales force. The monthly subscription fees typically charged are proving to be a more sustainable source of revenue than the advertising model prevalent among online firms in the early 2000s. Social networks are powerful drivers: Many services offer incentives for referring friends (which is more appealing when the product is free). And freemium is more successful than 30-day free trials or other limited-term offers, because customers have become wary of cumbersome cancellation processes and find indefinite free access more compelling.

But despite its popularity and clear benefits, freemium is still poorly understood. It has inherent challenges, as demonstrated by the many start-ups that have tried but failed to make it work.

Here are six questions that start-ups considering a freemium model should consider:

1) What Should be Free?

Let' say you've created a digital product that has 20 features and you've chosen five that will be free to anyone who registers on your site. Users who want the other 15 will have to pay. How do you know whether you've made the right choices? And if you suspect that you haven't, what should you do?

Recall that one of the chief purposes of freemium is to attract new users. If you're not succeeding with that goal, it probably means that your free offerings are not compelling enough and you need to provide more or better features free. If you're generating lots of traffic but few people are paying to upgrade, you may have the opposite problem: Your free offerings are too rich, and it' time to cut back.

This kind of tweaking was evident at the New York Times website. After years of unrestricted access, in 2011 the paper began limiting users to 20 free articles a month; people had to subscribe if they wanted to read more. Over subsequent months the company realized it was still giving away too much and was getting too few subscribers as a result, so in 2012 it cut the number of free monthly articles to 10. Start-ups should expect to do similar tweaking to find the optimal balance between traffic and paying customers. The balancing act can be tricky: Users may revolt when asked to pay for things they are accustomed to getting free.

2) Do Customers Fully Understand the Premium Offer?

Communicating two sets of benefits complicates your marketing efforts. If customers don't clearly grasp what they would gain by upgrading, you will monetize fewer of them than you otherwise might.

Dropbox and LinkedIn are a study in contrasts. The former has attracted 200 million users with a simple proposition: Everyone who enters a username and a password gets two gigabytes of cloud-based storage free. If people run out of space, they can pay $9.99 a month (or, alternatively, $99 a year) for 100 GB of storage. The free version is adequate for basic documents, but anyone who wants to back up photos or other media quickly hits the limit, and the reasons to upgrade are obvious.

For many LinkedIn users, the advantages of upgrading are murkier. The free version of LinkedIn provides more than enough features and allows you to keep in touch with colleagues, but the value of an upgrade is not readily apparent. LinkedIn offers four premium subscriptions: some aimed at specific customer segments, such as recruiters or salespeople, and most featuring deeper search functionality, better e-mail capability, and more visibility into who has viewed your profile. Although LinkedIn is successful and was one of the first freemium companies to go public, it probably could monetize more users if the distinctions between its free and paid offerings were clearer.

3) What is Your Target Conversion Rate?

Imagine that you'e the CEO of a freemium start-up and you're handed a report showing your conversion rate (the percentage of free users who have upgraded to a premium plan) for the most recent quarter. What figure do you hope to see?

A rate of 1% is probably too low, especially if you rely on subscription revenue alone. (Some players, including the New York Times and LinkedIn, also collect online ad revenue.) It signals that either too much of what you're providing is free and users have little reason to upgrade, or that consumers don't understand or value your premium features.

But less obviously, a very high conversion rate isn' necessarily good.

Remember that one of the benefits of a freemium model is the ability to generate traffic. Suppose that 50% of the users of your free product, upgrade to premium. You might think that your model is working well; but perhaps your free product is not very compelling, which will limit your potential acquisitions. All other things being equal, you would do better to convert 5% of 2 million monthly visitors, for example, than to convert 50% of 100,000 visitors.

The best long-term strategy is generally to aim for a moderate conversion rate (most companies' range from 2% to 5%) coupled with a high volume of traffic. But, if you're targeting a small market, you should aim for a higher conversion rate.

4) Are You Prepared for the Conversion Life Cycle?

Let' assume you're attracting plenty of traffic and new users, and your conversion rate is 5%. You then want to forecast growth and revenue. Can you simply draw a couple of straight lines, on the assumption that the rate will hold steady?

No. Early adopters are less price-sensitive than others, so they are more likely to upgrade. And often they are people for whom the value proposition is unusually compelling.

For instance, recruiters were early adopters of LinkedIn, because their business depends on their ability to identify and connect with professionals.

So over time, conversion rates typically dip as the user base expands to include people who are more price-sensitive or who see less value in the service. Although freemium companies universally have a very low marginal cost for each new user, otherwise the model wouldn't make sense, those costs aren't zero. At a minimum, free users put demands on server space and customer service.

Companies that fail to understand these realities may feel a cash crunch as the number of free users grows and the cost of servicing them therefore rises. This is often the reason that companies launched with freemium models pivot away, converting to free time-limited trials or eliminating free offerings altogether.

Start-ups that have recently made such a switch include LogMeIn, whose software provides remote access to PCs, and SugarSync, a cloud storage company that competes with Dropbox.

5) Are Users Becoming Evangelists?

It's important to recognize the full value of your free users, which takes two forms: Some of them become subscribers, and some draw in new members who become subscribers.

In a Harvard Business School working paper and in ongoing research, it was found that a free user is typically worth 15% to 25% as much as a premium subscriber, with significant value stemming from referrals. It was also determined that firms can increase the value of referrals by carefully managing referral incentives and communications. Therefore, if you're considering a freemium model, pay close attention to why and how satisfied users might help your product go viral.

6) Are You Committed to Ongoing Innovation?

It' a mistake to see the freemium model merely as a customer acquisition tool and drop the free version when new customers stop coming in or when the upgrade rate dives.

Users who join late are typically harder to convert; therefore, in order to keep increasing upgrades, you'll need to keep increasing the value of your premiumservices. Smart companies view freemium not only as a revenue model but also as a commitment to innovation.

Dropbox is a good example. When it launched, in 2008, it was primarily a service for backing up files. Then it began offering shared folders, making it a collaboration tool. Newer features allowed for automatic syncing of smartphones and other devices and for automatic uploading of photos. Over time the user interface has improved as well. Each new feature thereby increased the value of the premium offering.

In today's digital era, with marginal costs of many products dropping, businesses will increasingly turn to the freemium model. Across industries the model is destined to grow more and more attractive; ranging from media: where publishers are forced to rely less on advertising revenue and more on subscriber revenue, to education: where companies may eventually seek to monetize mostly free online courses.

Companies can boost their odds of success by considering the six key questions above.

<u>NOTES</u>

NOTES

<u>Part IX: Support Our Youth 100%</u>

Building a New Black Wall Street, require absolute commitment, and our youth have to know that we support them without qualification, right or wrong in whatever their actions.

Consider this... An average community has a population of 30,000 people. With just a one dollar deposit at a local bank, we can change the life of a local unemployed black youth every month.

However, the question remains. Are you willing to give a random youth $30,000 (thirty thousand dollars) without any strings attached?

Here's the thing, we cannot attempt to control that which we have no influence, until we can influence our youth with some sort of wealth opportunities. Even then, our responsibility is to lead by example, which will inspire responsible choices with this new found wealth. Don't forget, a black youth is anyone who is a teenager or a college graduate.

To actually realize this initiative, open a dual signature trust account with your local bank and partner with a local community leader. The necessary credibility can be achieved by partnering with the bank's president, or a local politician, or local business owner.

The trust account automatically creates transparency, and allows for anyone to make anonymous deposits or donations.

At the end of every (30) thirty days, choose a random local youth for this giveaway. If the bank account generates more than $30,000 within that time, rollover the remaining money into the next (30) thirty days.

There are (48) forty-eight states in the Continental United States, with hundreds, if not thousands of local black communities within each state. This means that on our own, we can change the life of 4,800 unemployed black youth every (30) days. (48 states multiplied by a minimum of 100 black communities = 4,800 (four thousand, eight hundred). That's almost 60,000 (sixty thousand) black youth each and every year.

Just Remember... Without Strings... Without Programs... Without any Requirements !!!

Every (30) thirty days... we can give away $30,000 to actually show support for our children.

Part X: Security

Every Black Owned Business and Home should have video surveillance.

A basic video surveillance system is a lifesaver on many fronts, for the home and business. Protection from rape accusations and rape prevention should never be in the back of your mind. Protect yourself from lawsuit opportunity seekers, criminal prosecution, sexual harassment and police harassment.

Even an old desktop computer can be used to create a great video surveillance system by just adding one or two video cards for the cameras.

NOTES

Chapter 35: Commercial Security

Security is paramount for Building a New Black Wall Street.

Therefore, consider exploiting the opportunity of a Federal Firearms License. Such a license allows the purchase of weapons and ammunition in bulk, to seek and fulfill local municipal and federal contracts.

As a Private Contractor (corporations also) with a Federal Firearms License, you'll have the ability to bid on municipal, state and federal law enforcement department open contracts for firearms and ammunition, especially for practice rounds at training facilities.

Bonded Couriers are a great opportunity for security protection services for professional athletes and entertainers, because they're authorized to cross state lines with firearms.

Seek out Black Owned Gun Clubs or establish a local gun club. The ASAFO gun club of Georgia, and the Georgia Security Company are great resources for weapons training and firearms certification programs.

Indoor Shooting Range:

From an enterprise point of view, setting up an indoor shooting range is fairly easy if you start a security company. Such a commercial operation is not open to the public and therefore circumvents most requirements for an open to the public shooting range. Otherwise how else can your security company offer firearms certifications without a place to train.

NOTES

Chapter 36: Cyber Security

Online Security is just as important as real world security.

To build a New Black Wall Street, we cannot overlook or take for granted the vulnerability of online commerce. And being that I'm an advocate for WordPress as an easily managed online platform, there are great free and paid security plugins available.

These plugins offer protections against denial of service website attacks, login brute force attacks, ip address tracking, as well as a range of other important features for securing your website.

Here's a Great Resource for Paid WordPress plugins:

https://ThemeForest.net/category/wordpress

<u>NOTES</u>

Part XI: Your Legal Enterprise

In Building a New Black Wall Street, this book focuses primarily on the corporate structure for your business entity, because of the versatility of it's nature.

A sole proprietor, partnership or co-op as a business entity, do not have the functionality to share tangible ownership. The corporation on the other hand, is a legal person and therefore possesses inherent legal rights. The corporation can buy, sell and own real property. The corporation can separately own a business and license the name of an enterprise from another separately owned corporation that you've established. What you can do with a corporation is only limited by your creativity and by law of course.

A corporation can become a new source of monetary exchange for the Building of a New Black Wall Street.

Take a look at the following scenario for example, using eleven corporations that you setup:

1) Setup (10) ten C-class stock corporations for the purpose of raising $100,000 each. Those (10) ten corporations then trade shares with the (11th) eleventh corporation at 100,000 shares each, for a combined total of (1) one million shares of stock.

The real beauty of corporate law is that the valuation of a share of stock is initially determined by the corporation itself. Therefore, when setting up your corporation, start with one million shares. So in this example, we will give each share a par value of ($1) one dollar, thereby giving us a $1 million capitalization. The 100,000 shares being traded in this example, are only 10% of total shares authorized.

2) Then use the $1 million in Capital to Setup (6) six retail locations (food service -or- consumer goods)... combined cost so far is $300,000 (three hundred thousand) for equipment and inventory for the (6) six locations ($50,000 each). The remaining balance of $700,000 (seven hundred thousand) is used to cover debt maintenance and overhead costs. Package this enterprise as a chain or franchise and then sell at $2 million minimum !!!

Here's the thing. That $1 million capitalization can be leveraged into debt financing. The $2 million sale price is based on a 3 - 5 year projection of an ongoing business, including franchise and license fees.
Divide $2 million by the six individual locations, then divide that amount by five.

Nevertheless, the sale of this franchise can be internal or external. External being outside of the Black Wall Street Network.

3) That 11th corporation then buys back it's shares or buy new shares from the initial (10) ten corporations at a given Share price. Let's say a 100,000 share buyback at $2 per share = $2 million.

Remember now, those original shares were valued at pennies on the dollar, which now have a value of $200,000 for each of the original ten corporations. The 11th corporation was the sale vehicle, which can either be dissolved or used for other deals as a holding corporation.

Therefore, the value created in such stock scenarios are real, and a tangible asset that can be traded amongst ourselves in exchange for real estate and capital equipment such as cars and trucks. And as shareholders, it forces us to support one another to do the best work possible in maintaining this newly created value.

The choice in using the corporate stockholder structure, guarantees our children's future with the legacy of a New Black Wall Street. The state filing fee for a c-class stock corporation averages $150.00.

Who We are is What We Do... Now Let's Do This !!!

"Our Reality is Not Fiction"

<u>NOTES</u>

NOTES

<u>Part XII: Sample Documents</u>

NOTICE:

We wish we could provide an agreement that was tailored *exactly* to your business, this is not possible,but we feel that these documents provides you with the head-start that you need to get your deal moving. Nevertheless, we must make this disclaimer:

Do Not Use These Agreements 'As-Is.'

These Sample Documents / Agreements / Contracts are Not Legal Advice.

Read Thoroughly and Make All Appropriate Changes to Fit Your Requirements.

You Should Have Any Agreement Reviewed and Approved by a Qualified Attorney at Law.

Publisher Accepts No Liability for the Effectiveness of These Documents For Your Purposes.

Articles of Incorporation

Articles of Incorporation for [Company]

Note: This is a form for Articles of Incorporation for use in the state of California. The incorporation papers required by other states may be substantially different. We encourage you to use this document for educational purposes and to consult an attorney in your state of incorporation for issues related to forming a corporation.

Article 1

Give the complete name of the Corporation (not any abbreviated version).

1.1 The name of this corporation is **[Company Legal Name].**

Article 2

Note: Article 2 states that the corporation can engage in any lawful act. It is wise to state such a broad purpose because you do not want to limit the types of businesses the corporation may pursue. Certain types of corporations, such as non-profit corporations, may require special descriptions of the corporate purpose for tax or other statutory purposes. Please consult with your attorney for clarification.

2.1 The purpose of this corporation is to engage in any lawful act or activity for which a corporation may be organized under the General Corporation Law of [State] other than the banking business, the trust company business or the practice of a profession permitted to be incorporated by the [State] Corporations Code.

Article 3

Note: Article 3 has two options. Option 1 states that the corporation can only issue one class of shares, while Option 2 allows for multiple classes of shares. Option 2 is called a "Blank Check Preferred" provision. It is typically used to avoid the need for shareholder approval when the terms of a new class or series of Preferred Stock is submitted to the Secretary of State for approval. You should consult an attorney when deciding upon the classes of securities to be authorized and in any matters relating to securities. There are many traps to avoid when dealing with corporate securities, so always consult an attorney experienced in securities law if you need to make a decision concerning corporate securities.

[Option 1] The corporation is authorized to issue only one class of stock, to be designated Common Stock. The total number of shares of Common Stock presently authorized is [List number of shares].

[Option 2] This corporation is authorized to issue two classes of stock to be designated, respectively, "Common Stock" and "Preferred Stock." The total number of shares that the corporation is authorized to issue is [number of shares) shares.

______ shares will be Common Stock.

______ shares will be Preferred Stock.

The Preferred Stock may be issued from time to time in one or more series. The Board of Directors is hereby authorized, to fix or alter the dividend rights, dividend rate, conversion rights, voting rights, rights and terms of redemption (including sinking fund provisions), redemption price or prices, and the liquidation preferences of any wholly unissued series of Preferred Stock, and the number of shares constituting any such series and the designation thereof, or any of them; and to increase or decrease the number of shares of any series subsequent to the issuance of shares of that series, but not below the number of shares of such series then outstanding. In case the number of shares will be so decreased, the shares constituting such decrease will resume the status that they had prior to the adoption of the resolution originally fixing the number of shares of such series.

Article 4

Note: Article 4 states that the corporation will limit liability exposure of its directors, officers and agents to the full extent of law. In the absence of this provision, the officers and directors may still be entitled to indemnification by statute. Usually, a corporation will purchase insurance and agree to indemnify the directors or agents.

The liability of the officers and directors of this corporation for monetary damages will be eliminated to the fullest extent permissible under [State] law.

This corporation is authorized to provide indemnification of agents (as defined in the [State] Corporations Code) for breach of duty to the corporation and its shareholders through bylaw provisions or through Agreements with the agents, or through shareholder resolutions, or otherwise, in excess of the indemnification otherwise permitted by the [State] Corporations Code, subject to the limits on such excess indemnification set forth in the [State] Corporations Code.

Article 5

Note: Article 5 provides the name and address of the "agent for service of process." This agent can be a business or an individual. If you use an attorney, the agent is usually your attorney.• The agent is the person or entity that receives any documents served on the corporation as part of a lawsuit or other legal proceeding, and notice for taxes due and the like.

The name and address in the State of [State] of this corporation's initial agent for service of process is:

(Company Name)
(Address of Company)
City, State and Zip)

In witness of this, for the purpose of forming this corporation under the laws of
the State of [State], the undersigned, as sole incorporator of this corporation
has executed these Articles of Incorporation this [Month, Day, Year].

____

[Owner/Founder]

Sole Incorporator

I hereby declare that I am the person who executed the foregoing Articles of
Incorporation, which execution is my act and deed.

____

[Owner/Founder]

<u>Corporation - Bylaws</u>

[Company Legal Name]

Company Bylaws

Special Note*: Many provisions in this sample Bylaws are subject to state laws that vary from state to state. Accordingly, provisions of these Bylaws may not apply or may be incorrect for a corporation incorporated in your state. That said, it's your company – how do you want it to be?*

This first section gives the principal address of the Corporation.

1. Offices

The principal executive office of the Corporation shall be located in **[City], [County], [State]**, and may have offices at other places as the Board of Directors may from time to time designate.

Note: The second section discusses rules related to regular and special shareholder meetings. The following paragraph sets the meeting place all shareholder meetings.

2. Shareholders' Meetings

2.1 All meetings of the shareholders shall be held at the principal executive office of the Corporation or at another place as the Board of Directors may determine.

Note: The next section sets the date for regular shareholder meetings.

2.2. The annual meeting of the shareholders shall be held on the [Day/Month] of each year at [Time]. If this day happens to be a legal holiday, then the meeting shall be held at the same time on the following business day.

The next section describes who can call a special shareholders meeting.

2.3. Special meetings of the shareholders may be called by the Chairman of the Board of Directors, the President of the Corporation or by one or more shareholders holding not less than ten (10) percent of the shares entitled to vote.

Note: Section 2.4 requires that notices of shareholder meetings comply with state law. You will have to insert the name of the state

2.4 Notice of annual and special meetings of the shareholders shall be given pursuant to the requirements of the Corporate Law of the State of [State], as it exists now or as it may be amended in the future.

Note: Actions taken at any shareholder meeting that is not a proper, regular, or special shareholder meeting may be valid if a majority of the shareholders attend the meeting in person or by proxy, and the non-attending shareholders do not object to such actions.

2.5 Actions taken at any meeting of the shareholders, no matter how called, or noticed, and wherever held, are as valid as if taken at a regularly noticed and called meeting, if a quorum is present, in person or by proxy, and if each of the absent persons entitled to vote signs a written waiver of notice or a consent to the holding of the meeting or an approval of the minutes. All such waivers, consents and approvals must be filed with the corporate records or made a part of the minutes. If a person attends a meeting and fails to object at the beginning to the holding of the meeting because it was not lawfully called, then such an appearance is a waiver of notice to that person. Such attendance is not a waiver of the right to object at the meeting to the consideration of matters required by the law or these Bylaws to be included in the notice but not so included.

The following paragraph defines "quorum" for voting purposes.

2.6 A quorum exists when a majority of shares entitled to vote is represented in person or by proxy. The Business may be transacted after withdrawal of enough shareholders to leave less than a quorum, so long as the action taken is approved by the number of shares required to constitute a quorum. A quorum is not needed to adjourn a meeting so long as a majority of the shares present, in person or by proxy, votes in favor of adjournment.

A shareholder can demand that the Directors be elected by ballot.

2.7 The Directors need not be elected by ballot unless a shareholder so demands at the meeting and before the commencement of voting.

Only the shareholders of record are entitled to vote except if provided otherwise by state law or in the Articles of Incorporation.

2.8 Only holders of shares at the close of business on the record date are entitled to notice and to vote, except as provided by the Articles of Incorporation, by consent agreement, or by the General Corporation Law.

The shareholders can have others vote on their behalf by proxy. The proxy can only be valid for 11 months and is subject to applicable state laws.

2.9 Every shareholder entitled to vote may authorize another to act by proxy with respect to the voting of such shares by filing a written proxy signed by such person with the Secretary of the Corporation. A proxy shall be valid for no more than eleven (11) months from the date of its execution, unless otherwise provided on the face of the proxy. All proxies shall be subject to the Corporate Laws of the State of [State].

3. Directors

Section 3 covers the rules related to the meetings of the Board of Directors, and the number of Directors on the Board.

The Board of Directors has the authority to manage the Corporation and exercise all corporate powers.

3.1 Subject to the provisions and limitations of the Corporate Law of the State of [State], and the Articles of Incorporation, or by any agreement of the outstanding shares pertaining to the business of this Corporation, so long as it remains a close Corporation, business and affairs of the Corporation shall be managed and all corporate powers exercised by or under the direction of the Board of Directors.

Note: You want an ODD number of Directors to break voting ties—usually 5-7 Directors is normal.

3.2 The number of Directors cannot be reduced to less than five (5) after issuance of shares unless such a Bylaw is adopted.

Note: The Directors will be elected annually by the shareholders and serve for a one year term.

3.3 Directors shall be elected at the annual meeting of the shareholders and serve until the next annual meeting and until their successors stand qualified to assume office.

Note: If a Director dies or resigns, or otherwise vacates a Directorship, the other Directors can elect a replacement. The shareholders have to approve a Director elected by the other Directors. If the Directors do not fill a vacancy on the Board, the shareholders may act to do so.

3.4 (1) Vacancies on the Board may be filled upon a vote of the majority of the Directors then in office, whether a quorum or not, or by a sole remaining Director,
except for a vacancy caused by the removal of a Director, or as otherwise provided in the Articles of Incorporation or these Bylaws. (2) Vacancies caused by the removal of the Directors may only be filled by approval of the shareholders as defined in Section [Enter section] of the Corporate Law of the State of [State], unless the Articles of Incorporation are amended or a Bylaw adopted in the future by the shareholders to provide that vacancies occurring because of removal may be filled by the Board. Any vacancy not filled by the Board that it is authorized to fill may be filled by the shareholders. Any such election by written consent requires the consent of the majority of the shareholders entitled to vote, however no vacancy caused by removal shall be filled by written consent except by the unanimous written consent of all the shareholders entitled to vote in the Directors' election.

3.5 Any Director or the entire Board of Directors may be removed from office in the manner provided by law.

3.6 Meetings of the Board of Directors may be called by the Chairman of the Board, the President, the Vice President, the Secretary, or any two Directors. Regular annual meetings of the Board of Directors shall be held without notice and immediately following and in the same location as the annual meeting of shareholders.

3.7 Meetings of the Board of Directors shall be held at the Corporation's principal executive office, or at any place designated by the Board of Directors and contained in the notice.

206

3.8 Notice of any special meeting of the Board of Directors shall be given by first-class mail, postage prepaid, to all the Directors four (4) days in advance of such meeting or by telephone or telegraph two (2) days in advance of the meeting.

Actions taken at any meeting of the Board of Directors that is not a (properly noticed) special meeting, may be valid if the Directors waive the notice requirement in writing or by attending the meeting without protest.

3.9 A Director who signs a waiver of notice, or a consent to the holding of a meeting, or an approval of the minutes of that meeting, or who attends the meeting without protest, thereby waives his right to notice of the meeting. All such waivers, consents, or approvals shall be made a part of the corporate record, filed and included in the minutes of the meeting.

It's important to define under what conditions a decision may be approved... 2/3, simple majority, unanimous, etc.

3.10 A quorum shall consist of a [2/3 / simple majority / unanimous vote] of the authorized number of Directors. Every act or decision done or made by a majority of the Directors present at a meeting of the Board is the act of the Board, except as provided by sections in these Bylaws, or Bylaw. Any meeting where a quorum is present may transact business after a withdrawal of the Directors if the vote for approval of an action constitutes a majority of the required quorum for that meeting.

The next section allows the Directors to take action by written consent.

3.11 Action required to be taken at a meeting of the Board may be taken instead by unanimous written consent of the Directors. Such consents shall be filed with the minutes of Board proceedings.

Section 4 establishes the corporate officers and the duties of each. Initially, the Corporation will have a President, Vice President, Secretary, and Treasurer who will serve on the Board.

4. Officers

4.1 The Corporation shall have officers including a President, Vice President, Secretary, Treasurer, and other officers as the Board of Directors from time to time, deems necessary. An officer may hold more than one office in the corporation, except that the President may not simultaneously serve as the Vice President or Secretary. The Board in its determination may leave any office vacant. All officers serve at the pleasure of the Board, which shall fix their compensation and term of employment.

Section 4.2 defines the President's duties.

4.2 The President shall be the chief executive officer of the Corporation and shall act in such a manner, and be responsible for such duties, appropriate to that officer.

However, the President shall always be under the supervisory power of the Board. The President shall be the presiding officer for the shareholders and Board of Directors meetings.

The next section describes the Vice President's responsibilities.

4.3 The Vice President shall be responsible for assuming the duties of the President upon the latter's inability to serve. The Vice President shall also have such other duties as the President or Board may determine.

The following section describes the duties of the Secretary.

4.4 The Secretary shall issue all notices demanded by the law or these Bylaws and shall keep the minutes of all the shareholders and Board of Directors proceedings. The Secretary shall also have such other duties as the President or Board may determine.

This next section states the duties of the Treasurer.

4.5 The Treasurer shall be responsible for all funds received by the Corporation and shall be the custodian of the corporate securities. The Treasurer shall also maintain accurate books and records of account of the assets and liabilities of the Corporation. The Treasurer shall also have such other duties as the President or the Board may determine.

5. Corporate Records / Reports

The corporation is required to keep accurate and complete corporate and financial records.

5.1 The Corporation shall maintain accurate books and records of assets and liabilities, and shall keep minutes of all proceedings involving shareholders, Board of Directors and Board committees, and shall keep at its principal executive office a record of the shareholders and the number and class of shares held by each. All books, records, and minutes must be kept in written form, with the exception of those books and records that are capable of being kept in a form convertible into written form.

The shareholders and Directors can inspect the corporate records.

5.2 The record of shareholders, the books and records of assets and liabilities, and the minutes of meetings and proceedings, shall be open for inspection by any shareholder upon written request. Each and every Director shall have the unqualified right to, at reasonable times, inspect and copy all Corporate documents of any kind, and to inspect all Corporate properties and holdings.

The corporation may have to provide an annual report to the shareholders if required to do so by state law. The following provision waives such a requirement.

5.3 The annual report to shareholders provided for in Section [x] (Enter section) of Corporate Law of the State of [x] (State), is hereby waived.

208

6. Indemnification of Corporate Agents

Officers, Directors, and other agents of the corporation will be indemnified by the corporation for legal expenses arising out of their efforts on behalf of the corporation.

Each and every agent of the Corporation shall be indemnified against legal expenses, judgments, fines, settlements and other amounts, reasonably incurred by such person after having been made or threatened to be made a party to a legal action. Payment of such amounts may also be made in advance if expenses are reasonably likely to be incurred by a Corporate agent in defense of any such action.

7. Execution of Instruments

The Board of Directors may authorize other individuals to sign documents on behalf of the corporation. Some state laws acquire certain signatures for special documents, so this article does not give the authorization to sign every document on behalf of the corporation.

The Board of Directors may by resolution determine the officers and agents to execute any corporate instrument or document, or to sign the Corporate name, within the law, and such execution and signing shall be binding on The Corporation.

The next article covers issues related to the issuance and transfer of corporate shares.

8. Issuance / Transfer of Shares

Every shareholder will get a certificate, signed by a corporate officer, evidencing his / her ownership of corporate shares.

8.1 Every Corporate shareholder shall be issued a certificate certifying the number and class of shares owned and contain any statement required by the provisions of the Corporate Law of the State of [State]. Every certificate shall Be signed by the Chairman of the Board, or the President or Vice President and by the Treasurer or Secretary of the Corporation, and the corporate seal shall be affixed thereto.

The transfer of shares can be accomplished by endorsing the certificate and recording the transfer with the corporation. You should note that state law may affect the ability to transfer shares at a corporation.

8.2 A transfer of shares may be made upon the signature of the owner and the delivery of the certificate, but to be effective, such transfer must be entered in the corporate records, complete with the names of the parties, the certificate registration, the number of shares involved and the date of transfer, and the old certificate must be surrendered and canceled.

The corporation will keep track of who owns how many shares.

8.3 The Corporation has the duty to record the transfer of shares, to cancel surrendered certificates, and to issue new certificates to new owners.

Section 9 discusses the rules relating to amending these Bylaws.

9. Amendment of Bylaws

Subject to state law, the shareholders can amend the Bylaws by vote. Also, the Directors can amend the Bylaws if not restricted from doing so.

9.1 These Bylaws may be amended or repealed, and new Bylaws adopted, upon approval by the shareholders entitled to vote, subject to the provisions of the Corporate Law of the State of [State]. Except for limitations imposed by the Articles of Incorporation on the Board of Directors' power to amend, repeal or adopt Bylaws, such actions may be taken by approval of the Board. However, such Bylaws may not contain any language in conflict with the law, or the Articles of Incorporation.

Only the shareholders can amend these Bylaws to change the number of Directors. A small minority (16 2/3%) can block such an amendment.

9.2 A Bylaw changing the number of Directors can be adopted only by approval of the outstanding shares, and any such change that reduces the number of Directors below five (5) cannot be adopted if the votes cast against its adoption are equal to more than sixteen and two-thirds (16 2/3) percent of the outstanding shares entitled to vote.

The following certificate should be completed and signed by the Corporate Secretary once the Board acts to approve the Corporate Bylaws.

Certificate of Secretary

I certify that I am the Secretary of [Company] and the attached Bylaws were duly adopted by the Board of Directors of the Corporation on [Month, Day, Year] at a meeting duly held.

____

Date

____

Secretary [Company]

<u>Corporation - Resolution Authority</u>

Resolution of The Directors
Of
Transfer of Shares

WHEREAS _____ •(the "Transferor") is currently the registered and beneficial owner of•_____ •shares (the "Transferred Shares") in the capital stock of _____ (the "Corporation");

NOW THEREFORE BE IT RESOLVED THAT the Directors of the Corporation hereby approve and consent to the transfer by the Transferor to _____ of the Transferred Shares.

The foregoing resolution is hereby consented to by the signatures of all the directors of the Corporation.

____

DATE

<u>NOTES</u>

<u>Board of Director Agreement</u>

SHAREHOLDER AGREEMENT

Note: Unanimous Shareholders Agreement by the sole Shareholder in a Corporation limiting powers of Directors of Corporation to govern the business and affairs of Corporation.

THIS UNANIMOUS SHAREHOLDER AGREEMENT made as of _____(Date) between _____, of _____ (the "Shareholder") and _____, of _____ (the "Director").

WHEREAS:

(the "Corporation") is a corporation incorporated under the laws of _____; and the Shareholder is the registered owner of all the issued and outstanding shares of the Corporation; and the Director has agreed to serve as a director of the Corporation at the request of the Shareholder and in consideration of the execution and delivery of the within Agreement by the Shareholder; and the Shareholder, acting under authority contained in _____ (the "Act"), has agreed to enter into this Unanimous Shareholder Agreement and will enter into agreements in identical form with any other directors of the Corporation (collectively the "Directors") so as to restrict the rights, powers and discretion of the directors of the Corporation to manage the business and affairs of the Corporation and so as to provide that the Shareholder shall assume the rights, powers and duties of such directors and thereby relieve such directors of their duties and liabilities to the fullest extent permitted by the Act;

NOW THEREFORE THIS INDENTURE WITNESSES AS FOLLOWS:

1. The powers of the Directors, including the Director, to manage the business and affairs of the Corporation, whether such powers arise from the Act, the articles or the by-laws of the Corporation, or otherwise, are hereby restricted to the fullest extent permitted by law.

2. In accordance with the Act and paragraph 1 hereof, the Shareholder shall have, enjoy, exercise and perform all the rights, powers and duties of the Directors to manage the business and affairs of the Corporation.

3. In the exercise of the rights, powers and duties granted and transferred hereunder, the Shareholder shall be subject to the same duties and liabilities

to which Directors would have been subject in the exercise of such rights and powers had this Agreement not been made.

4. The rights, powers and duties granted or transferred hereby to the Shareholder shall be exercised or performed to the extent appropriate, by instrument in writing executed by the Shareholder and any transferee of any shares of the Corporation registered in the name of the Shareholder. Subject to the Act, any such transferee shall be deemed to be a party to this Agreement and shall be governed hereby in the same manner and to the same extent as the Shareholder. The Shareholder shall cause a reference to this Agreement to be noted conspicuously on any share certificate issued by the Corporation.

5. Notwithstanding that the rights, powers and duties of directors of the Corporation to manage the business and affairs of the Corporation are hereby vested in the Shareholder, the Director, so long as he shall continue as a director of the Corporation, shall act in an advisory capacity to the Corporation, and in consideration thereof and of the within Agreement, the Shareholder hereby undertakes and agrees to indemnify and save harmless the Director and his heirs and legal representatives, respectively, from and against all costs, charges and expenses, including all amounts paid to settle any action or satisfy any judgment reasonably incurred by or on behalf of the Director in respect of any civil, criminal or administrative action or proceeding to which the Director is made a party (or any such proceeding which might be threatened and in respect of which the Director is threatened to be made a party) by reason of his being or having been a director of the Corporation or by
reason of any breach by the Shareholder of the rights, powers, duties and liabilities expressed herein to be assumed by the Shareholder.

6. This Agreement shall continue in full force and effect until terminated by notice in writing given by either party to the other, provided that such termination shall not affect any obligation of either party arising prior to the date of termination, including any obligation to indemnify by reason of any matter which has arisen or any circumstances which have occurred prior to the termination.

7. This Agreement shall enure to the benefit of the Director and his heirs and legal representatives and shall be governed in accordance with the laws of the State of _____ and the laws of the United States of America applicable therein.

IN WITNESS WHEREOF the parties hereto have duly executed this Agreement.

____

Date

____

Signature

____

Date

____

Signature

<u>NOTES</u>

<u>Stock Option Agreement</u>

THIS AGREEMENT made as of _____ between _____, of _____
(the "Corporation") and _____, of _____ (the "Optionee").

WHEREAS the Corporation wishes to grant to the Optionee and the Optionee
wishes to accept from the Corporation, an option to purchase _____ shares in
the capital stock of the Corporation (the "Optioned Shares");

NOW THEREFORE THIS AGREEMENT WITNESSES that in
consideration of the premises and for other good and valuable consideration,
the receipt and sufficiency of which is hereby acknowledged, the Corporation
hereby grants to the Optionee an option (the "Option") to purchase the
Optioned Shares at a purchase price (the "Purchase Price") of _____ per share
for an aggregate Purchase Price of _____, upon and subject to the following
terms and conditions:

1.   **Option Exercise Period**. The Option may be exercised by the
Optionee in whole (but not in part) at any time from the date hereof until the
day preceding the earlier of (i) _____, (ii) the death of the Optionee, or (iii)
_____, (the earliest of which dates shall be the "Termination Date") and shall
terminate on the Termination Date unless exercised by the Optionee prior
thereto.

2.   **Exercise of Option**. The Optionee shall, for the purposes of exercising
the Option, give to the Corporation notice in writing thereof (the "Notice"),
accompanied by a certified check or bank draft payable to the Corporation in
the amount of the Purchase Price.

3.   **Transfer of Optioned Shares**. Upon compliance by the Optionee of
all of the terms and conditions of this Agreement and upon receipt by the
Corporation of (i)   the Notice, and (ii) payment of the Purchase Price, the
Corporation shall issue to the Optionee one or more stock certificates
representing the Optioned Shares. The Corporation shall also cause the
Corporation's directors to consent to the sale and transfer of the Optioned
Shares to the Optionee.

4.   **Non-Assignability of Option**. The Option is personal to the
Optionee. Accordingly, the Optionee may not sell, assign or otherwise transfer
the Option or any of its rights under this Agreement without the prior written
consent of the Corporation, which consent may be unreasonably or arbitrarily
withheld.

5.   **Entire Agreement**. This Agreement expresses the entire agreement
between the parties concerning the subject matter hereof and supersedes all
previous agreements, whether written or oral, between the parties respecting
the subject matter hereof.

6.   **Successors and Assigns**. This Agreement shall be binding upon the parties hereto and their respective heirs, executors, administrators and successors and permitted assigns.

7.   **Governing Law**. This Agreement shall be governed by and construed in accordance with the laws of the State of _____.

IN WITNESS WHEREOF the parties hereto have executed this Agreement as of the date first above written.

Per:_______________________________

____
Name:

____
Title:

____
Witness

Stock Power to Transfer

FOR VALUE RECEIVED, the undersigned hereby sells, assigns and transfers unto ______ (______) ______ shares of ______ stock of ______ standing in the name of the undersigned on the books of the said Corporation represented by Certificate(s) No(s). ______.

The undersigned hereby irrevocably constitute and appoint ______ attorney to transfer the said stock on the books of the said Corporation, with full power of substitution in the premises.

____

Date

____

Witness

Stock Redemption Agreement

This is a standard introductory paragraph that lists the parties to the Agreement and the date the Agreement is being entered into. You need to enter the date of the Agreement, the names of the parties, the specific type of organization, and their addresses.

Effective Date: **[Date]** between **[Shareholder Name]**, ("Shareholder") a **[State of residence]** Resident, residing at **[Address]** and **[Company Legal Name]**, ("Company") a **[State of organization or residence]** [Corporation / Partnership / Sole Proprietorship / Resident) located at **[Address]**, **[City]**, **[State] [Zip Code]**.

Summary

Enter the total number of shares that the Shareholder owns.

The Shareholder presently owns _____ shares of the issued and outstanding capital stock of the Company (the "Shares").

Enter the total number of shares that the Company is redeeming or buying from the Shareholder. This may be all or part of the total number of shares listed above.

The Shareholder wishes to sell to the Company, and the Company wishes to redeem from the Shareholder, _____ Shares (the "Subject Shares") on the terms and conditions set forth in this Agreement.

In consideration for the mutual promises, covenants, and Agreements made below, the parties, intending to be legally bound, agree as follows:

Agreement

For the first insert in Section 1, indicate the total price being paid. For the second insert indicate the price being paid for each of the shares being redeemed.

1. Sale Redemption of Shares

The Shareholder hereby sells to the Company, and the Company hereby redeems from the Shareholder, all of the Subject Shares for an aggregate purchase price of $[xx] (or $[xx] per Subject Share).

2. Payment of Purchase Price; Delivery of Shares

Simultaneously with the execution and delivery of this Agreement by the Company and the Shareholder:

(1) The Company shall pay the purchase price for the Subject Shares to the Shareholder in cash or by cashier's check; and

(2) the Shareholder shall deliver to the Company the stock certificate evidencing the Subject Shares, duly endorsed to the Company.

Each state has different requirements for the redemption of stock. You need to either verify the requirements in your state, or check with an attorney.

For the first insert in Section 3, indicate the name of your state's statute relating to corporations. For example, in California insert California Corporations Code. Enter your state of incorporation for the second insert.

3. Compliance with State Corporation's Laws

The Company's Board of Directors has determined that the redemption of the Subject Shares is in compliance with the financial conditions required by the state of [State] in connection with the repurchase of the shares of stock of a [State] corporation.

This is a standard Representations and Warranties section that basically says that the Shareholder has not sold or otherwise encumbered the stock.

4. Representations Warranties

The Shareholder represents and warrants to the Company that:

(1) s/he is the owner, beneficially and of record, of all of the Subject Shares free and clear of all liens, encumbrances, security Agreements, options and restrictions, and

(2) s/he has full power to transfer the Subject Shares to the Company without obtaining the consent or approval of any third party.

5. Expenses

The Company shall pay all costs and expenses incurred or to be incurred in negotiating and preparing this Agreement and in closing and carrying out the transactions contemplated by this Agreement.

If there is a lawsuit or proceeding involving this Agreement, the losing party agrees to pay the winning party his or her costs and expenses, including reasonable attorney fees.

6. Attorney Fees

If either party is required to retain the services of any attorney to enforce or otherwise litigate or defend any matter or claim arising out of or in connection with this Agreement, then the prevailing party shall be entitled to recover from the other party, in addition to any other relief awarded or granted, its reasonable costs and expenses (including attorneys' fees) incurred in the proceeding.

The following section states that this Agreement is intended to be the only Agreement between these parties regarding this particular matter, and that no other documents or communications, whether oral or written, are binding. Therefore, it is very important to make sure that everything the parties have agreed to and want to include is accounted for in the body of this Agreement.

7. Entire Agreement

The parties acknowledge that this Agreement expresses their entire understanding and Agreement, and that there have been no warranties, representations, covenants or understandings made by either party to the other except such as are expressly set forth in this section. The parties further acknowledge that this Agreement supersedes, terminates and otherwise renders null and void any and all prior Agreements or contracts, whether written or oral, entered into between the Company and the Shareholder with respect to the matters expressly set forth in this Agreement.

8. Binding Effect

This Agreement shall be binding upon and shall inure to the benefit of the parties in this Agreement and their respective heirs, legal representatives, successors and assigns.

9. Notices

All notices, demands or consents required or permitted under this Agreement shall be in writing and shall be delivered or mailed certified return receipt requested to the respective parties at the addresses set forth above or at such other address as such party shall specify to the other party in writing. Any notice required or permitted to be given by the provisions of this Agreement shall be conclusively deemed to have been received on the day it is delivered to that party by U.S. Mail with Acknowledgment of Receipt or by any commercial courier providing equivalent acknowledgment of receipt.

In Section 10, you must decide which state's laws govern this Agreement. Generally, it is your (company's) state of residence. Insert that state in all three inserts.

10. Governing Law

This Agreement shall be governed by the laws of the State of [State] applicable to Agreements made and fully performed in [State] by [State] residents.

If any part of this Agreement is unenforceable or invalid, the balance of the Agreement should be enforced. Basically, ignore any sections that are invalid.

11. Severability

If any provision of this Agreement is found invalid or unenforceable under judicial decree or decision, the remainder shall remain valid and enforceable according to its terms. Without limiting the previous, it is expressly understood and agreed that each and every provision of this Agreement that provides for a limitation of liability, disclaimer of warranties, or exclusion of damages is intended by the parties to be severable and independent of any other provision and to be enforced as such. Further, it is expressly understood and agreed that if any remedy under this Agreement is determined to have failed of its essential purpose, all other limitations of liability and exclusion of damages set forth in this section shall remain in full force and effect.

Section 12 requires all changes to this Agreement, including any waivers, to be in writing and signed by the party against whom compliance is sought. Also, if one party waives a promise or condition such as a deadline, that doesn't mean that the promise or condition is automatically waived again.

12. Waiver, Amendment, Modification

No waiver, amendment or modification, including those by custom, usage of trade, or course of dealing, of any provision of this Agreement will be effective unless in writing and signed by the party against whom such waiver, amendment or modification is sought to be enforced. No waiver by any party of any default in performance by the other party under this Agreement or of any breach or series of breaches by the other party of any of the terms or conditions of this Agreement shall constitute a waiver of any subsequent default in performance under this Agreement or any subsequent breach of any terms or conditions of that Agreement. Performance of any obligation required of a party under this Agreement may be waived only by a written waiver signed by a duly authorized officer of the other party, that waiver shall be effective only with respect to the specific obligation described in that waiver.

13. Agreement Preparation

Both parties understand and expressly state that this Agreement was prepared by the Shareholder. The Company declares and states that it has read this Agreement, understand its terms, and has been advised to seek recourse to other and independent counsel to assure itself that this Agreement is fair. To the degree deemed necessary and appropriate, the Shareholder has sought such independent counsel.

Understood, Agreed & Accepted

We have carefully reviewed this contract and agree to and accept its terms and conditions. We are executing this Agreement as of the Effective Date first written above.

_______________________________   _______________________________

Shareholder   [Company Legal Name]

______________________________   ______________________________
Shareholder   [Owner / Founder], [Title]

______________________________   ______________________________
Name   Title

Spousal Consent

The undersigned is the spouse of [Shareholder] ("Shareholder") a party to the foregoing Stock Redemption Agreement (the "Agreement") between Shareholder and [Company] a [State of incorporation] corporation ("Company"). I have read and approve the provisions of the Agreement and consent to the execution of it by my spouse. I have been advised by the Company to obtain legal representation in connection with this Spousal Consent, and either I have done so or voluntarily chosen not to do so. I also hereby give my consent to and agree to be bound by the terms of the Agreement to the extent of my interest (whether by community property or otherwise) in any of the matters covered by the Agreement.

____
[Date]

____
(Signature of spouse)

____
(Signature of attorney)

Share Purchase Agreement (1)

Note: Share Purchase Agreement to be used when one shareholder (the Purchaser)• wishes to buy out all of the shares of a company from a his or her co- shareholder (the Vendor).

THIS AGREEMENT made as of _____ between _____, of _____ (the "Purchaser") and _____, of _____ (the "Vendor").

WHEREAS the Vendor is the registered and beneficial owner of _____ (the "Purchased Shares") in the capital stock of _____ (the "Corporation");

AND WHEREAS the Vendor wishes to sell to the Purchaser and the Purchaser agrees to purchase from the Vendor the Purchased Shares in accordance with the terms and conditions of this Agreement;

THIS AGREEMENT WITNESSES that in consideration of the covenants, agreements, warranties and payments herein set out and provided for, the parties hereto covenant and agree as follows.

Article 1

Purchased Shares and Purchase Price

1.1   Subject to the terms and conditions hereof, the Vendor agrees to sell to the Purchaser and the Purchaser agrees to purchase from the Vendor the Purchased Shares, effective _____ (the "Closing Date").

1.2   The purchase price payable by the Purchaser to the Vendor for the Purchased Shares shall be _____ and shall be payable on closing by certified check.

Article 2

Representations and Warranties of the Vendor

2.1   The Vendor covenants, represents and warrants as follows and acknowledges that the Purchaser is relying upon such covenants, representations and warranties in connection with the purchase by the Purchaser of the Purchased Shares:

2.2 The Vendor covenants, represents and warrants as follows and acknowledges that the Purchaser is relying upon such covenants, representations and warranties in connection with the purchase by the Purchaser of the Purchased Shares:

(a)   No person, firm or corporation has any agreement or option, or any right or privilege capable of becoming an agreement or option for the purchase from the Vendor of any of the Shares.

(b)   The Vendor is the registered and beneficial owner of the Shares, with good and marketable title thereto, free and clear of any pledge, lien, charge, encumbrance or security interest of any kind and the Vendor has the power and authority and right to sell the Shares in accordance with the terms of this Agreement.

(c)   The Vendor is not and will not be a non-resident alien within the meaning of the *Internal Revenue Code* of 1986, as amended.

2.3   The covenants, representations and warranties of the Vendor contained in this Agreement and contained in any document or certificate given pursuant hereto shall survive the closing of the purchase and sale of the Purchased Shares herein provided for and, notwithstanding such closing, or any investigation made by or on behalf of the Purchaser, shall continue in full force and effect for the benefit of the Purchaser for a period of three (3) years following closing of the transaction provided for herein after which time the Vendor shall be released from all obligations and liabilities hereunder in respect of such representations and warranties except with respect to any claims made by the Purchaser in writing prior to the expiration of such period.

Article 3

Indemnification

3.1   The Vendor agrees to indemnify and save harmless the Purchaser and the Corporation of and from any loss whatsoever arising out of, under or pursuant to:

(a)   any material loss suffered by the Purchaser or the Corporation as a result of any breach or inaccuracy of representation, warranty or covenant contained in this Agreement; and

(b)   all claims, demands, costs and expenses reasonably incurred in respect of the foregoing.

Article 4

General

4.1   The closing shall take place at 11 o'clock a.m. on the Closing Date at the address of the Purchaser.

4.2   Each of the parties hereto will from time to time at the other's request and expense and without further consideration, execute and deliver such other instruments of transfer, conveyance and assignment and take such further action as the other may require to more effectively complete any matter provided for herein.

4.3   Any notice, direction or instrument required or permitted to be given to the Vendor hereunder shall be in writing and may be given by mailing the same postage prepaid or delivering the same addressed to the Vendor at the address of the Vendor first above mentioned.

4.4   Any notice, direction or other instrument required or permitted to be given to the Purchaser hereunder shall be in writing and may be given by mailing the same postage prepaid, or delivering the same addressed to the Purchaser at the address of the Purchaser first above mentioned.

4.5   Any notice, direction or other instrument aforesaid, if delivered shall be deemed to have been given or made on the date on which it was delivered or it mailed shall be deemed to have been given or made on the third business day following the day on which it was mailed.

4.6   The Parties may change their addresses for service from time to time by notice given in accordance with the foregoing.

4.7   Time shall be of the essence of this Agreement.

4.8   This Agreement, including the Schedules hereto, constitutes the entire agreement between the parties hereto. There are not and shall not be any verbal statements, representations, warranties, undertakings or agreements between the parties and this Agreement may not be amended or modified in any respect except by written instrument signed by the parties hereto.

4.9   This Agreement shall be construed and enforced in accordance with, and the rights of the parties shall be governed by, the laws of the State of

______.

4.10   This Agreement shall enure to the benefit of and be binding upon the parties hereto and their respective heirs, legal personal representatives, successors and assigns.

4.11   The parties acknowledge that the recitals herein are true and correct in all material respects.

IN WITNESS WHEREOF the parties hereto have executed this Agreement as of the date first above written.

____

Witness

____

Witness

Per:____

____

Name

____

Title

Share Purchase Agreement (2)

Note: Unanimous Shareholders Agreement between two Shareholders in a Corporation. Significant modifications will be required if there are more than two Shareholders in the Corporation.

THIS AGREEMENT made as of _____ among _____, of _____ ("_____"), and _____, of _____ ("_____") and _____, with its principal place of business at _____ (the "Corporation").

WHEREAS the Corporation was incorporated under the laws of _____;

AND WHEREAS the Shareholders own all of the issued and outstanding Common Shares in the following proportion:

Per: _______________________________   Per: _______________________________

Per: _______________________________   Per: _______________________________

AND WHEREAS the Shareholders have agreed to execute and deliver this Agreement as a Shareholders' Agreement as they are desirous of entering into certain arrangements regarding the purchase and sale of their Common Shares and to restrict in part the powers of the Directors to manage the business and affairs of the Corporation in the manner hereinafter described.

NOW THEREFORE THIS AGREEMENT WITNESS that in consideration of the respective covenants and agreements of the parties herein contained, it is agreed by and between the parties as follows.

Article 1

Definitions

1.1   In this Agreement, the following words and phrases shall have the following respective meanings unless the context otherwise provides:

(a)   **"Agreement"** means this Agreement and any Schedules hereto;

(b)   **"Common Share"** means a common share in the capital of the Corporation;

(c) "**Director**" means any director of the board of directors of the Corporation and "**Board of Directors**" means the board of directors of the Corporation;

(d) "**Prime Rate**" means a revolving rate of interest commonly known as the prime rate of interest announced from time to time by ______ as a reference rate then in effect for determining interest rates;

(e) "**Proportionate Shareholdings**" when used in connection with any Shareholder, means a fraction the numerator of which is the number of Common Shares held by such Shareholder and the denominator of which is the total number of issued and outstanding Common Shares;

(f) "**Section**" and "**Subsection**" refer to a section or subsection of this Agreement;

(g) "**Shareholder**" means any of ______, ______ and any person who becomes the holder of one or more Common Shares in accordance with the provisions of this Agreement;

(h) "**Shareholder's Loan**" means any loan made by a Shareholder to the Corporation in accordance with the provisions of this Agreement.

Article 2

Purpose and Intent

2.1 The parties shall cause the Corporation to carry on the business of a ______ and to generally carry on all ancillary and related activities which in the mutual opinion of the parties will enhance the Corporation's income and profit.

2.2 The parties agree that the Corporation shall operate under the name of " ______ ".

2.3 The Shareholders will irrevocably instruct their nominees and representatives at all the meetings of the Shareholders and insofar as permitted by law their nominees or representatives on the Board of Directors always to vote and act in accordance with the terms of this Agreement so as to give this Agreement full force and effect and to carry out its intent.

Article 3

Organization

3.1 The Corporation shall be organized as follows:

(a) There shall be two (2) Directors on the Board of Directors, consisting of one (1) nominee of each Shareholder. The first members of the Board of Directors shall be ______ as nominee of ______ and ______ as nominee of ______.

(b) The Corporation shall have three (3) officers, namely, President, Secretary and Treasurer. The parties agree that the following persons will be appointed to hold the following offices of the Corporation:

President - ________________________

Secretary - ________________________

Treasurer - ________________________

(c)   All checks and other banking documents, deeds, transfers, contracts, agreements and other documents that are required to be executed by the Corporation from time to time shall be executed on its behalf by any one of the Shareholders.

(d)   All share certificates issued or to be issued by the Corporation shall be endorsed with a memorandum as follows:

"This certificate is subject to a Shareholders' Agreement dated _____, a copy of which is filed with the Secretary of the Corporation, and the shares represented by this certificate cannot be sold, transferred, assigned or otherwise disposed of or mortgaged, pledged, hypothecated, charged or otherwise encumbered except pursuant to the terms of the said Shareholders' Agreement."

(e)   The by-laws of the Corporation shall provide or shall be deemed hereby to be amended to provide amongst other things, as follows:

(i)   the presence of two (2) Directors shall be required to constitute a quorum at any meeting of the Board of Directors;

(ii)   any resolution of the Board of Directors shall require affirmative votes of at least two (2) Directors;

(Iii)   the presence of two (2) Shareholders holding Common Shares, having voting rights and representing in person or by proxy one hundred percent (100%) of all issued Common Shares shall be required to constitute a quorum at any meeting of Shareholders;

(iv)   any resolution of the Shareholders shall require the affirmative votes of one hundred percent (100%) of all issued Common Shares entitled to voting rights at the meeting at which such resolution is being passed;

(v)   each Director shall have the right at any time and from time to time to call a meeting of the board of directors on not less than seven (7) days' notice;

(vi)   any Shareholder shall have the right at any time or from time to time to call a meeting of the Shareholders on not less than seven (7) days' notice;

(vii)   the Chairman presiding at meetings of the Board of Directors shall have the right to vote in his capacity as Director in the first instance, but shall have no second or casting vote in case of an equality of votes;

(viii)   the Chairman presiding at meetings of the Shareholder shall have the right to vote in the first instance in his capacity as a Shareholder and as a proxy if so appointed but shall have no second or casting vote in case of an equality of votes.

Article 4

Conduct of Business

4.1 The parties agree that the powers of the directors will be restricted and, except with the written consent of all of the Shareholders:

(a)   no dividends shall be declared;

(b)   no management or consulting fees shall be paid;

(c)   no additional shares in the capital stock of the Corporation shall be issued or allotted;

(d)   there shall be no material change in the nature of the business of the Corporation nor any action taken which may lead to or result in such material change;

(e)   the Corporation shall not directly nor indirectly make loans or advances, give guarantees for, invest in, or give security for or guarantee the debts of any other corporation or person;

(f)   the Corporation shall not sell, lease, exchange or dispose of its undertaking or any part thereof as an entirety or substantially as an entirety;

(g)   the Corporation shall not hypothecate, mortgage, pledge or otherwise encumber its assets or any of them except as may be required by its bankers in connection with its normal banking activities and arrange lines of credit;

(h)   the number of Directors shall not be increased nor decreased;

(i)   if at any time or from time to time additional shares in the capital of the Corporation are to be allotted, issued or sold, then they shall be allotted, issued and sold to the Shareholders pro rata in relation to their then existing Proportionate Shareholdings; and

(j)   there will be no amendments to any of the Corporation's by-laws or the Articles of Incorporation.

Article 5

Financing

5.1 The parties agree that they will actively pursue and work towards attaining satisfactory bank credit and financing for the Corporation, it being the intention of the parties that such financing be sought in the highest amount necessary so that the equity investment required by the Shareholders should be kept to a minimum.

5.2 The Shareholders shall be jointly and severally liable with respect to any guarantees or other security given by any of the Shareholders, to secure any loans or advances made to the Corporation by any third party. In the event any Shareholder is called upon to honor any such guarantee or other security and so does, then such Shareholder shall have the right to recover any money so paid in excess of the amount which would have been required on the basis of Proportionate Shareholdings, jointly and severally from the Corporation and the Shareholders.

5.3   Notwithstanding the foregoing, if bank credit and financing cannot be arranged in an amount sufficient for the Corporation to carry on its business in a proper manner, upon unanimous consent of the Board of Directors, all further monies required shall be advanced to the Corporation as a Shareholder's Loan by the Shareholders, pro rata in relation to their then existing Proportionate Shareholdings.

5.4   Any Shareholder's Loans, to the extent to which they have been advanced by the Shareholders in proportion to their respective Proportionate Shareholdings, shall bear no interest unless and until the Shareholders agree to the contrary, in which case such loans shall bear such rate of interest as is from time to time agreed upon. Except as expressly set forth below, none of the Shareholder's Loans shall be due or payable to or called by any of the parties.

5.5   Any Shareholder having outstanding a Shareholder's Loan which bears to all Shareholders' Loans then outstanding a greater proportion than the respective Proportionate Shareholding of such Shareholder shall be called the "Credit Shareholder" and any Shareholder having outstanding a Shareholder's Loan which bears to all Shareholders' Loans then outstanding a lesser proportion that the respective Proportionate Shareholding of such shareholder shall be called the "Debit Shareholder". If for any reason Shareholders' Loans outstanding to the Shareholders at any time or from time to time are not exactly in the same proportions as the respective Proportionate Shareholdings of the Shareholders, that portion of the Shareholder Loans outstanding to the Credit Shareholder in excess of its Proportionate Shareholding shall be payable to it out of monies available for distribution by the Corporation, and in any such case any payments made by the Corporation out of any monies available for distribution to the Shareholders shall be firstly applied by the Corporation to bring the Shareholders' Loans outstanding to the appropriate amount necessary so that the Shareholders' Loans are exactly in the same proportion as the respective Proportionate Shareholdings of the Shareholders.

5.6   If at any time or from time to time any Shareholder defaults in advancing forthwith its proportionate share of any monies which may at any time be required by the Corporation, then such Shareholder shall be referred to herein as the "Defaulting Shareholder" and the others shall be referred to herein as the "Non-defaulting Shareholders". In the event of default as aforesaid and provided such default continues for a period of five (5) days after written notice thereof to the Defaulting Shareholder by the Non-defaulting Shareholders, the Non-defaulting Shareholders shall have the following rights:

5.7   Any Non-defaulting Shareholder may advance to the Corporation the amount so required to be advanced by the Defaulting Shareholder and such amount shall constitute a debt owing to such Non-defaulting Shareholder by the

Defaulting Shareholder and shall be repaid forthwith by the Defaulting Shareholder to the Non-defaulting Shareholder, and until repaid, shall bear interest at the Prime Rate plus three percent (3%) per annum calculated monthly on the amount from time to time owed to the Non-defaulting Shareholder by the Defaulting Shareholder as aforesaid and, until so repaid, such amounts, together with interest thereon as aforesaid, shall, to the extent thereof, be and constitute a first lien and charge on and against the Common Shares of the Defaulting Shareholder, on and against the Shareholder Loans of the Defaulting Shareholder, and on and against all other interest of the Defaulting Shareholder in the Corporation.

5.8 Any Non-defaulting Shareholders may, at its option, borrow from any lender acting in good faith, on such terms and conditions, and at such rate of interest, as may be agreed upon between the Non-defaulting Shareholder and such lender, on behalf of the Corporation and the Defaulting Shareholder, an amount equal to the amount which would be required to be advanced to the Corporation by the Defaulting Shareholder to cure the default, and to advance such amount to the Corporation on behalf of the Defaulting Shareholder and to charge the Defaulting Shareholder all costs and expenses reasonably incurred by the Non-defaulting Shareholder in connection with the amount so borrowed, and interest on the amount so borrowed and advanced at the same rate as that charged by such lender on the amount from time to time outstanding. All such costs and expenses and all such advances and interest thereon at the rate aforesaid shall, to the extent thereof, be and constitute a first lien and charge on and against the Defaulting Shareholder's interest in the Corporation by way of shares or advances.

5.9 If the default of the Defaulting Shareholder shall continue for a period of forty-five (45) days or more, thereafter, the Non-defaulting Shareholder shall have the right to acquire in full the said Defaulting Shareholder's aggregate shareholdings in, and Shareholder's Loans to, the Corporation for a purchase price therefor equal to the outstanding Shareholder's Loans made by the Defaulting Shareholder to the Corporation, plus the sum of One Dollar ($1.00) and the purchase of the Defaulting Shareholder's loans and shares as aforesaid shall be subject to the following terms and conditions:

(a)   One Dollar ($1.00) shall be the down payment, and

(b)   the balance of the purchase price, without interest, shall be payable in full only after the Corporation has repaid out of surplus funds on hand to the Non-defaulting Shareholder, all monies owed to the Non-defaulting Shareholders by the Corporation, including the amount of the Shareholder's Loans so purchased by the Non-defaulting Shareholder from the Defaulting Shareholder. The Defaulting Shareholder shall upon such payment execute all necessary share transfers and other resolutions and documents in order to fully and effectually transfer the shares of the Defaulting Shareholder to the Non-defaulting Shareholder.

5.10 The Non-defaulting Shareholder is hereby irrevocably authorized, instructed and directed for, and on behalf of and as attorney for the Defaulting Shareholder to execute any and all documents required to be executed by the Corporation or the Defaulting Shareholder for the purposes set out in Article 5.

5.11   All Shareholder's Loans shall be upon the express understanding that unless specific terms for such loans are unanimously agreed to by the Shareholders, same will be on the following terms and conditions:

(a)   all advances and contributions shall be evidenced by bonds, debentures, security agreements, or promissory notes (the "Shareholder's Debt Instrument") in the principal amount advanced by each of the Shareholders;

(b)   there shall be a separate series of Shareholder's Debt Instruments issued by the Corporation upon the occasion of each advance of funds to the Corporation by the Shareholders; and

(c)   Shareholder's Debt Instruments shall bear no interest unless unanimously agreed otherwise by the Shareholders.

5.12   The Shareholders agree that at the request of the Board of Directors, they will subordinate all Shareholder's Loans (and any interest thereon) to conventional financing or other borrowing by the Corporation to the extent required by the Board of Directors.

Article 6

Administration

6.1   Proper books of account shall be kept by the Corporation, and entries shall be made therein of all such matters, terms, transactions and other things as are usually written and entered in books of account kept by others engaged in an enterprise of a similar nature and each of the Shareholders shall have free access at all times to inspect, examine and copy them and shall at all times furnish to the other, correct information, accounts and statements of and concerning all such transactions without concealment or suppression.

6.2   A separate bank account shall be opened and maintained for the Corporation in the name of the Corporation or in such other name or names as may from time to time be agreed upon by the parties, at such bank or banks as the parties may from time to time agree upon. All monies received from time to time on account of the business of the Corporation shall be paid immediately into such bank account for the time being in operation and in the same form of drafts, checks, bills or cash in which they are received and all disbursements on account of the Corporation shall be made by check on such bank account.

6.3   Receipts and revenues of the business of the Corporation from any source whatsoever shall be applied and distributed in the following order of priority, no distribution being made in any category set forth below unless and until the preceding category has been satisfied in full, unless the Shareholders otherwise unanimously agree in writing:

(a) the payments of all debts, obligations, liabilities, costs and expenses in connection with or on account of the business of the Corporation, if any;

(b) the repayment of Shareholder Loans;

(c) the distribution of the monies remaining, if any, in such manner as is mutually agreeable after consultation with the Corporation's accountants, to the Shareholders in proportion to their Proportionate Shareholdings.

Article 7

First Right of Refusal

7.1   In the event that any Shareholder (the "Seller") receives a bona fide offer (the "Offer") from a person, firm, or corporation dealing at arm's length which is not directly or indirectly controlled by any of the other parties, to purchase all or any part of the Common Shares owned or controlled by the Seller which the Seller is prepared to accept, then the Seller shall forthwith send to the other Shareholders (the "Offerees") notice in writing of its desire or intention to sell such shares accompanied by a copy of the Offer.

7.2   Upon receipt of notice in accordance with the foregoing provisions of this Article 7, each Offeree shall have fifteen (15) days from the date of receipt within which to give the Seller notice (the "Intent to Buy") that it desires and agrees to so purchase the shares referred to in the Offer on the same terms and conditions as are contained in the Offer, provided that:

(a)   if the Offeree shall have given an Intent to Buy, the Offeree shall
          purchase
all of the Common Shares of the Seller referred to in the Offer;

(b)   if the Offeree shall not have given an Intent to Buy within the time provided, then the Offeree shall be deemed for all purposes to have refused to purchase the Common Shares of the Seller; and

(c)   if more than one Offeree shall have given an Intent to Buy, then such Offerees shall purchase all of the Common Shares of the Seller referred to in the Offer pro rata in proportion to the such Offerees Proportionate Shareholdings.

7.3   In the event that each Offeree elects not to purchase or is deemed to have refused to purchase the Common Shares referred to in the Offer then the Seller may accept the Offer and proceed to sell the Common Shares referred to in the Offer but only at the price and on and in accordance with the terms and conditions contained in the Offer provided that, if the transaction contemplated by the Offer is not completed within a period of twenty-one (21) days after the expiration of the last day upon which the Offeree has the right to give an Intent to Buy, then the Seller shall not thereafter sell the said Common Shares unless and until it again complies with the provisions contained in this Section 7.

7.4   Any transaction between the Seller and the Offeree effected pursuant to the provisions of this Section shall be completed not later than the fifteenth (15th) day after which the Offeree has become obligated to purchase the said Common Shares.

7.5   No sale under this Section to a person who is not a Shareholder at the time of such sale, shall be completed until the purchaser of such Common Shares agrees in writing to be bound by the terms of this Agreement.

Article 8

Compulsory Buy-Sell

8.1   Any Shareholder (the "Offeror") may, at any time, make a written Offer (the "Offer") to any other Shareholder (the "Offeree"), which Offer shall contain both an offer to purchase all and not less than all of the Common Shares held by the Offeree, and an offer to sell to the Offeree all but not less than all of the Common Shares held by the Offeror. Upon such an Offer being received by the Offeree, the Shareholders shall not do or cause to be done or permit to be done by the Corporation anything except in the ordinary and usual course of business of the Corporation.

8.2   The Offer shall stipulate a price for each share to be purchased and shall also contain all other terms and conditions attached to such Offer to purchase, provided that none of the other terms and conditions shall conflict in any way with the terms of this Agreement. Notwithstanding any other provision contained herein, it is agreed that the purchase price contained in the Offer shall provide for a payment in cash or by certified check of at least twenty-five percent (25%) of the total purchase price (including the deposit to be credited towards the purchase price), at the time of the completion of the purchase transaction and that the balance of any such purchase price shall be evidenced by a promissory note and be paid over a period of two (2) years from the date of closing of the said purchase transaction in twenty-four (24) equal monthly installments of principal together with interest monthly calculated at the Prime Rate per annum on the outstanding principal sum from time to time, provided that the note shall be fully open as to additional payments of principal at any time or times without notice or bonus, and provided further that in the event of any default in payment, which default continues for a period of ten (10) days after written notice thereof, the entire balance shall immediately become due and payable.

8.3   The Offeree shall, within fifteen (15) days of the date on which the Offer is delivered, elect to either:

(a)   accept the Offer made by the Offeror to purchase all the Common Shares of the Offeree at the price and upon the conditions contained in the Offer, by an acceptance in writing executed by the Offeree, in which event the Offeree shall be bound to sell all of the Offeree's Common Shares to the Offeror at the price and upon the terms and conditions contained in the Offer; or

(b)   accept the Offer made by the Offeror to sell all of the Offeror's Common Shares by a notification in writing executed by the Offeree, in which event the Offeree shall be bound to purchase from the Offeror all of the Offeror's Common Shares at the price and upon the terms and conditions contained in the Offer.

8.4   An Offer made pursuant to this Agreement must be delivered by personal service to the Offeree, and a copy mailed or delivered to the Corporation's solicitor, and must be accompanied by a certified check drawn in favor of the Corporation's solicitor in trust as a deposit, in an amount equal to ten percent (10%) of the total purchase price offered for the Common Shares of the Offeree. The deposit monies shall be placed in an interest earning account or deposit certificate with the bank of the Corporation's solicitor, to be credited on account of the total purchase price, or to be returned without deduction in the event the Offeree elects to purchase the Common Shares of the Offeror, in which case the Offeree shall deliver in its place its certified check drawn in favor of the Corporation's solicitor in trust as a deposit in an amount equal to ten percent (10%) of the total purchase price for all the Common Shares of the Offeror. The funds so received in trust as a deposit shall be applied against the purchase price and shall be delivered on closing. If the purchaser fails to complete the purchase, the vendor may retain such deposit as liquidated damages and not as a penalty.

8.5   In the event the Offeree fails or refuses to deliver an acceptance either under Subsection 8.3(a) or 8.3(b) within the time limit prescribed for such communication, the Offeree shall be deemed to have communicated to the Offeror an acceptance of the Offer made by the Offeror to purchase all the Common Shares of the Offeree at the price and upon the conditions contained in the Offer under Subsection 8.3(a).

8.6   Upon the formation of a contract by an acceptance or deemed acceptance of the Offer to purchase all the Common Shares of the Offeree under Subsection 8.3(a), the Offeror, as purchaser, shall purchase from the Offeree and the Offeree, as vendor, shall convey, transfer and assign to the Offeror all of the Common Shares of the Offeree, at and for the price set out in the Offer and under the terms and conditions set out therein and in this Agreement.

8.7   Upon the formation of a contract by an acceptance of the Offer to purchase all of the Common Shares of the Offeror under Subsection 8.3(a), the Offeree, as purchaser, shall purchase from the Offeror and the Offeror, as vendor, shall convey, transfer and assign to the Offeree all the Common Shares of the Offeror at and for the price set out in the Offer and under the terms and conditions set out therein and in this Agreement.

8.8   The completion of the sale pursuant to this Section shall be at any time mutually agreed upon by the parties within thirty (30) days of the formation of a contract hereunder. Should the parties be unable to mutually agree on a time, then the date for completion of the sale shall be the thirtieth (30th) day following the date on which the contract was formed. The completion of the sale shall take place at the offices of the Corporation's solicitors on the day specified for the closing. In the event the said thirtieth (30) day falls on a weekend or statutory holiday, the closing date shall be the next following business day.

8.9   When there is a sale of shares pursuant to an Offer made pursuant to this Section 8, the purchase price shall be paid in accordance with the terms and conditions contained in the said Offer, subject to any overriding terms and conditions which may be contained in this Agreement.

Article 9

Bankruptcy, Insolvency

9.1   In the event of bankruptcy, insolvency, winding-up or liquidation of a Shareholder, or if a receiver is appointed in respect of the whole or substantially the whole of such Shareholder's Common Shares and Shareholder Loans, or in the event of the transfer, voluntary or involuntary, by a Shareholder of its said shares to any creditor, in total or partial satisfaction of any debt, obligation, judgment or other liability (any such assignee, trustee, receiver or transferee being referred to as the "Special Transferee", and the said Shareholder being referred to as the "Insolvent Shareholder", and each of the other Shareholders being referred to as the "Solvent Shareholder"), the Solvent Shareholder shall have the sole exclusive and irrevocable option exercisable by written notice delivered to the Special Transferee within thirty (30) days subsequent to such an event and the Insolvent Shareholder shall be deemed to have granted such option prior to the event or appointment to purchase the Insolvent Shareholder's Common Shares and Shareholder's Loan at a purchase price equal to eighty percent (80%) of the aggregate of (i) the net book value of such Common Shares, calculated by multiplying the net worth of the Corporation as set forth in the Corporation's most recent fiscal year end balance sheet by the Insolvent Shareholder's Proportionate Shareholding, and (ii) the principal and accrued interest on such Shareholder's Loan. Ten percent (10%) of the said purchase price shall be payable in cash to the Special Transferee within thirty (30) days from the date the option is exercised, and the balance shall be payable in twenty- four (24) equal monthly installments together with interest at a rate of eight percent (8.0%) per annum, calculated monthly, on the outstanding principal balance from time to time.

Article 10

Death of a Shareholder

10.1   Upon the death of any Shareholder (the "Deceased"), any other Shareholder may elect in writing delivered to the legal representative of the Deceased and to the other Shareholders within thirty (30) days of the date of death of the Deceased to have the sale provisions of this Article apply (an "Election").

10.2   In the event that an Election is made in accordance with the foregoing, the Deceased's legal representative (the "Vendor"), shall sell all of the Common Shares beneficially owned or controlled by the Vendor to the Corporation upon and subject to the terms and conditions hereinafter set forth.

10.3   Upon the unanimous consent of the board of directors, the Corporation shall place and maintain in good standing a policy of term insurance on the lives of each of Shareholder, in amounts to be agreed upon, which amounts shall be proportionately adjusted simultaneously with the estimation of the fair market value of the Common Shares of the Corporation as determined in accordance with Section 10.5, or such other amount as the Shareholders may agree upon.

10.4   Each of the Shareholders shall use their best efforts to permit the Corporation to obtain and maintain any such life insurance, including but not limited to, attending for physical examinations, answering such questions as may be reasonably necessary and executing consents to the placing of such insurance coverage.

10.5   Each year, within thirty (30) days of the date upon which the Corporation's annual financial statements are available for review by the

Shareholders, the shareholders, upon consultation with the Corporation's accountants, shall estimate and duly note in writing, the fair market value of the outstanding Common Shares. In the event of a disagreement, the opinion of the Corporation's accountants shall prevail.

10.6   In the event that the Vendor owns any preference shares of the Corporation, and an Election is made in accordance with this Article, the Corporation shall redeem such shares within sixty (60) days of the date of death of the Deceased at the redemption price of such shares plus any dividends which have been declared thereon prior to the date of death of the Deceased and which remain unpaid.

10.7   In the event that the Vendor owns any Common Shares and the Deceased was insured pursuant to this Article and an Election is made in accordance with this Article, the Corporation shall purchase such Common Shares for cancellation for a purchase price equal to the Proportionate Shareholdings of the Deceased multiplied by the fair market value of all of the issued and outstanding Common Shares of the Corporation, as last noted and determined in accordance with Section 10.5. The purchase of the Common Shares as aforesaid shall be completed forthwith upon receipt by the Corporation of the insurance proceeds referred to in Section 10.3; provided that any portion of the purchase price which exceeds the insurance proceeds received by the Corporation shall be payable in twenty-four (24) equal consecutive monthly payments commencing thirty (30) days after closing, with interest thereon at the Prime Rate per annum, calculated and payable monthly, provided that the Corporation shall have the privilege to prepay or repay the whole or any part of such balance at any time and from time to time without notice or bonus.

10.8   In the event that the Vendor owns any Common Shares and the Deceased was not insured pursuant to this Article and an Election is made in accordance with this Article, the Corporation shall purchase such Common Shares for cancellation for a purchase price equal to the Proportionate Shareholdings of the Deceased multiplied by the fair market value of all of the issued and outstanding Common Shares of the Corporation, as last noted and determined in accordance with Section 10.5. The purchase price as aforesaid shall be payable in twenty-four (24) equal consecutive monthly payments commencing thirty (30) days after the date of death of the Deceased, with interest thereon at the Prime Rate per annum, calculated and payable monthly, provided that the Corporation shall have the privilege to prepay or repay the whole or any part of such balance at any time and from time to time without notice or bonus.

Article 11

Prohibition on Share Transfers

11.1   Unless otherwise specifically provided for in this Agreement, no Shareholder without the prior written consent of each of the other Shareholders will sell, assign, transfer, pledge, mortgage, hypothecate, charge or otherwise transfer or encumber any Common Shares now or hereinafter beneficially owned by such Shareholder.

11.2   For the purposes of this Agreement, any transfer, sale, assignment, transmission, bequest, inheritance, mortgage, encumbrance or other disposition of shares of any corporate shareholder having the result (directly or indirectly and either immediately or subject to the happening of any contingency) of changing the identity of the person or persons exercising or who might exercise control of any corporate Shareholder (from the applicable party exercising control of any such corporate Shareholder as of the date of execution of this Agreement) shall be deemed to be a transfer by such corporate Shareholder of its interest hereunder notwithstanding whether such change shall be voluntary or involuntary on the part of such corporate Shareholder. However, this covenant shall not apply to transfers or sales of Common Shares to an immediate member of the family of a Shareholder of such corporate Shareholder, nominees, companies owned or controlled by a Shareholder of such corporate Shareholder, or any trust which may be established for the benefit of any shareholder of such corporate Shareholder, or a member of his immediate family, provided that at the time of any such transfer or sale, any successor or assign shall, in writing, agree to be bound by the terms and provisions of this Agreement and further provided that in the event of a transfer or sale of Common Shares to a corporation owned or controlled by a shareholder of such corporate Shareholder, the shareholder of such corporate Shareholder shall covenant not to transfer the shares of any such transferee corporation to any persons who are not members of his immediate family.

Article 12

Sale Provisions

12.1   In this Article the selling Shareholder is referred to as the "Vendor" and the purchaser is referred to as the "Purchaser". In the event of a sale or transfer of shares in the Corporation pursuant to Sections 8 and 10, and not in any other case, the following provisions shall apply unless otherwise agreed upon by the Shareholders or unless any other provision contained herein applies specifically to such a sale or transfer, in which case, the provision applying specifically to such a sale or transfer shall apply:

(a)   Upon payment of the monies payable upon closing, the Vendor shall execute and deliver a transfer of his shareholdings in the capital of the Corporation to the Purchaser or as he or she may, in writing, direct and upon such payment, the Purchaser is hereby irrevocably appointed and constituted attorney for the Vendor with full power and authority to execute and deliver such transfers and other documents as may be necessary or desirable to complete such transaction of purchase and sale.

(b)   Unless otherwise herein provided, until payment in full of the unpaid balance of the purchase price, unless proceeds derived from the following are used to repay the indebtedness of the Purchaser to the Vendor, neither the Purchaser nor the Corporation shall:

(i)   transfer, redeem, assign, hypothecate or otherwise deal with any shares in the capital of the Corporation;

(ii)   declare any dividends;

246

(iii)   issue or sell any shares in the capital of the Corporation;

(iv)   increase or decrease the capital of the Corporation;

(v) dispose of the whole or a substantial part of the Corporation's assets or undertaking;

(vi)   take any proceedings for the winding-up, reorganization or dissolution of the Corporation;

(vii)   repay any Shareholders' Loans;

(viii)   increase, except for increases to compensate for reasonable cost of living increases from time to time, any salary or other remuneration payable to the Purchaser or other officers or directors of the Corporation, or any other person or persons, other than bona fide full-time active employees of the Corporation other than the Purchaser, nor will the Corporation by means of any directors' fees, new bonus or pension plan and/or new contract or commitment increase in any amount the benefits and compensation of any director, officer, or Shareholder of the Corporation;

(ix)   carry on the business of the Corporation other than diligently and substantially in the same manner as prior to such sale;

(x)   make any commitments for capital expenditures other than in the ordinary course of business;

(xi)   dispose of any of the Corporation's capital assets other than in the ordinary course of business;

(xii)   increase any indebtedness other than that incurred in the ordinary course of business or incurred pursuant to existing contracts;

(xiii)   amend the Articles of Incorporation or by-laws of the Corporation if such amendment has a material affect on the sold shares;

(xiv)   fail to keep insured against all risks as prior to such sale all property, real and personal, owned, leased, or used by the Corporation or fail to use, operate, maintain and repair such property as it was previously used.

(xv)   In the event of default of any of the above provisions, the Vendor shall have the right to require the rectification thereof, and if such breach is not rectified within ten (10) days of a written request for rectification, any balance of the purchase price outstanding shall immediately become due and payable.

(c)   If at the time of such sale the Vendor shall be liable or responsible for any debts, liabilities or obligations incurred by or on behalf of the Corporation as guarantor or otherwise, the Purchaser shall cause any and all such guarantees of indebtedness of the Corporation to any bank, or other lender to be delivered up and cancelled, and shall use his best efforts to cause any and all other guarantees of any of the Corporation's other contractual obligations to be delivered up and cancelled but if these others are not available then the Purchaser shall indemnify the Vendor against and save him harmless from all claims arising out of such guarantees or other obligations.

(d)   At the time of such sale, the Vendor shall receive from the Corporation a release of any and all claims which it may have against him and the Vendor shall deliver to the Corporation a release of any and all claims which he may have against it and the Purchaser, as a shareholder, director or employee, save and except any claims arising out of a portion of the purchase price remaining unpaid and any guarantees or obligations for which a release was not obtained pursuant to Section 12(c) above.

(e) All of the Corporation's costs and expenses relating to the sale of the shares shall be paid equally by the Vendor and Purchaser.

(f)   If at the time of sale, pursuant to the provisions of this Section, the Corporation shall be indebted to the Vendor upon closing, the Purchaser shall purchase such indebtedness from the Vendor for a purchase price and consideration equal to the amount of such indebtedness and accrued interest, if any, which purchase price shall be paid as follows:

(i)   the balance of any insurance proceeds remaining after utilizing the amount required to complete the purchase of the Vendor's common shares pursuant to the survivorship provisions shall be fully utilized towards the purchase of such indebtedness;

(ii)   a sum equivalent to twenty-five percent (25%) of the balance of the indebtedness not satisfied by insurance proceeds as aforesaid, shall be paid in cash or certified check on closing;

(iii)   the remainder owing shall be paid in twenty-four (24) equal monthly installments of principal together with interest monthly at the Prime Rate per annum on the outstanding principal sum from time to time, provided that the Purchaser shall have the privilege to prepay or repay the whole or any part of such balance at any time and from time to time without notice or bonus, and provided further, that in the event of any default in payment, which default continues for a period of ten (10) days, the entire balance shall immediately be due and payable.

(g) If shares of the Corporation are sold pursuant to the survivorship provisions herein, any interests in the life insurance policies on the life of the survivor held by the personal representatives of the deceased shall forthwith upon the closing of the sale be transferred and assigned by them, as owners of such policies, to the insured or as the insureds may direct.

(h)   While monies are due and owing by the Purchaser to the Vendor, the Purchaser will supply annual financial statements of the Corporation to the Vendor, annually within ninety (90) days of the Corporation's fiscal year end.

(i) The date scheduled for closing may be at any earlier date agreed to and fixed by the parties, but in no case will it be later than thirty (30) days after the Agreement has been reached for the sale or transfer of shares. The transaction shall be completed at the offices of the Corporation's solicitors at 2:00 p.m. on

248

the date arranged for the closing, or at such other location or times as the parties may decide. In the event the said thirtieth (30th) day falls on a weekend or statutory holiday, the closing date shall be the next following business day.

(j) The Vendor and any nominees of the Vendor shall resign from the Board of Directors and from any office or employment with the Corporation.

(k) Any amount payable under the Agreement of Purchase and Sale or other agreed transaction shall be paid by way of cash or by way of certified check.

(l) If upon the date determined for the completion of such a transaction the Vendor shall be indebted to the Corporation, the amount shall be verified by the accountant of the Corporation, and the Purchaser shall be entitled out of the purchase price to pay, satisfy and discharge all or any portion of such indebtedness and to receive and to take a credit against the amount owing on closing to the Vendor for his shares for an amount or amounts so paid on account of any such indebtedness.

(m) The Vendor shall contemporaneously with the closing of the subject transaction execute and deliver to the Purchaser all notices, documents and other materials reasonably necessary to complete the transaction.

(n) Between the date of any offer and the date of closing of any ensuing transaction, neither the Vendor nor the Purchaser shall do or cause or permit to be done anything except in the ordinary course of business of the Corporation.

Article 13

Arbitration

13.1 If any dispute arises between the parties concerning this Agreement, that dispute shall be submitted to binding arbitration. The arbitration shall be conducted according to the Commercial Arbitration Rules of the American Arbitration Association. The arbitrator's award may be confirmed and entered as a final judgment in any court of competent jurisdiction and enforced accordingly. The costs of arbitration shall be borne equally by the parties.

Article 14

Notices

14.1 Any notice or other writing required or permitted to be given hereunder or for the purposes hereof (a "Notice") shall be sufficiently given and delivered to the party to whom it is given or mailed, by prepaid registered mail, addressed to such party:

if to ___________________ - ___________________

if to ___________________ - ___________________

if to the Corporation - ___________________

or at such other address as the parties to whom such writing is to be given shall have last notified in writing all other parties of a change of address for the purposes of this provision. Any notice mailed as aforesaid shall be deemed to have been given and received on the third business day following the date of its mailing. Any notice personally delivered to the party hereto to whom it is addressed shall be deemed to have been given and received on the day it is personally delivered, provided that if such day falls on a weekend or statutory holiday, then the notice shall be deemed to have been given and received on the business day next following such day. In the event of a postal disruption, notices hereunder must be personally delivered.

Article 15

General Provisions

15.1   Time shall be of the essence of this Agreement and every part thereof.

15.2   No waiver on behalf of any party or breach of any of the covenants, conditions and provisions herein contained shall be effective or binding upon such party unless the same shall be expressed in writing and any waiver so expressed shall not limit or affect such party's rights with respect to any other future breach.

15.3   Each of the parties covenants and agrees that he, his heirs, executors, administrators, successors and assigns will sign such further agreements, assurances, waivers and documents, attend such meetings, enact such by-laws or pass such resolutions and exercise such votes and influence, do and perform or cause to be done and performed such further and other acts and things that may be necessary or desirable from time to time in order to give full effect to this Agreement and every part thereof.

15.4   The headings of the sections of this Agreement are inserted for convenience only and do not constitute part of this Agreement.

15.5   This Agreement shall be binding upon and enure to the benefit of the parties and their respective heirs, executors, administrators, successors and assigns.

15.6   All words and pronouns relating thereto shall be read and construed as the number and gender of the party of parties referred to in each case require and the verb shall be construed as agreeing with the required word and pronoun.

15.7   If any covenant or other provision of this Agreement is invalid, illegal o incapable of being enforced by reason of any rule of law or public policy, all other conditions and provisions of this Agreement shall, nonetheless remain in full force and effect and no covenant or provision shall be deemed dependent upon any other covenant or provision unless so expressed herein.

15.8   This Agreement expresses the final Agreement between the parties with respect to all matters herein and no representations, inducements, promises or agreements or otherwise between the parties not embodied herein shall be of any force and effect. This Agreement shall not be altered, amended or qualified except by a memorandum in writing, signed by all of the parties, and any alteration, amendment or qualification thereof shall be null and void and shall not be binding upon any such party unless made and recorded as aforesaid.

15.9 This Agreement shall be construed and enforced in accordance with, and the rights of the parties shall be governed by, the laws of ______.

IN WITNESS WHEREOF the parties have executed this Agreement as of the date and year first above written.

____
Witness

____
Witness

Per: _______________________________________

____
 Name:

____
Title

Share Purchase Warrant

Note: Warrant to Purchase Shares given by a Corporation to a person.

To Subscribe for and Purchase Common Shares of _____

THIS CERTIFIES that, for value received, _____ (or registered assigns succeeding to ownership hereof pursuant to the provisions of paragraph 2 hereof) is entitled to subscribe for and purchase from _____, a corporation organized and existing under the laws of _____ (the "Corporation"), for a total purchase price of _____, at any time from the date hereof to _____, up to _____ Common Shares (as defined below) in the capital of the Corporation as fully paid and non-assessable Common Shares of the Corporation, subject, however, to the provisions and upon the terms and conditions hereinafter set forth.

1. **Exercise of Warrants**. The rights represented by this Warrant may be exercised by the holder hereof, in whole or in part (but not as to a fractional share of a Common Share), by the surrender of this Warrant, with the attached Purchase Form duly executed, at the principal office of the Corporation at _____ (or such other office or agency of the Corporation as it may designate by notice in writing to the holder hereof at the address of such holder appearing on the books of the Corporation at any time during the period within which the rights represented by this warrant may be exercised) and upon payment to it for the account of the Corporation, by cash or by certified or bank cashier's check, of the purchase price. The Corporation agrees that the shares so purchased shall be and be deemed to be issued to the holder hereof as the record owner of such shares as of the close of business on the date on which this Warrant shall have been surrendered and payment made for such shares as aforesaid. Certificates for the shares so purchased shall be delivered to the holder hereof within a reasonable time, not exceeding ten (10) days, after the rights represented by this Warrant shall have been so exercised and, unless this Warrant has expired, a new Warrant representing the number of shares, if any, with respect to which this Warrant shall not then have been exercised shall also be issued to the holder hereof within such time.

2. **Transferability of Warrant**. This Warrant is transferable on the books of the Corporation at its office described above by the holder hereof in person or by duly authorized attorney, upon surrender of this Warrant together with the Purchase Form attached hereto, duly executed. Upon the surrender of this Warrant to the Corporation in proper form for transfer, as required hereby, the Corporation shall issue a new warrant or new warrants in the same form and of like tenor as this Warrant representing the right to subscribe for and purchase, in the aggregate, the number of Common Shares which may be subscribed for and purchased hereunder and, individually, the number of Common Shares the right

to purchase which has been so transferred to each transferee and which has been retained by the transferor, if any.

3. Covenants of the Corporation. The Corporation hereby agrees as follows:

(a)   all shares which may be issued upon the exercise of the rights represented by this Warrant will, upon issuance, be validly issued, fully paid and non-assessable and free from any and all taxes, liens and charges with respect to the issue thereof.

(b)   during the period within which the rights represented by this Warrant may be exercised, the Corporation will at all times have authorized and reserved a sufficient number of its Common Shares to provide for the exercise of the rights represented by this Warrant.

(c)   in the event the Corporation files a prospectus in order to become a Reporting Issuer, the Corporation shall include in such prospectus a full disclosure and qualification with respect to all of the shares which may be issued upon the exercise of the rights represented by this Warrant, such that all of the shares which may be issued upon the exercise of the rights represented by this Warrant will be qualified by the prospectus.

(d)   the Corporation will carry on and conduct is business in a proper, efficient and businesslike manner and in accordance with good business practice; will keep or cause to be kept proper books of account in accordance with generally accepted accounting practice; and will, if and whenever required in writing by the holder of this Warrant, provide to the holder of this Warrant all annual statements of the Corporation furnished to its shareholders after the date hereof.

4. Adjustment of Subscription Rights. The above provisions are, however, subject to the following:

(a)   if shares of the Corporation are reclassified or the capital is otherwise reorganized and if the holder of this Warrant has not exercised its right of purchase prior to the effective date of such capital reorganization, upon the exercise of such right the holder of this Warrant shall be entitled to receive and shall accept in lieu of the number of shares then subscribed for by it but for the same aggregate consideration payable therefor, the number of shares or other securities of the Corporation resulting from such capital reorganization that such holder would have been entitled to receive on such capital reorganization if, on the effective date hereof, it had been the registered holder of the number of shares so subscribed for.

(b)   if there is a consolidation, amalgamation or merger of the Corporation or a sale of the property and assets of the Corporation as or substantially as an entirety to any other company, and if the holder of this warrant has not exercised its right of purchase prior to the effective date of such consolidation, amalgamation, merger or sale, upon the exercise of such right the holder of this Warrant shall be entitled to receive and shall accept in lieu of the number of shares then subscribed for by it but for the same aggregate consideration payable therefor, the number of shares or other securities or property of the Corporation or of the company resulting from such merger, amalgamation or consolidation or to which such sale may be made, as the case may be, that such holder would have been entitled to receive on such consolidation, amalgamation, merger or sale if, on the record date or the effective date thereof, as the case may be, it had been the registered holder of the number of shares so subscribed for. In any case, the necessary adjustments shall be made in the application of the provisions et forth in this Warrant with respect to the rights and interests hereafter of the holder of the Warrant to the end that the provisions et forth in this Warrant shall thereafter correspondingly be made applicable, as nearly as may reasonably be, in relation to any shares or other securities or property to which the holder hereof is entitled on the exercise of its purchase rights thereafter. Any such adjustment shall be made by and set forth in a supplemental Warrant entered into and approved by the board of directors of the Corporation and shall for all purposes hereof be conclusively deemed to be an appropriate adjustment.

(c)   the adjustments provided for in this paragraph 4 are cumulative. After any adjustment pursuant to this paragraph, the term "shares" where used in the preceding subparagraphs of this paragraph 4 shall be interpreted to mean the shares which, as a result of all previous adjustments pursuant to this paragraph, the holder hereof would have been entitled to receive upon the exercise of this Warrant, and the number of shares indicated in any subscription made pursuant to this Warrant shall be interpreted to mean the number of shares which, as a result of all previous adjustments pursuant to this paragraph, the holder hereof would have been entitled to receive upon the full exercise of this Warrant entitling the holder thereof to purchase the number of shares so indicated.

(d)   if any question arises with respect to the adjustment provided for in this paragraph, such question shall be referred to the auditors of the Corporation and their determination shall be binding upon the Corporation and the holder of this Warrant.

5.   **Authorized Shares**. As a condition precedent to the taking of any action which would require an adjustment pursuant to paragraph 4 of this Warrant, the Corporation shall take any corporate action which may be necessary in order that the Corporation has issued and reserved in its authorized capital and may validly and legally issue as fully paid and non-assessable, all of the shares which the holder of this Warrant is entitled to receive on the full exercise hereof.

6.   **Consent of Holder Required**. The Corporation shall not, without the prior written consent of the holder of this Warrant:

(a)   pay dividends by the issue of shares in the capital of the Corporation;

(b)   issue any shares in the capital of the Corporation;

(c)   issue any securities convertible into shares in the capital of the Corporation other than those in existence at the date hereof;

256

(d)   grant to any party an interest in or option to purchase any shares in the capital of the Corporation;

(e)   purchase, redeem or otherwise acquire any shares in the capital of the Corporation; or

(f)   make any loans, advances to or investments in any person, firm or corporation not dealing at arm's length with the Corporation, other than in the normal course of business.

7.   Common Shares. As used herein the term "Common Shares" shall mean and include the common shares of the Corporation authorized on the date of the original issue of the Warrants and shall also include any shares of any class of the Corporation thereafter authorized which shall not be limited to a fixed sum or percentage in respect of the rights of the holders thereof to participate in dividends and in the distribution of assets upon the voluntary or involuntary liquidation, dissolution or winding up of the Corporation; provided, however, that the shares purchasable pursuant to this Warrant shall include only shares of such class referred to in the first paragraph hereof and designated as Common Shares in the Corporation's Articles of Incorporation on the date of the original issue of this Warrant or, in case of any reorganization, reclassification, amalgamation or sale of assets of the character referred to in paragraph 4 hereof, the shares, securities or assets provided for in such paragraph.

8.   No Fractional Shares. Upon the exercise of this Warrant, whether in whole or in part, the Corporation shall not be required to issue any fractional shares or script certificates evidencing any fractional interest in shares. In any case where, pursuant to the terms of this Warrant, the holder hereof would be entitled, except for the provisions of this paragraph 8, to receive a fractional share, the number of shares issuable upon such exercise shall be rounded to the next larger whole share if, but only if, such fractional share interest is one-half (1/2) or greater; if such fractional share interest is less than one-half (1/2), it shall be disregarded.

9.   Exchange of Warrant. This Warrant is exchangeable, upon the surrender hereof by the holder hereof at the office or agency of the Corporation referred to in paragraph 1 hereof, for new Warrants of like tenor representing in the aggregate the right to subscribe for and purchase the number of Common Shares which may be subscribed for and purchased hereunder, each such new Warrant to represent the right to subscribe for and purchase such number of Common Shares as shall be designated by such holder hereof at the time of such surrender.

10.   Mutilated or Missing Warrants. Upon receipt of evidence satisfactory to the Corporation of the loss, theft, destruction or mutilation of this Warrant and, in the case of any such loss, theft or destruction, upon delivery of a bond or indemnity satisfactory to the Corporation, or, in the case of any such mutilation, upon surrender or cancellation of this Warrant, the Corporation will issue to the holder hereof a new warrant of like tenor, in lieu of this Warrant, representing the right to subscribe for and purchase the number of Common Shares which may be subscribed for and purchased hereunder.

11. Governing Law. This Warrant shall be governed by and construed in accordance with the laws of the State of _______ and the laws of the United States of America applicable therein.

IN WITNESS WHEREOF, the Corporation has caused this Warrant to be signed by its duly authorized officers under its corporate seal, and this Warrant to be dated.

____
Per:

____
Name:

____
Title:

Purchase Form

[to be signed only upon Exercise of this Warrant]

The undersigned hereby exercises the within Warrant for the purchase of _____ Common Shares covered by such warrant and in accordance with the terms and conditions thereof, and herewith makes payment of the exercise price in full.

The Corporation is instructed to issue certificates for such shares and any new Warrant to which the undersigned may be entitled on partial exercise hereof in the name of the undersigned and to deliver the same at the address indicated.

____
Name:

____
Social Security Number:

____
Address

____

Purchaser's Signature

____

Signature Guaranteed By

[Signature must conform exactly with the name of the registered owner on the front of this Warrant and must be signed and guaranteed by a financial institution satisfactory to the Corporation]

Assignment Form

FOR VALUE RECEIVED, the undersigned hereby sells, assigns and transfers unto _____ the rights represented by the attached Warrant of _____ (the "Corporation") and appoints the Secretary of the Corporation attorney to transfer said rights on the books of said Corporation, with full power of substitution in the premises.

____

Date

____

Witness

Non-Disclosure Agreement

Note: This agreement is fairly tightly formatted – you should be able to get it all onto 2 pages (print both sides and have a handy NDA on one sheet of paper.)

This Non-Disclosure Agreement is entered into as of **[Month, Day, Year]**, by **[Name of the Entity receiving the confidential Information]**, a **[State] [Corporation / Partnership / Sole Proprietorship / individual]** with its principal place of business / residing at **[Address]** (Receiving Company), in favor of **[Company providing the Information]**, a **[State] [Corporation / Partnership / Sole Proprietorship / Individual]** with its principal place of business / residing at **[Address], [City], [State] [Zip Code]** (Disclosing Company).

Note: For the first insert, state the general purpose the confidential Information is going to be used for. For example, study and evaluation. For the second insert, state the specific purpose; for example, if the Information is being supplied to a potential investor, the purpose would be to possibly invest in the Disclosing Company.

1.   For purposes of [Enter purpose], the Receiving Company acknowledges that it may be furnished with or may otherwise receive or have access to Information or material which relates to past, present or future products, software, research development, inventions, processes, techniques, designs or technical information and data, marketing plans, financial statements, pro formas, and so on, relating to the business affairs and operations of the Disclosing Company (the "confidential Information") to [Enter specific purpose of use].

Note: Not only is the Receiving Company prohibited from disclosing the confidential Information, but any discussions between the Receiving Company and the Disclosing Company as well.

2.   The Receiving Company agrees not to disclose the confidential Information or any discussions or contracts with the Disclosing Company that have occurred or are intended, other than as provided for in the following section.

3. It is acknowledged by the Receiving Company that the Information to be furnished is in all respects confidential in nature, and that any disclosure or use of the same by the Receiving Company, except as provided in this Agreement, may cause serious harm or damage to the Disclosing Company, and its owners and officers. Therefore, the Receiving Company agrees that the Receiving Company will not use the Information furnished for any purpose other than as stated above, and agrees that the Receiving Company will not either directly or indirectly by agent, employee, or representative, disclose this Information, either in whole or in part, to any third party; provided, however that (1) the Information furnished may be disclosed only to those directors, officers and employees of the Receiving Company and to the Receiving Company's advisors or their representatives who need such Information for the purpose of evaluating any possible transaction (it being understood that those directors, officers, employees, advisors and representatives shall be informed by the Receiving Company of the confidential nature of such Information and shall be directed by the Receiving Company to treat such Information confidentially), and (2) any disclosure of the Information may be made to which Disclosing Company consents in writing.

4. Neither party shall take or cause to be taken any physical forms of Proprietary Information (nor make copies of same) without the other party's written permission.

Note: If the Information is otherwise available, then it's not confidential Information, and, therefore not covered by this Agreement.

5. The previously stated obligations do not apply to any Information that (1) is publicly known; (2) is given to a party by someone else who is not obligated to maintain confidentiality; or (3) a party had already developed prior to the day this Agreement is signed, as evidenced by documents.

Note: Indicate when the confidential Information should be returned; generally, this is set at three days.

6. Within [Enter number] days after the close of the negotiations, the Receiving Company will return to the Disclosing Company all records, reports, documents, and memoranda furnished and will not make or retain any copy of them.

I have carefully reviewed this contract and agree to and accept its terms and conditions. I am executing this Agreement as of the day and year first written above.

Receiving Company:

____ Signature

____ Name

Non-Disclosure - Mutual

Mutual Non-Disclosure Agreement

Effective Date: **[Date]** by and between **[Company] Inc.]** (Company), located at **[Address], [City], [State] [Zip Code]** and **[Recipient]**, Inc. (Recipient), located at **[Address], [City], [State] [Zip Code].**

1. Purpose. Company and Recipient wish to explore a business opportunity of mutual interest and in connection with this opportunity, Company may disclose to Recipient certain confidential technical and business information which Company desires Recipient to treat as confidential.

2. "Confidential Information" means any information disclosed to Recipient by Company, either directly or indirectly in writing, orally or by inspection of tangible objects, including without limitation the Company's operating plans. Confidential Information may also include information disclosed to Company by third parties. Confidential Information shall not, however, include any information which Recipient can establish

* was publicly known and made generally available in the public domain prior to the time of disclosure to Recipient by Company;

* becomes publicly known and made generally available after disclosure to Recipient by Company through no action or inaction of Recipient; or

* is in the possession of Recipient, without confidentiality restrictions, at the time of disclosure by Company as shown by Recipient's files and records immediately prior to the time of disclosure.

3. Non Use / NonDisclosure. Recipient agrees not to use any Confidential Information for any purpose except to evaluate and engage in discussions concerning a potential business relationship between Recipient and Company or to perform work for Company. Recipient agrees not to disclose any Confidential Information to third parties or to employees of Recipient, except to those employees who are required to have the information in order to evaluate or engage in discussions concerning the contemplated business relationship. Recipient shall not reverse engineer, disassemble or decompile any prototypes, software or other tangible objects which embody Company's Confidential Information and which are provided to Recipient hereunder.

4. Maintenance of Confidentiality. Recipient agrees that it shall take all reasonable measures to protect the secrecy of and avoid disclosure And unauthorized use of the Confidential Information. Without limiting the foregoing, Recipient shall take at least those measures that Recipient takes to protect its own most highly confidential information and shall have its employees, if any, who have access to Confidential Information sign a nonuse and nondisclosure agreement in content substantially similar to the provisions hereof, prior to any disclosure of Confidential Information to such employees. Recipient shall not make any copies of Confidential Information unless the same are previously approved in writing by Company. Recipient shall reproduce Company's proprietary rights notices on any such approved copies, in the same manner in which such notices were set forth in or on the original. Recipient shall immediately notify Company in the event of any unauthorized use or disclosure of the Confidential Information.

5. No Obligation. Nothing herein shall obligate Company or Recipient to proceed with any transaction between them, and each party reserves the right, in its sole discretion, to terminate the discussions contemplated by this Agreement concerning the business opportunity.

6. No Warranty. All confidential information is provided as is. Company makes no warranties, express, implied or otherwise, regarding its accuracy, completeness or performance.

7. Return of Materials. All documents and other tangible objects containing or representing Confidential Information and all copies thereof which are in the possession of Recipient shall be and remain the property of Company and shall be promptly returned to Company upon Company's request.

8. No License. Nothing in this Agreement is intended to grant any rights to Recipient under any patent, mask work right or copyright of Company, nor shall this Agreement grant Recipient any rights in or to Confidential Information except as expressly set forth herein.

9. Term. This Agreement shall survive until such time as all Confidential Information disclosed hereunder becomes publicly known and made generally available through no action or inaction of Recipient.

10. Remedies. Recipient agrees that any violation or threatened violation of this Agreement will cause irreparable injury to the Company, entitling Company to obtain injunctive relief in addition to all legal remedies.

11. Recipient Information. Company does not wish to receive any confidential information from Recipient, and Company assumes no obligation, either express or implied, with respect to any information disclosed by Recipient.

12. Miscellaneous. This Agreement shall bind and inure to the benefit of the parties hereto and their successors and assigns. This Agreement shall be governed by the laws of the State of [State], without reference to conflict of laws principles. This document contains the entire agreement between the parties with respect to the subject matter hereof. Any failure to enforce any provision of this Agreement shall not constitute a waiver thereof or of any other provision hereof. This Agreement may not be amended, nor any obligation waived, except by a writing signed by both parties hereto.

13. Severability. In the event any term of this Agreement is found by any court to be void or otherwise unenforceable, the remainder of this agreement shall remain valid and enforceable as though such term were absent upon the date of its execution.

____

[Company] [Recipient]

____

[Owner/Founder] [Recipient]

____

Date

<u>Non-Disclosure - Formal</u>

Non-Disclosure / Non-Circumvention Agreement

Note: This agreement presumes that your company is the party in possession of the Confidential Information. The following is a standard introductory paragraph that lists the date and the parties to the Agreement. If you do not know whether the Recipient is a corporation, or partnership, and / or its state of incorporation, or partnership, leave this area blank and fill it in when the Agreement is signed.

This Non-Disclosure and Non-Circumvention Agreement is entered into as of:

Effective Date **[Date]** *between* **[Company Legal Name]**, ("[Company]"), [State] [Corporation/Partnership/Sole Proprietorship] *and* **[Recipient]**, ("Recipient") [State] [Corporation/Partnership/Sole Proprietorship]. [Recipient Address]

Summary

Note: In Section 1 of this Recital, [Company] is stating that the information he is about to impart is unique and commercially valuable.

1. [Company] has developed certain Confidential Information (as defined in Section 1 of the Agreement below) that is proprietary to [Company] and that [Company] believes has substantial value for commercial exploitation.

Note: Section 2 of this Recital states that [Company] will share the information but subject to the terms, conditions, and limitations of this Agreement. By agreeing to the terms, conditions and limitations that follow, the party receiving the information must be careful to comply with all of [Company]'s demands.

2. [Company] is willing to disclose the Confidential Information to the Recipient for the limited purpose, and subject to the terms and conditions, set forth in this Agreement.

Agreement

Note: Section 1 of this Agreement defines both the nature of the confidential information and the scope of the information covered. You should delineate the requested information as thoroughly as possible so as to avoid any confusion or ambiguity.

The first insert should include a broad description of the information you seek to protect such as "the proposed business concepts and plans of [Company]." The second insert should be fairly inclusive and include as much information as possible. (i.e., Inventions, discoveries, processes, and know-how; computer software code, designs, routines, algorithms, and structures; product information; research and development information; information related to actual and potential customers; financial data and information; business plans; marketing materials and strategies; and any information regarding the foregoing [Company] discloses to the Recipient.)

1. Definition of Confidential Information

For purposes of this Agreement, the term "Confidential Information" means all information disclosed to the Recipient by or on behalf of [Company] either directly or indirectly and either in writing or orally, relating to: [Insert appropriate language]. Confidential Information shall include, without limitation: [Insert appropriate language]. Despite the foregoing, Confidential Information does not include: (1) information already in possession of the Recipient at the time of [Company]'s disclosure; (2) information that is now or later becomes part of the public domain, unless such information becomes part of the public domain as a result of any action or inaction on the part of the Recipient; or (3) information received by the Recipient from a third party, unless such third party has been directed by [Company] to retain such information on a confidential basis.

Note: Section 2 describes the permissible uses the Recipient may make of the confidential information and states that the Recipient may not disclose the information to third parties. In the brackets in Section 2, describe exactly what the reasons are that you are providing (information to the Recipient).

2. Use of Confidential Information

The Recipient shall use the Confidential Information exclusively for the purpose of: [evaluating potential business relationships and opportunities with [Company] / preparing sales and marketing materials for [Company] / advising [Company]]. Except as required by law, the Recipient shall not disclose any Confidential Information to any third party excepting employees of the Recipient who have expressly agreed in writing to be bound by the terms of this Agreement or make use of any Confidential Information in any manner without [Company]'s prior written consent, that may be given or withheld by [Company] in his sole discretion.

Note: Where the previous section prohibits the Recipient from disclosing the information to third parties, Section 3 prohibits the Recipient from using the information in any manner not agreed upon by the parties. For the first insert, enter the time frame that should be made for as long as you anticipate the information remaining non-public. Try not to go overboard and set a ten or fifteen year period unless the circumstances require it.

3   Non-Circumvention

In consideration of [Company]'s disclosure of the Confidential Information, the Recipient shall not at any time prior to the date immediately preceding the [first / second / third / fourth / fifth] anniversary date of this Agreement, attempt in any manner to commercially exploit [the proposed business concepts and plans of [Company] / [Company]'s business concepts, including x, y, and z] or any of the Confidential Information without [Company]'s prior written consent, that may be given or withheld by [Company] in his sole discretion.

Note: Section 4 merely acknowledges that [Company], not the Recipient, owns the information, and that [Company] may request the return of the information at any time.

4   Ownership Return of Confidential Information

The Recipient acknowledges that the Recipient has no Ownership or proprietary rights in the Confidential Information. Upon [Company]'s request, the Recipient shall immediately return to [Company] all Confidential Information provided to it, and shall retain no materials relating thereto, including copies of, notes on, or abstracts of, any Confidential Information.

Note: Section 5 is a standard paragraph that says the Recipient has no rights other than stated above to the information and that neither party is obligated to further contract with the other.

5   Further Agreements

Nothing contained in this Agreement shall be deemed, by implication or otherwise, to convey to the Recipient any rights in any Confidential Information, nor shall this Agreement be deemed a commitment of any kind by either [Company] or the Recipient to enter into any further Agreements with each other with respect to any Confidential Information.

6   General Provisions

Note: The General Provisions that follow are fairly standard. These provisions enhance the balance of the Agreement by explaining issues such as notice, assignment, legal remedies, waiver, and attorney fees.

6.1 Independent Contractors. The relationship between both parties established by this Agreement is that of independent contractors, and nothing contained in this Agreement shall be construed to give either party the power to direct and control the day-to-day activities of the other. Neither party is an agent, representative or partner of the other party. Neither party shall have any right, power or authority to enter into any agreement for, or on behalf of, or incur any obligation or liability of, or to otherwise bind, the other party. This Agreement shall not be interpreted or construed to create an association, agency, joint venture or partnership between the parties or to impose any liability attributable to such relationship upon either party.

Note: You must decide which state governs this Agreement and where any legal action would be taken. Generally, it is your (company's) state of residence.

6.2 Governing Law Jurisdiction. This agreement and the parties' actions under this Agreement shall be governed by and construed under the laws of the state of [State], without reference to conflict of law principles. The parties hereby expressly consent to the jurisdiction and venue of the federal and state courts within the state of [State]. Each party hereby irrevocably consents to the service of process in any such action or proceeding by the mailing of copies thereof by registered or certified mail, postage prepaid, to such party at its address set forth in the preamble of this Agreement, such service to become effective thirty (30) days after such mailing.

Note: This Agreement is intended to be the only Agreement, and that no other documents or communications are binding. Therefore, it is very important to make sure that everything [Company] and [Client] have agreed to be included in this Agreement. Otherwise, it is as if it was not agreed to.

6.3 Entire Agreement. This Agreement, including the attached exhibits, constitutes the entire Agreement between both parties concerning this transaction, and replaces all previous communications, representations, understandings, and Agreements, whether verbal or written between the parties to this Agreement or their representatives. No representations or statements of any kind made by either party, which are not expressly stated in this Agreement, shall be binding on such parties.

Note: Any changes to this Agreement must be in writing and signed by the party against whom that writing is to be used.

6.4 All Amendments in Writing. No waiver, amendment or modification of any provisions of this Agreement shall be effective unless in writing and signed by a duly authorized representative of the party against whom such waiver, amendment or modification is sought to be enforced. Furthermore, no provisions in either party's purchase orders, or in any other business forms employed by either party will supersede the terms and conditions of this Agreement.

6.5 Notices. Any notice required or permitted by this Agreement shall be deemed given if sent by registered mail, postage prepaid with return receipt requested, addressed to the other party at the address set forth in the preamble of this Agreement or at such other address for which such party gives notice hereunder. Delivery shall be deemed effective three (3) days after deposit with postal authorities.

6.6 Costs of Legal Action. In the event any action is brought to enforce this Agreement, the prevailing party shall be entitled to recover its costs of enforcement including, without limitation, attorneys' fees and court costs.

6.7 Inadequate Legal Remedy. Both parties understand and acknowledge that violation of their respective covenants and Agreements may cause the other irreparable harm and damage, that may not be recovered at law, and each agrees that the other's remedies for breach may be in equity by way of injunctive relief, as well as for damages and any other relief available to the non-breaching party, whether in law or in equity.

6.8 Arbitration. Any dispute relating to the interpretation or performance of this Agreement shall be resolved at the request of either party through binding arbitration. Arbitration shall be conducted in [County], [State] in accordance with the then-existing rules of the American Arbitration Association. Judgment upon any award by the arbitrators may be entered by any state or federal court having jurisdiction. Both parties intend that this Agreement to arbitrate be irrevocable.

6.9   Delay is Not a Waiver. No failure or delay by either party in exercising any right, power or remedy under this Agreement, except as specifically provided in this Agreement, shall operate as a waiver of any such right, power or remedy.

Note: Neither party will be blamed if there is a problem resulting from something beyond its control, such as an earthquake, flood, war.

6.10   Force Majeure. In the event that either party is unable to perform any of its obligations under this Agreement or to enjoy any of its benefits because of any Act of God, strike, fire, flood, governmental acts, orders or restrictions, Internet system unavailability, system malfunctions or any other reason where failure to perform is beyond the reasonable control and not caused by the negligence of the non-performing party (a "Force Majeure Event"), the party who has been so affected shall give notice immediately to the other party and shall use its reasonable best efforts to resume performance. Failure to meet due dates resulting from a Force Majeure Event shall extend such due dates for a reasonable period. However, if the period of nonperformance exceeds sixty (60) days from the receipt of notice of the Force Majeure Event, the party whose ability to perform has not been affected may, by giving written notice, terminate this Agreement effective immediately upon such notice or at such later date as is therein specified.

Note: This section limits the ability of either party to transfer any of its rights or delegate any of its duties to third parties.

You want to make sure that you can sell your business along with all of the relationships you have developed along the way. (Often these relationships can add tremendous value to your business and you want to make sure that all of your agreements can be transferred to the new owners.) I wouldn't want to seek (let alone pay for) permission to sell my company.

Generally, neither party may assign their respective rights to a third party; however, with the possible exception of assignment to a successor corporation or partnership, either party may transfer its rights or obligations under this Agreement without the approval of the other party. This Agreement would be binding on the 3

However, you may want to limit each other's ability to pass along this deal to another possibly unknown and possibly unfriendly entity. The second paragraph prevents unauthorized transfer of responsibilities...

CHOOSE one or the other of these two following paragraphs.

6.11   Assignability &Binding Effect. Except as expressly set forth within this Agreement, neither party may transfer or assign, directly or indirectly, this Agreement or its rights and obligations hereunder without the express written permission of the other party, not to be unreasonably withheld; provided, however, that both parties shall have the right to assign or otherwise transfer this Agreement to any parent, subsidiary, affiliated entity or pursuant to any merger, consolidation or reorganization, provided that all such assignees and transferees agree in writing to be bound by the terms of this Agreement prior to such assignment or transfer. Subject to the foregoing, this Agreement shall be binding upon and inure to the benefit of the parties hereto, their successors and assigns.•

Note: This paragraph DOES NOT ALLOW either party to transfer its rights to a successor company without prior approval.

6.11   Non-Assignability &Binding Effect. Except as otherwise provided for within this Agreement, neither party may assign any of its rights or delegate any of its obligations under this Agreement to any third party without the express written permission of the other. Any such assignment is deemed null and void.

Note: If any part of this Agreement is unenforceable or invalid, the balance of the Agreement should still be enforced. Basically, ignore any sections that are invalid.

6.12   Certain Sections Invalid. If any provisions of this Agreement are held by a court of competent jurisdiction to be invalid under any applicable statute or rule of law, they are to that extent to be deemed omitted and the remaining provisions of this Agreement shall remain in full force and effect.

Note: The headings of the various sections are meant to explain or otherwise give meaning to those sections; they are for convenience only.

6.13   Headings. The titles and headings of the various sections and sections in this Agreement are intended solely for convenience of reference and are not intended for any other purpose whatsoever, or to explain, modify or place any construction upon or on any of the provisions of this Agreement.

Note: Even after the termination of the Agreement, the parties may still have certain responsibilities such as keeping information confidential.

6.14   Survival of Certain Provisions. The warranties and the indemnification and confidentiality obligations set forth in this Agreement shall survive the termination of the Agreement by either party for any reason.

Understood, Agreed & Approved

We have carefully reviewed this contract and agree to and accept all of its terms and conditions. We are executing this Agreement as of the Effective Date above.

____

[Company]

____

[Recipient]

____

[Owner/Founder], [Title]

____

[Recipient] [Title]

____

Date

Non-Disclosure - Confidentiality

Confidentiality / Non-Disclosure Agreement

I understand that this statement is a Proprietary Information Agreement (Agreement) with **[Company]**, Inc. and its affiliated companies **[Company]**. I understand further that:

The Agreement contains material restrictions on my right to disclose or use, during or subsequent to my association, information learned or developed by me during my association with [Company].

[Company] considers this Agreement to be vitally important to the protection of its business. [Company] intends to enforce the terms of the Agreement and to seek appropriate injunctions or restraining orders, as well as monetary damages, should I violate the Agreement.

I have been advised to consult an attorney regarding any questions I have, and that the employees and agents of [Company] are not authorized to, and will not, give me legal advice concerning this Agreement.

For the specific purposes of receiving or submitting proposals, business plans, providing (including, but not limited to) pre-release product evaluations, product testing, performing specific services or concept / product formulation, I agree as follows:

1. Definitions: As used in this Agreement:

*   **"Company"** includes [Company] and all its present and future subsidiaries, affiliates and alliance partners;

*   **"Intellectual Property"** means any and all Inventions, Works of Authorship, Patents, Trademarks, and Copyrights which (i) relate directly to the business of [Company] or to the actual or demonstratively anticipated research or development of [Company], or (ii) result from any work performed by me for [Company], or (iii) any [Company] equipment, supply, facility or trade secret information is used to develop or improve, or (iv) are not developed entirely on my own time;

*   **"Inventions"** means any and all discoveries, improvements, ideas, concepts, creative works, and designs, whether or not they are in writing or reduced to practice and whether or not they are patentable;

*   **"Works of Authorship"** mean those works fixed in any tangible medium of expression from which they can be perceived, reproduced or otherwise communicated, either directly or with the aid of a machine or device, whether or not they are copyrightable; and

*   **"Confidential Information"** means any and all information which is not generally known and which is proprietary to [Company] or any of its clients,

consultants, licensors, licensed dealers or distributors.•• Confidential Information includes, without limitation, business plans, customer lists, consultants, financial information, and trade secrets about [Company] and its products and information or other proprietary information relating to designs, formulas, developmental or experimental work, know-how, products, processes, computer programs, source codes, data bases, designs, schematics, other original works of authorship, or other subject matter related to [Company]'s research and development, manufacturing, engineering, purchasing, finance, marketing, promotion, distribution and selling activities, whether now existing, acquired, developed or made available anytime in the future to [*Company*].• All information which I have a reasonable basis to consider confidential or which is treated by [*Company*] as confidential shall be presumed to be Confidential Information, whether originated by me or by others.• I agree that any Confidential Information acquired by me is the property of [*Company*].

2. Confidentiality: I agree at all times during the term of my association with (or employment by) [*Company*] and from then on to hold in strictest confidence, and not to use, except for the benefit of [*Company*], or to disclose, transfer or reveal, directly or indirectly to any person or entity any Confidential Information without the prior written authorization of [*Company*].

3. Third Party Information: I recognize that [*Company*] has received, and in the future will receive confidential or proprietary information from third parties, subject to a duty on [Company]'s part to maintain the confidentiality of such information and to use it only for certain limited purposes. I agree that I owe [*Company*] and such third parties, during the term of my association and from then on, a duty to hold all such confidential or proprietary information in the strictest of confidence and not to disclose it to any person, firm or corporation (except as necessary in carrying out my work for [*Company*] consistent with [*Company*]'s agreement with such third party) or to use it for the benefit of anyone other than for [*Company*] or such third party (consistent with [*Company*]'s agreement with such third party) without the express written authorization of [*Company*]. Any such information shall be considered Confidential Information for the purposes of this agreement.

4. Non-Circumvention. In consideration of [*Company*]'s disclosure of Confidential Information, I shall not at any time prior to the date immediately preceding the third anniversary date of this Agreement, attempt in any manner to commercially exploit the proposed business concepts and plans of [*Company*] or any of the Confidential Information without [*Company*]'s prior written consent, that may be given or withheld by [*Company*] at it's sole discretion.

5. Return of Materials: At the request of [*Company*] or upon the termination of my association with or employment by [Company], I will immediately deliver to my immediate contact or supervisor at [*Company*] all papers, notes, data, reference materials, sketches, drawings, memoranda, documentation, software, tools, apparatus and any other materials furnished to me by [*Company*] or which were prepared or made, in whole or in part, by me at any time during my association with or employment by [*Company*], together with the attached Termination Certification, which I agree to sign and deliver.

6. Trade Secrets of Others: I understand that it is the firm policy of [*Company*] to maintain the rights of any party with whom I have a confidentiality or proprietary rights agreement.• I will not disclose to [*Company*] or induce [*Company*] to use the proprietary information of others. I do not have any existing obligation to others which might be inconsistent with any of the provisions in this Agreement, except for those obligations identified on a separate page and attached to this Agreement.

7. At Will Employment, Surviving Terms: My association with or employment by [*Company*] is "at will" or per the terms of an attached specific agreement between myself and [Company], and may be terminated by me or [*Company*] at any time or according to the attached agreement; however, my obligations in this agreement will survive the termination of my association with or employment by [*Company*].

8. Notice: I authorize [*Company*] to notify others, including customers of [*Company*] and my future employers or associates, of the terms of this Agreement and my responsibilities.•

9. Injunctive Relief: I understand that in the event of a breach or threatened breach of this agreement by me, [Company] may suffer irreparable harm and consequently will be entitled to injunctive relief to enforce this agreement.

10. Attorney's Fees: I agree that if any legal action or other proceeding is brought for the enforcement of this Agreement, or because of an alleged dispute, breach, default or misrepresentation in connection with any provision of this Agreement, [*Company*] shall be entitled to recover reasonable attorney's fees and other costs incurred in that action or proceeding, in addition to any other relief to which [*Company*] may be entitled.

11. General: My obligations under this Agreement are binding upon my heirs, assigns and legal representatives. This Agreement is governed by the laws of California. If any provision of this Agreement is more restrictive than permitted by law in any jurisdiction in which enforcement is sought, this Agreement will be limited only to the extent necessary to bring this Agreement within the law of such jurisdiction and other provisions of the Agreement will remain in full force.

I have read and understood this Agreement, and I agree to its terms and conditions.

____
Name   Title

____
Company

____
Date

Termination Certification

Note:If/when it come time to end the NDA relationship, you can use this form – for example you agree that you will not continue to pursue a business relationship..

This is to certify that I do not have in my possession, nor have I failed to return, any devices, records, data, notebooks, notes, reports, proposals, lists, correspondence, specifications, drawings, blueprints, sketches, materials, equipment, other documents or property, or reproductions of any aforementioned items belonging to [Company], its subsidiaries, affiliates, successors or assigns (together, the "Company").

I further certify that I have complied with all the terms of [Company]'s Agreement Concerning Non-Disclosure of Company Information signed by me, including the reporting of any inventions and original works of authorship (as defined in this document), conceived or made by me (solely or jointly with others) covered by that agreement.

I further agree that, in compliance with the Agreement Concerning Non-Disclosure of Company Information, I will preserve as confidential all trade secrets, confidential knowledge, data or other proprietary information relating to products, processes, know-how, designs, formulas, developmental or experimental work, computer programs, data bases, other original works of authorship, customer lists, business plans, financial information or other subject matter pertaining to any business of [Company] or any of its clients, consultants or licensees.

____

Date

____

Signature

____

Name (typed or printed)

<u>Contract</u>

Agreement

Note: Basic Template for an Agreement between two parties. Add provisions as appropriate.

THIS AGREEMENT dated as of **Effective Date of Agreement (ie. July 1, 2000)** between **Name of Party 1**, of **Address of Party 1** (the "1st Party") and **Name of Party 2**, of **Address of Party** 2 (the "2nd Party").

IN CONSIDERATION of the mutual covenants and conditions hereinafter set forth and for other good and valuable consideration, the receipt and sufficiency of which is hereby acknowledged, the parties agree as follows:

1.   **List 1st Term of Agreement**

2.   **List 2nd Term of Agreement**

3.   **List Additional Terms of Agreement**

4.   This Agreement is sets forth the entire agreement between the parties relating to the subject matter hereof and stands in the place of any previous agreement, whether oral or in writing. The parties agree that no amendment to this Agreement shall be binding upon the parties unless it is in writing and executed by both parties.

5.•   This Agreement shall enure to the benefit of and be binding upon the respective heirs, executors, administrators and assigns of each of the parties hereto.

6.   This Agreement may be executed in one or more counterparts, each of which when so executed shall be deemed to be an original and such counterparts together shall constitute one and the same instrument.

7.   The parties acknowledge that this Agreement may be negotiated and transmitted between the parties by means of a facsimile machine and that the terms and conditions agreed to are binding upon the parties. Upon the Agreement being accepted, copies of the facsimile will be validated by both parties forthwith.

IN WITNESS WHEREOF this Agreement has been executed by the parties hereto as of the date first above written.

____
Witness

____
1st Party

____
Witness

____
2nd Party

<u>Contract - Assignment</u>

Note:This introductory paragraph lists the date and the parties and contains the necessary language of the Assignment.• Make sure to spell out enough detail concerning the underlying contract and attach a copy of the contract to this Assignment.

Effective Date: **[Date],** In consideration of the sum of $**[xxx]**, I, **[Owner / Founder]**, hereby assign to: **[Name of Assignee]** of [**Address, City and Stat**e], all my right, title and interest in and to the contract entitled.

[Contract Name] dated **[Month, Day, Year]**, entered into between **[Company Legal Name]** and **[myself / Company]**.

A copy of the contract is attached to this Assignment, and involves (*the "Work for Hire" website development project for [Company] / a brief description of the purpose of the contract*).

General Provisions

Note:The General Provisions that follow are fairly standard. These provision enhance the balance of the Agreement by explaining issues such as notice, assignment, legal remedies, waiver, and attorney fees.

Independent Contractors. The relationship between both parties established by this Agreement is that of independent contractors, and nothing contained in this Agreement shall be construed to give either party the power to direct and control the day-to-day activities of the other. Neither party is an agent, representative or partner of the other party. Neither party shall have any right, power or authority to enter into any agreement for, or on behalf of, or incur any obligation or liability of, or to otherwise bind, the other party. This Agreement shall not be interpreted or construed to create an association, agency, joint venture or partnership between the parties or to impose any liability attributable to such relationship upon either party.

Note:You must decide which state governs this Agreement and where any legal action would be taken. Generally, it is your (company's) state of residence.

Governing Law Jurisdiction. This agreement and the parties' actions under this Agreement shall be governed by and construed under the laws of the state of [State], without reference to conflict of law principles. The parties hereby expressly consent to the jurisdiction and venue of the federal and state courts within the state of [State].

Each party hereby irrevocably consents to the service of process in any such action or proceeding by the mailing of copies thereof by registered or certified mail, postage prepaid, to such party at its address set forth in the preamble of this Agreement, such service to become effective thirty (30) days after such mailing.

Note:This Agreement is intended to be the only Agreement, and that no other documents or communications are binding. Therefore, it is very important to make sure that everything [Company] and [Client] have agreed to is included in this Agreement. Otherwise, it is as if it was not agreed to.

Entire Agreement. This Agreement, including the attached exhibits, constitutes the entire Agreement between both parties concerning this transaction, and replaces all previous communications, representations, understandings, and Agreements, whether verbal or written between the parties to this Agreement or their representatives. No representations or statements of any kind made by either party, that are not expressly stated in this Agreement, shall be binding on such parties.

Note:Any changes to this Agreement must be in writing and signed by the party against whom that writing is to be used.

All Amendments in Writing. No waiver, amendment or modification of any provisions of this Agreement shall be effective unless in writing and signed by a duly authorized representative of the party against whom such waiver, amendment or modification is sought to be enforced. Furthermore, no provisions in either party's purchase orders, or in any other business forms employed by either party will supersede the terms and conditions of this Agreement.

Note:All notices between the parties must be in writing and either delivered in person or by certified or registered mail, return receipt requested.

Notices. Any notice required or permitted by this Agreement shall be deemed given if sent by registered mail, postage prepaid with return receipt requested, addressed to the other party at the address set forth in the preamble of this Agreement or at such other address for which such party gives notice hereunder. Delivery shall be deemed effective three (3) days after deposit with postal authorities.

Note:In the event of a lawsuit or any legal proceeding involving this Agreement, the losing party will have to pay the winning party his or her costs and expenses, including reasonable attorney fees.

Costs of Legal Action. In the event any action is brought to enforce this Agreement, the prevailing party shall be entitled to recover its costs of enforcement including, without limitation, attorneys' fees and court costs.

Note:Legal remedies, i.e., money damages, may not be sufficient; therefore, both parties agree to equitable remedies such as an injunction where the breaching party would be required to do or not to do something.

Inadequate Legal Remedy. Both parties understand and acknowledge that violation of their respective covenants and Agreements may cause the other irreparable harm and damage, that may not be recovered at law, and each agrees that the other's remedies for breach may be in equity by way of injunctive relief, as well as for damages and any other relief available to the non-breaching party, whether in law or in equity.

Note:Assuming the parties wish to use Arbitration in the event of a dispute, the following section should be included. You take your chances with an arbitrator, but it keeps legal costs down and keeps you out of a drawn out legal process.

Arbitration. Any dispute relating to the interpretation or performance of this Agreement shall be resolved at the request of either party through binding arbitration. Arbitration shall be conducted in [County], [State] in accordance with the then-existing rules of the American Arbitration Association. Judgment upon any award by the arbitrators may be entered by any state or federal court having jurisdiction. Both parties intend that this Agreement to arbitrate be irrevocable.

Note:Merely delaying to bring an action that one party has a right to bring does not cause that party to lose or waive his right to pursue that action.

Delay is Not a Waiver. No failure or delay by either party in exercising any right, power or remedy under this Agreement, except as specifically provided in this Agreement, shall operate as a waiver of any such right, power or remedy.

Note:Neither party will be blamed if there is a problem resulting from something beyond its control, such as an earthquake, flood, war.

Force Majeure. In the event that either party is unable to perform any of its obligations under this Agreement or to enjoy any of its benefits because of any Act of God, strike, fire, flood, governmental acts, orders or restrictions, Internet system unavailability, system malfunctions or any other reason where failure to perform is beyond the reasonable control and not caused by the negligence of the non-performing party (a "Force Majeure Event"), the party who has been so affected shall give notice immediately to the other party and shall use its reasonable best efforts to resume performance. Failure to meet due dates resulting from a Force Majeure Event shall extend such due dates for a reasonable period. However, if the period of nonperformance exceeds sixty (60) days from the receipt of notice of the Force Majeure Event, the party whose ability to perform has not been affected may, by giving written notice, terminate this Agreement effective immediately upon such notice or at such later date as is therein specified.

Note: This section limits the ability of either party to transfer any of its rights or delegate any of its duties to third parties.

You want to make sure that you can sell your business along with all of the relationships you have developed along the way. (Often these relationships can add tremendous value to your business and you want to make sure that all of your agreements can be transferred to the new owners.) I wouldn't want to seek (let alone pay for) permission to sell my company. Generally, neither party may assign their respective rights to a third party; however, with the possible exception of assignment to a successor corporation or partnership, either party may transfer its rights or obligations under this Agreement without the approval of the other party. However, you may want to limit each other's ability to pass along this deal to another possibly unknown and possibly unfriendly entity. The second paragraph prevents unauthorized transfer of responsibilities. CHOOSE one or the other of these two following paragraphs.

Assignability & Binding Effect. Except as expressly set forth within this Agreement, neither party may transfer or assign, directly or indirectly, this Agreement or its rights and obligations hereunder without the express written permission of the other party, not to be unreasonably withheld; provided, however, that both parties shall have the right to assign or otherwise transfer this Agreement to any parent, subsidiary, affiliated entity or pursuant to any merger, consolidation or reorganization, provided that all such assignees and transferees agree in writing to be bound by the terms of this Agreement prior to such assignment or transfer. Subject to the foregoing, this Agreement shall be binding upon and inure to the benefit of the parties hereto, their successors and assigns.•

Note: This paragraph DOES NOT ALLOW either party to transfer its rights to a successor company without prior approval.

Non-Assignability & Binding Effect. Except as otherwise provided for within this Agreement, neither party may assign any of its rights or delegate any of its obligations under this Agreement to any third party without the express written permission of the other. Any such assignment is deemed null and void.

Note:If any part of this Agreement is unenforceable or invalid, the balance of the Agreement should still be enforced. Basically, ignore any sections that are invalid.

Certain Sections Invalid.

Certain Sections Invalid. If any provisions of this Agreement are held by a court of competent jurisdiction to be invalid under any applicable statute or rule of law, they are to that extent to be deemed omitted and the remaining provisions of this Agreement shall remain in full force and effect.

Note:The headings of the various sections are meant to explain or otherwise give meaning to those sections; they are for convenience only.

Headings. The titles and headings of the various sections and sections in this Agreement are intended solely for convenience of reference and are not intended for any other purpose whatsoever, or to explain, modify or place any construction upon or on any of the provisions of this Agreement.

Note:Even after the termination of the Agreement, the parties may still have certain responsibilities such as keeping information confidential.

Survival of Certain Provisions. The warranties and the indemnification and confidentiality obligations set forth in this Agreement shall survive the termination of the Agreement by either party for any reason.

Understood, Agreed & Approved

We have carefully reviewed this contract and agree to and accept all of its terms and conditions. We are executing this Agreement as of the Effective Date above.

Date:_______________________________

Name:_______________________________

The foregoing is hereby accepted and approved by:

Name:_______________________________

Contract - Services

Service Agreement

Note: This is a standard introductory paragraph that lists the date and the parties to the Agreement.

Effective Date **[Date]** by and between **[Company Legal Name]**, ("Company") with offices located in **[Address] [City] [State] [Zip Code]** and **[Customer Name]**, ("Customer") with offices located in **[Address, City and State] [Zip Code]** (herein after referred to as "customer".)

Note: The following paragraph sets forth the basic obligations of the serving Company to maintain the Customer's equipment. You will note that the Service Company will only be required to Service equipment you specify on "Attachment A". Make sure that the list of equipment is complete before you sign the Agreement.

[Company] agrees to Service and provide all labor and furnish all parts necessary to maintain Customer's equipment (hereinafter referred to as "Equipment") listed on Attachment A, in proper operating order according to the following terms and Conditions:

1 Term of the Agreement

Note: This first section establishes the duration of the Agreement. Many times Service agreements are used in conjunction with equipment lease arrangements. In that case the duration of the Service Agreement may correspond to the term of the lease.

This Agreement shall commence on the Effective Date and shall remain in full force and effect for a Term of [xx months/years] [and automatically renew for an additional xx months/years unless notice of termination is provide in writing by either party prior to 30 days from the end of the Term], or until terminated according to the provisions of this Agreement.

Note: Section 1.2 gives either party the right to terminate this Agreement if the other fails to perform its obligations.

1.2 If either party shall neglect or fail to perform any of its obligations under this Agreement, and such failure continue for a period of ten (10) calendar days after written notice of complaint, the other party shall have the right to immediately terminate this Agreement.

Note: Section 1.3 allows the Service Company to terminate its obligations thirty days after the Customer fails to make any required payments.

1.3 [Company] may, at its option, immediately terminate this Agreement, or temporarily suspend all of its responsibilities stated in this Agreement, for payment delinquency in any amount in excess of thirty (30) calendar days.

Note: Section 2 establishes what equipment will be covered by this Agreement. Remember, make sure to double check the list of equipment and attach the list as Attachment A.

2   Equipment Eligible for Service

All Equipment to be included under this Agreement, along with the charge for this Agreement, is listed on Attachment A.

3   Service Location

Note: Section 3 establishes the location where the servicing will be performed. The following two sections require that servicing be performed at the Servicing Company's facility. You may want servicing performed at your location. If so, add the appropriate language in this section.

3.1 The Equipment to be Serviced must be delivered by the Customer to [Company] repair facility during Company's normal business hours.

Note: If you are required to bring the equipment to the Servicing Company's facilities, you will have to bring all interconnecting cords and cables.

3.2 All interconnecting cords and cables must accompany the Equipment to be Serviced.

4   Charges / Payment

Note: This paragraph sets forth a monthly payment plan with the first payment due one month after you enter into this Agreement. You can establish any type of payment plan you desire, so don't feel obligated to use a monthly payment schedule. You should negotiate acceptable payment terms and servicing charges with the Servicing Company and include those terms in this section.

Monthly Service Charges for this Agreement shall be reflected on the monthly lease invoice. Payment shall be made by Customer to [Company]. Monthly Maintenance Charges for the first month of the term of this Agreement (plus any pro rata portion) shall be due on the first day of the month following the date of delivery of the listed Equipment, with all subsequent payments due in advance on the first day of each subsequent month during the term of this Agreement.

5   Exclusions

Note: Often a Servicing Company will not service equipment under all circumstances. The following section delineates some conditions which must be fulfilled before [Company] will be obligated to perform services.

[Company] shall not be obligated to provide the Services required by this Agreement:

Note: Section 5.1 is included to protect the Servicing Company from problems created by some other maintenance or Servicing Company.

5.1 If the Equipment has been modified or repaired by anyone other than an authorized [Company] Service Center, or if the Equipment contains non-[Company] parts.

Note: Section 5.2 protects the Servicing Company from problems caused by things such as power surges. Basically, it Note: protects the Servicing Company from things beyond its control.

5.2 If the Equipment requires repair of damages caused by external factors, including, but not limited to: loss or damage resulting from the elements, misuse, abuse, or the operation of the Equipment in improper environments, such as, but not limited to, locations having defective or inadequate power source, static electricity, or excessive interference caused by external sources.

Note: Sometimes government bodies establish regulations that set standards for equipment. An example would be fire code regulations that require a certain type of sprinkler system. The following section protects the Servicing Company from being forced to provide service if a government body establishes regulations that necessitate changes to equipment.

5.3 If extra Service is required to comply with changes in the regulations of any governmental body or agency.

Note: Section 5.4 protects the Servicing Company from being forced to service equipment that may not have been covered by this Agreement. If the serial numbers have been removed, how is the Servicing Company to know if the equipment was part of the original Agreement?

5.4 If the serial numbers of the Equipment have been tampered with or are missing.

6   Services Not Provided

Note: Section 6 sets further limits on the servicing companies obligations.

This Agreement shall not require [Company] to provide:

Note: Section 6.1 excludes routine maintenance from the Servicing Company's obligations. You may want to negotiate some form of maintenance requirement with the Servicing Company that is different from that imposed by this provision. For example, you may want to have your computer hard disks checked periodically to insure that you will not lose important data.

6.1   Routine maintenance, such as, but not limited to, periodic cleaning of printer heads, ribbon replacement, blotter replacement or blotter roller replacement.

Note: In the next two sections, the Servicing Company declines to be obligated to replace everyday products or to be responsible for servicing the external casing of the equipment.

6.2   Consumable items such as, but not limited to, paper, ribbons, diskettes, oil, fuel, water, tapes, toner, lamps, tires, etc..

6.3   Refinishing or replacement of any external cosmetic plastic or plated parts including the cabinet and cabinet parts.

7   Limited Warranty & Limitation of Liability

Note: Section 7 is an important one. It establishes the limits of liability for the Servicing Company.

Note: Section 7.1 includes a "best efforts" term. Basically, it protects the Servicing Company from responsibility for things outside its control. For example, the Servicing Company would not breach this agreement if it failed to supply replacement parts that are unavailable.

7.1 [Company] agrees to use its "best efforts" to provide the maintenance required under this Agreement in a prompt manner, but in no event shall [Company] be liable for any damages or liabilities, directly or indirectly caused by the Equipment not being repaired properly, by length of down time, temporary shortages or unavailability of the replacement parts, or temporary unavailability of qualified Service personnel at [Company]'s Service Center.

Note: These next two sections set forth the sole warranty of the Company for defective replacement parts. The first section establishes the warranty while the second section disclaims or excludes other possible warranties the Customer could exercise. Remember to try and negotiate better warranty terms for yourself.

7.2 All replacement parts, components, modules, or units (hereinafter collectively referred to as "part[s]") supplied under this Agreement are warranted against defects in workmanship and material. If this Agreement is still in effect, [Company]'s sole responsibility under this warranty shall be to repair or replace any part(s), discovered to be defective. If within thirty (30) calendar days from the date of installation of parts(s), this Agreement is not in effect and a defect is discovered, [Company]'s sole responsibility will be to provide replacement part(s) at no cost, but labor provided will be charged to Customer at [Company]'s Service rates and terms in effect.

Note: Section 7.3 contains the Uniform Commercial Code (adopted in all states except Louisiana), and requires that a disclaimer of warranties be conspicuous.

7.3 Except for the limited warranties stated above, [Company] disclaims all warranties of any kind with regard to the subject matter hereof, the Service to be provided by [Company], and parts and other material to be supplied by [Company], including without limitation, any implied warranty of merchantability or fitness for a particular purpose.

Note: Section 7.4 limits the Servicing Company's liability for breach of this Agreement. For example, if your business shuts down because of an equipment failure and the Servicing Company is in some way responsible for that failure, the Servicing Company would not be liable for any business lost as a consequence.

7.4 [Company] shall have no liability or responsibility to the Customer or any other person or entity with respect to any liability, loss or damage caused or alleged to be caused directly or indirectly by [Company] computer equipment or software sold or Service provided by [Company], including, but not limited to, any interruption of Service, loss of business or anticipatory profits or consequential damages resulting from the use of operation of the equipment. In no event shall [Company] be liable for loss of profits, or any indirect, special, or consequential damages arising out of any breach of this Agreement or any warranty provided herein.

Note: The next two sections are included to account for different laws in some states.

7.5 Some states do not allow the limitation or exclusion of incidental or consequential damages, so the above limitation(s) or exclusion(s) may not apply to the Customer.

7.6 The warranties granted herein give the Original Customer specific legal rights, and the Original Customer may have other rights which vary from state to state.

8   General Provisions

Note: The General Provisions that follow are fairly standard. These provision enhance the balance of the Agreement by explaining issues such as notice, assignment, legal remedies, waiver, and attorney fees.

8.1 Independent Contractors. The relationship between both parties established by this Agreement is that of independent contractors, and nothing contained in this Agreement shall be construed to give either party the power to direct and control the day-to-day activities of the other. Neither party is an agent, representative or partner of the other party. Neither party shall have any right, power or authority to enter into any agreement for, or on behalf of, or incur any obligation or liability of, or to otherwise bind, the other party. This Agreement shall not be interpreted or construed to create an association, agency, joint venture or partnership between the parties or to impose any liability attributable to such relationship upon either party.

Note: You must decide which state governs this Agreement and where any legal action would be taken. Generally, it is your (company's) state of residence.

8.2   Governing Law Jurisdiction. This agreement and the parties' actions under this Agreement shall be governed by and construed under the laws of the state of [State], without reference to conflict of law principles. The parties hereby expressly consent to the jurisdiction and venue of the federal and state courts within the state of [State]. Each party hereby irrevocably consents to the service of process in any such action or proceeding by the mailing of copies thereof by registered or certified mail, postage prepaid, to such party at its address set forth in the preamble of this Agreement, such service to become effective thirty (30) days after such mailing.

Note: This Agreement is intended to be the only Agreement, and that no other documents or communications are binding. Therefore, it is very important to make sure that everything [Company] and [Client] have agreed to is included in this Agreement. Otherwise, it is as if it was not agreed to.

8.3 Entire Agreement. This Agreement, including the attached exhibits, constitutes the entire Agreement between both parties concerning this transaction, and replaces all previous communications, representations, understandings, and Agreements, whether verbal or written between the parties to this Agreement or their representatives. No representations or statements of any kind made by either party, which are not expressly stated in this Agreement, shall be binding on such parties.

Note: Any changes to this Agreement must be in writing and signed by the party against whom that writing is to be used.

8.4 All Amendments in Writing. No waiver, amendment or modification of any provisions of this Agreement shall be effective unless in writing and signed by a duly authorized representative of the party against whom such waiver, amendment or modification is sought to be enforced. Furthermore, no provisions in either party's purchase orders, or in any other business forms employed by either party will supersede the terms and conditions of this Agreement.

Note: All notices between the parties must be in writing and either delivered in person or by certified or registered mail, return receipt requested.

8.5 Notices. Any notice required or permitted by this Agreement shall be deemed given if sent by registered mail, postage prepaid with return receipt requested, addressed to the other party at the address set forth in the preamble of this Agreement or at such other address for which such party gives notice hereunder. Delivery shall be deemed effective three (3) days after deposit with postal authorities.

Note: In the event of a lawsuit or any legal proceeding involving this Agreement, the losing party will have to pay the winning party his or her costs and expenses, including reasonable attorney fees.

8.6 Costs of Legal Action. In the event any action is brought to enforce this Agreement, the prevailing party shall be entitled to recover its costs of enforcement including, without limitation, attorneys' fees and court costs.

Note: Legal remedies, i.e., money damages, may not be sufficient; therefore, both parties agree to equitable remedies such as an injunction where the breaching party would be required to do or not to do something.

8.7 Inadequate Legal Remedy. Both parties understand and acknowledge that violation of their respective covenants and Agreements may cause the other irreparable harm and damage, that may not be recovered at law, and each agrees that the other's remedies for breach may be in equity by way of injunctive relief, as well as for damages and any other relief available to the non-breaching party, whether in law or in equity.

Note: Assuming the parties wish to use Arbitration in the event of a dispute, the following section should be included. You take your chances with an arbitrator, but it keeps legal costs down and keeps you out of a drawn out legal process.

8.8 Arbitration. Any dispute relating to the interpretation or performance of this Agreement shall be resolved at the request of either party through binding arbitration. Arbitration shall be conducted in [County], [State] in accordance with the then-existing rules of the American Arbitration Association. Judgment upon any award by the arbitrators may be entered by any state or federal court having jurisdiction. [Company] and [Client] intend that this Agreement to arbitrate be irrevocable.

Note: Neither party will be blamed if there is a problem resulting from something beyond its control, such as an earthquake, flood, war.

8.9 Force Majeure. In the event that either party is unable to perform any of its obligations under this Agreement or to enjoy any of its benefits because of any Act of God, strike, fire, flood, governmental acts, orders or restrictions, Internet system unavailability, system malfunctions or any other reason where failure to perform is beyond the reasonable control and not caused by the negligence of the non-performing party (a "Force Majeure Event"), the party who has been so affected shall give notice immediately to the other party and shall use its reasonable best efforts to resume performance.• Failure to meet due dates resulting from a Force Majeure Event shall extend such due dates for a reasonable period.• However, if the period of nonperformance exceeds sixty (60) days from the receipt of notice of the Force Majeure Event, the party whose ability to perform has not been affected may, by giving written notice, terminate this Agreement effective immediately upon such notice or at such later date as is therein specified.

Note: This section limits the ability of either party to transfer any of its rights or delegate any of its duties to third parties. You want to make sure that you can sell your business along with all of the relationships you have developed along the way. (Often these relationships can add tremendous value to your business and you want to make sure that all of your agreements can be transferred to the new owners.) I wouldn't want to seek (let alone pay for)• permission to sell my company. Generally, neither party may assign their respective rights to a third party, however, with the possible exception of assignment to a successor corporation or partnership, either party may transfer its rights or obligations under this Agreement without the approval of the other party. However, you may want to limit each other's ability to pass along this deal to another possibly unknown and possibly unfriendly entity. The second paragraph prevents unauthorized transfer of responsibilities.

Note: CHOOSE one or the other of these two following paragraphs.

8.10 Assignability &Binding Effect. Except as expressly set forth within this Agreement, neither party may transfer or assign, directly or indirectly, this Agreement or its rights and obligations hereunder without the express written permission of the other party, not to be unreasonably withheld; provided, however, that both parties shall have the right to assign or otherwise transfer this Agreement to any parent, subsidiary, affiliated entity or pursuant to any merger, consolidation or reorganization, provided that all such assignees and transferees agree in writing to be bound by the terms of this Agreement prior to such assignment or transfer. Subject to the foregoing, this Agreement shall be binding upon and inure to the benefit of the parties hereto, their successors and assigns.

Note: This paragraph DOES NOT ALLOW either party to transfer its rights to a successor company without prior approval.

8.10 Non-Assignability &Binding Effect. Except as otherwise provided for
within this Agreement, neither party may assign any of its rights or delegate any of its obligations under this Agreement to any third party without the express written permission of the other. Any such assignment is deemed null and void.

Note: Merely delaying to bring an action that one party has a right to bring does not cause that party to lose or waive his right to pursue that action.

8.11 Delay is Not a Waiver. No failure or delay by either party in exercising any right, power or remedy under this Agreement, except as specifically provided in this Agreement, shall operate as a waiver of any such right, power or remedy.

Note: If any part of this Agreement is unenforceable or invalid, the balance of the Agreement should still be enforced. Basically, ignore any sections that are invalid.

8.12 Certain Sections Invalid. If any provisions of this Agreement are held by a court of competent jurisdiction to be invalid under any applicable statute or rule of law, they are to that extent to be deemed omitted and the remaining provisions of this Agreement shall remain in full force and effect.

Note: The headings of the various sections are meant to explain or otherwise give meaning to those sections; they are for convenience only.

8.13 Headings. The titles and headings of the various sections and sections in this Agreement are intended solely for convenience of reference and are not intended for any other purpose whatsoever, or to explain, modify or place any construction upon or on any of the provisions of this Agreement.

Note: Even after the termination of the Agreement, the parties may still have certain responsibilities such as keeping Note: information confidential.

8.14 Survival of Certain Provisions. The warranties and the indemnification and confidentiality obligations set forth in the Agreement shall survive the termination of the Agreement by either party for any reason.

Understood, Agreed & Approved

We have carefully reviewed this contract and agree to and accept all of its terms and conditions. We are executing this Agreement as of the Effective Date above.

___________________________   ___________________________
[Company]   [Customer]

___________________________   ___________________________
[Owner/Founder]   [Customer Officer]

___________________________   ___________________________
Date   Date

Attachment - A

Equipment

*	[Equipment A]	$[100]	per month
*	[Equipment B]	$[100]	per month
*	[Equipment C]	$[100]	per month

NOTES

<u>Waiver Agreement</u>

Waiver of Condition

Note: Waiver of a condition contained in an Agreement by one party in favor of the other. To be used in a situation where completion of an agreement is conditional upon one or more events which must occur.

TO: **Name of Party Receiving benefit of Waiver of Condition (as in Original Agreement)**

We refer to the **(Described Agreement)** which is the subject matter of this Waiver of Condition (ie. Consulting Agreement) dated _____, **(Date of• Agreement)** which is the subject matter of this Waiver of Condition (the "Original Agreement") between **Name of Party Waiving Condition (as in Original Agreement)** (the "1st Party") and **Name of Party Receiving benefit of Waiver of Condition (as in Original Agreement)** (the "2nd Party") pursuant to which the parties hereto entered into an agreement relating to Brief Description of Nature of Original Agreement (ie. the Consulting Services to be provided by the 2nd Party to the 1st Party).

We also refer to the condition contained in the Original Agreement which provides that the Original Agreement is conditional upon Describe Condition Being Waived (ie. the approval of the board of directors of the 1st Party) (the "Waived Condition").

You are hereby notified that the 1st Party hereby waives the Waived Condition, provided that this Waiver of Condition does not constitute, nor shall it be construed of interpreted as constituting, a waiver of any other term or condition contained in the Original Agreement other than the Waived Condition.

Dated: _____, Effective Date of Waiver of Condition (ie. July 1, 2000)

____

Witness

____

Name of Party Waiving Condition (as in Original Agreement)

Indemnity Agreement

*Note: Indemnity Agreement to be given to Landlord by someone who
is indemnifying the Landlord against non-payment by Tenant.*

THIS AGREEMENT made as of ____between ____, of ____(the
"Landlord") and ____, of ____("Indemnifier").

WHEREAS the Landlord is entering into a lease of certain premises
described as ____with ____(the "Lease");

AND WHEREAS the Landlord has agreed to enter into the Lease on the
condition that the Landlord receive an indemnity from the Indemnifier, upon
the terms and conditions set out in this Agreement;

AND WHEREAS in order to induce the Landlord to enter into the Lease,
the Indemnifier has agreed to provide an indemnity;

NOW THEREFORE• THIS AGREEMENT WITNESSES that in
consideration of the premises, the covenants and agreements herein contained
and for other good and valuable consideration, the receipt and sufficiency of
which is hereby acknowledged, the parties hereto agree as follows:

1.   The Indemnifier hereby agrees with the Landlord:

(a)   to make the due and punctual payment of all rent, additional rent and
other monies and charges of any kind whatsoever payable under the Lease
during the term thereof and any extension or renewal of the term;

(b)   to effect prompt and complete performance of all obligations contained
in the Lease on the part of the Tenant to be kept, observed and performed; and

(c)   to indemnify and save the Landlord harmless from any loss, costs or
damages arising out of any failure by the Tenant to pay the aforesaid rent,
additional rent and monies and charges or resulting from any failure by the
Tenant to observe or perform any of the obligations contained in the
Lease.

2.   This Indemnity is absolute and unconditional and the obligations of the
Indemnifier shall not be released, discharged, mitigated, impaired or affected
by:

(a)   any extensions of time, indulgences or modifications which the
Landlord extends to or makes with the Tenant in respect of the performance
of any of the obligations of the Tenant under the Lease;

(b) any waiver by or failure of the Landlord to enforce any of the terms, covenants and conditions contained in the Lease;

(c) any assignment of the Lease by the Tenant or any consent which the Landlord gives to any such assignment;

(d) any amendment to the Lease or any waiver by the Tenant of any of its rights under the Lease;

(e) the expiration of the term or the termination of the Lease for any reason whatsoever;

(f) • any loss of or in respect of any security received by the Landlord from the Tenant or from any other person, firm or corporation, whether or not occasioned or contributed to by or through the act, omission, default or neglect of the Landlord; or

(g) any act or omission of the Landlord or any other person whereby the Indemnifier would or might otherwise be released or have its obligations hereunder discharged, mitigated, impaired or affected in any way whatsoever, it being agreed that nothing but payment and satisfaction in full of all monies and charges payable under the Lease and the due performance and observance of all terms, covenants and conditions on the part of the Tenant to be paid and performed shall release the Indemnifier of its obligations hereunder.

3. The Indemnifier hereby expressly waives notice of the acceptance of this Indemnity and all notice of non-performance, non-payment or non-observance on the part of the Tenant of the terms, covenants and conditions contained in the Lease.

4. In the event of a default under the Lease, the Indemnifier waives any right to require the Landlord to:

(a) proceed against the Tenant or any other indemnifier or pursue any rights or remedies against the Tenant or any other indemnifier with respect to the Lease;

(b) proceed against or exhaust any security held by the Landlord from the Tenant or any other person; or

(c) pursue any other remedy whatsoever in the Landlord's power.

(d) The Landlord has the right to enforce this Indemnity regardless of the acceptance of additional security from the Tenant and regardless of any release or discharge of the Tenant by the Landlord or by others or by operation of any law.

5. Without limiting the generality of the foregoing, the liability of the Indemnifier under this Indemnity shall continue in full force and effect and shall not be or be deemed to have been waived, released, discharged, impaired or affected by reason of the release or discharge of the Tenant in any receivership,

bankruptcy, winding-up or other creditors' proceedings or the rejection, disaffirmance or disclaimer of the Lease in any proceeding and shall continue with respect to the periods prior thereto and thereafter, for and with respect to the terms as if the Lease had not been disaffirmed or disclaimed. The liability of the Indemnifier shall not be affected by any repossession of the Premises by the Landlord.

6.   No action or proceeding brought or instituted under this Indemnity and no recovery in pursuance thereof shall be a bar or defense to any further action or proceeding which may be brought under this Indemnity by reason of any further default hereunder or in the performance and observance of the terms, covenants and conditions contained in the Lease.

7.   No modification of this Indemnity shall be effective unless the same is in writing and is executed by both the Indemnifier and the Landlord.

8.   The Indemnifier shall, without limiting the generality of the foregoing, be bound by this Indemnity in the same manner as though the Indemnifier were the Tenant named in the Lease. Notwithstanding the foregoing, or any performance in whole or in part by the Indemnifier of its obligations hereunder or of the Tenant under the Lease, the Indemnifier shall not have any entitlement to any of the benefits to which the Tenant is entitled under the Lease.

9.   If two or more individuals, corporations, partnerships or other business associations (or any combination of two or more thereof) execute this Indemnity as Indemnifier, the liability of each such individual, corporation, partnership or other business associations hereunder is joint and several. In like manner, if the Indemnifier named in this Indemnity is a partnership or other business association, the members of which are by virtue of statutory or general law subject to personal liability, the liability of each such member is joint and several.

10.   All of the terms, covenants and conditions of this Indemnity extend to and are binding upon the Indemnifier, his or its heirs, executors, administrators, successors and assigns, as the case may be, and enure to the benefit of and may be enforced by the Landlord its successors and assigns.

11.   The obligations of the Indemnifier hereunder shall be assignable by the Landlord and an assignment of the Lease shall constitute an assignment of the obligations of the Indemnifier unless the said obligations of the Indemnifier are specifically excepted from such assignment of the Lease.

12.   In the event of the termination of the Lease for any reason whatsoever including, without limitation, any termination resulting from the bankruptcy, insolvency, winding-up or similar situation of the Tenant, then at the option of the Landlord the Indemnifier shall enter into a written agreement with the

Landlord for a term commencing at the date of such termination and expiring on the date on which the Lease would have expired if it had run its full term without default by the Tenant and without such termination. Such agreement shall contain the same terms and conditions as are contained in the Lease which would apply to and be in force for that portion of the term of Lease which by the original terms of the Lease would have remained unexpired at the date of such termination.

EXECUTED by the parties hereto as of the date first written above.

Witness

Witness

<u>License Agreement - Product</u>

Product Licensing Agreement

Note: This is a standard introductory paragraph that lists the parties to the Agreement and the date the Agreement is being entered into. You need to enter the date of the Agreement, the names of the parties, the specific type of organization, and their addresses.

Effective Date **[Date]** Between **[Company Legal Name]**, ("[Company]") a [State of organization or residence] (Corporation / Partnership / Sole Proprietorship / Resident), located at **[Address] [City], State] [Zip Code]** and **[Licensee]**, ("Licensee") a **(State of organization or residence) [Corporation / Partnership / Sole Proprietorship / Resident)** located at **[Address]**.

1. Summary

Note: the Licensor is the owner of the item(s) being licensed and owns or will own any changes made by the Licensee as well.

Note: Enter the name(s) of the item(s) being licensed. Complete exhibit A which is a thorough description of the item(s).

The Licensor is the owner of a certain item now known as "[Describe items]," as more fully described in Exhibit A attached hereto, together with all modifications, all improvements thereto (including all those made by the Licensee), all patents and all copyrights and trademarks originated by the Licensee used in connection therewith (collectively, the "Property").

Note: Insert the specific geographic area(s) where the Licensee will be able to manufacture, distribute and sell the Property.

The Licensee desires to acquire from the Licensor, and the Licensor is willing to transfer to the Licensee, all rights in and to the Property pursuant to the Licensor's grant to the Licensee of an exclusive license to manufacture, distribute and sell the Property throughout [Describe Territory] (the "Territory") on the terms and subject to the conditions of this Agreement.

In consideration for the mutual promises, covenants, and Agreements made below, the parties, intending to be legally bound, agree as follows:

2. Grant of License

Note: The Licensee can pretty much do anything with the Licensed Products in the Territory. While it may manufacture the Products outside the Territory, it can not sell or distribute them there.

2.1 Grant of Exclusive License. The Licensor hereby grants to the Licensee an exclusive license (the "License") to manufacture, distribute and sell, and to sublicense the manufacture, distribution and sale of, Licensed Products (defined below) in the Territory. The Licensee may manufacture Licensed Products outside the Territory; provided, however, that in no event shall the Licensee distribute or sell Licensed Products outside the Territory. Except as otherwise provided in Sections 9 and 11, the License specifically includes the right to exclude any person from manufacturing, distributing and selling Licensed Products in the Territory.

2.2 Licensed Products. The term "Licensed Products" means all products sold by the Licensee, any Affiliate or Subsidiary (as such terms are defined in Exhibit A), or any sublicensee of the Licensee during the term of this Agreement that are based on the Property.

3. Term Termination

3.1 Term. The term of this Agreement shall commence on the date stated above and shall continue until terminated as provided below.

Note: Obviously, it is much easier for the Licensee to terminate than the Licensor. You should carefully review these termination provisions deleting and / or adding where appropriate. Most are not commented as they are fairly straightforward.

Note: Insert the termination notice required by the Licensee, generally 30 days.

3.2 Termination. This Agreement may be terminated by the Licensee at any time upon [Enter time) prior notice to the Licensor, and by the Licensor:

3.2.1 Upon any material breach of this Agreement by the Licensee that is not remedied within 30 days after the Licensee's receipt of notice of such breach;

3.2.2 If the Licensor does not receive payment of the advance against royalties in accordance with Section 3.2;

3.2.3 Pursuant to Section 3.2.9.

Note: You should include this provision where the Licensee has agreed to present the Products at a certain trade show or fair. For example, if the Product was a toy, the Licensee might be required to present it at the New York City Toy Show.

Note: Insert the year and name of the show or fair where the Licensee must present the Product.

3.2.4   If the Licensee does not present the Licensed Products at the [Year] [Enter Tradeshow];

Note: Insert the date on or before that the Company must ship Products to its customers.

3.2.5   If the Licensee does not ship the Licensed Products to its customers on or before [Date];

Note: Insert a time frame, for example, during 1996.

3.2.6   The Licensee notifies the Licensor of its intent not to manufacture the Licensed Products during [Enter time frame);

Note: Insert the time period in the next section, for example 12 months. If the Licensee doesn't manufacture or sell during this period, then the Licensor can terminate the Agreement.

3.2.7   If the Licensee does not manufacture and sell the Licensed Products for any consecutive [Enter time period) period;

3.2.8   If the Licensee files a petition in bankruptcy, is adjudicated a bankrupt, becomes insolvent, makes an arrangement or assignment for the benefit of creditors, or discontinues its business, or if a receiver or custodian is appointed for the Licensee or its business, or if a petition in bankruptcy is filed against the Licensee that is not dismissed within 90 days after the date of such filing; or

Note: For the first insert in the next section, enter the first year that the minimum guarantee applies. Normally this is the second year of the License. For the second insert, state the amount of the minimum annual guarantee.

3.2.9   The Licensor may terminate this Agreement if within 30 days after the end of any calendar year beginning with [Enter Year], the Licensee has not paid to the Licensor royalties of at least [Enter amount) from the sale of Licensed Products during such calendar year (the "Minimum Guarantee").

Note: The following termination provisions are fairly routine. Rather than comment on each one on all of the time periods, we have inputted standards for you; of course you can change them if you so desire. Basically, they all relate to when money is due the Licensor by the Licensee; depending on the nature of the money, the due times will vary.

3.3 Effect of Termination. Upon termination of this Agreement by either party:

3.3.1. All rights granted to the Licensee under this Agreement shall revert to the Licensor free and clear of any lien, security interest or other encumbrance, and the Licensee and its Affiliates and Subsidiaries shall as soon as practicable cease the manufacture, distribution, sale, promotion, advertising and marketing of the Licensed Products; provided, however, that for a period of 120 days after termination of this Agreement the Licensee and its Affiliates and Subsidiaries may complete any work in process and sell their existing inventories of the Licensed Products;

3.3.2 All portion of the advance against royalties described in Section 4.3 that has not been paid shall be immediately due and payable;

3.3.3 All royalty payments due pursuant to Section 4 (other than royalty payments, if any, for the 120 day period during which the Licensee and its Affiliates and Subsidiaries may complete their work in process and sell their existing inventories of Licensed Products) shall be paid to the Licensor within 30 days after the date this Agreement is terminated;

3.3.4 All other amounts due under this Agreement from either party to the other (except for amounts due from the Licensee's sublicensees that shall continue to be collected by the Licensee and paid to the Licensor in accordance with Sections 4) shall be paid within 150 days after the date this Agreement is terminated, at that time the Licensee shall submit to the Licensor a final account statement in accordance with Section 4.1.

4. Royalty

Note: For the first two inserts in Section 4.1, enter the royalty percentage to be paid to the Licensor. For the third insert, enter the maximum amount, either a fixed dollar or percentage, permitted for returns, discounts, allowances and credits. For the last insert, indicate the interest rate applied to late payments.

4.1 [x]% of the Net Sales. Except as otherwise provided in Section 4.2, the Licensee shall pay to the Licensor a royalty equal to [x]% of the Net Sales of all Licensed Products sold by the Licensee. The term "Net Sales" shall mean the gross sales price of all Licensed Products sold by the Licensee (and, with respect to 4.2, any sublicensee of the Licensee) less all returns and less reasonable discounts, allowances and credits not to exceed $[x] of such gross sales price.

Licensed Products shall be regarded as "sold" when either shipped or invoiced by the Licensee, whichever occurs first. Royalties shall be paid to the Licensor quarterly within 30 days after the end of each calendar quarter. The term "calendar quarter" shall mean the periods ending March 31, June 30, September 30, and December 31, in any given calendar year. Royalty payments shall be accompanied by account statements certified as accurate and complete by an authorized officer of the Licensee for the applicable calendar quarter setting forth the amount of gross sales, discounts, allowances and credits in the aggregate and separately for each Licensed Product by stock keeping number. Late payments of royalties shall bear interest at a rate of [Indicate interest rate) per annum, provided that such rate shall not exceed the maximum rate permitted by law.

Note: Section 4.2 deals with sales to affiliates, subsidiaries and sublicensees of the Licensee. We have written this section so as to protect the Licensor from below market sales to affiliates. Imagine what the Licensor's payments would be if the Licensee sold to an affiliate for one tenth of what the Product normally sold for. Section 4.2 ensures that the royalties resulting from the sales to affiliates are at least one half of what the Licensor normally gets or 50% of what the Licensee gets, whichever is greater.

Note: For the first insert, enter the royalty percentage to be paid to the Licensor (this should be the same percentage as stated in Section 4.1). For the second insert, enter the maximum amount, either a fixed dollar or percentage, permitted for returns, discounts, allowances and credits. (This should also match Section 4.1). The third insert is merely one half the Royalty; thus if the Royalty is 5%, this insert would be 2.5%.

4.2 Despite anything to the contrary contained in Section 4.1, royalties paid to the Licensor in connection with the sale of the Licensed Products by the Licensee to: (1) any Affiliate or Subsidiary shall be based on [x]% of the gross sales price of all Licensed Products sold by them less all returns and less reasonable discounts, allowances and credits not to exceed $[x] of such gross sales price; (2) any sublicensee shall be based on the greater of 50% of all royalties, including advances against royalties, paid to the Licensee by each such sublicensee or [x]% of the Net Sales of all the Licensed Products sold by each such sublicensee. The Royalties paid to the Licensor pursuant to this Section 4.2 shall be paid in accordance with Section 4.1 within 30 days after the end of the calendar quarter during which such royalties are collected by the Licensee.

Note: If the Licensee will be advancing Royalties to the Licensor, insert the amount of the advance for the first insert. For the second, insert the schedule for those payments.

4.3 Advance Against Royalties. The Licensee shall pay to the Licensor the sum of $[x] as a non-refundable advance against royalties from the sale of the Licensed Products in accordance with the following schedule:

*   [Enter schedule]

*   [Xxx]

*   [xxx]

Note: The Licensee does not have to pay royalties on Products sold in Close Out Sales, where products are sold at a 25% discount. If appropriate, you may wish to change the percentages.

4.4 Close Out Sales. The royalty provisions of this Agreement shall not apply to Close Out Sales by the Licensee or its sublicensees. The term "Close Out Sales" shall mean any sale of the Licensed Products at a net selling price of less than 75% of the Licensee's or its sublicensees customary wholesale price.

Note: This is a common and useful section assuring you of the right to audit their books.

4.5 Access to Books & Records. The Licensee shall keep complete and accurate books and records with respect to the manufacture, distribution and sale of Licensed Products. The Licensor shall have the right, through an independent accountant retained by the Licensor, to inspect the Licensee's books and records relating to the subject matter of this Agreement once per year during the term of this Agreement and for a period of two years thereafter on reasonable notice to the Licensee, during regular business hours at the place where such books and records are normally kept and to the extent reasonably necessary to determine the accuracy of any royalty payments to be made hereunder. The Licensee shall be entitled to rely on the financial reports submitted to it by its sublicensees' and the Licensee shall not be required to verify such reports by actual inspection of its sublicensees, books and records. However, the Licensee shall require its sublicensees to keep complete and accurate books and records with respect to the manufacture, distribution and sale of Licensed Products. The Licensee shall make available to the Licensor the results of any audit it conducts of its sublicensees. Any and all information obtained by the Licensor in such inspections and in the royalty reports provided under Section 4.1 shall be considered strictly confidential and shall not be released or disclosed to any person, except in connection with any action to enforce the rights of the Licensor under this Agreement.

5. Representations & Warranties; Indemnification

Note: Section 5 contains a number of fairly typical representations and warranties by both parties, along with standard indemnification provisions in the event of a breach of warranty or misrepresentation.

5.1 The Licensor represents and warrants to the Licensee that: (1) it is the owner of the Property and has the power to grant the License to the Licensee; (2) it has not granted to any other person a license to manufacture, distribute or sell the Property in the Territory; and (3) to the best of its knowledge, the Property does not infringe any patent, copyright, trademark or other proprietary right of any third party.

Note: In the event that the Licensor breaches any of the warranties contained in Section 5.1 to the Licensee, it will indemnify the Licensee, i.e., it will pay any and all damages and expenses resulting from that breach. In the event of such a claim, the Licensor can suspend payment of royalties.

5.2 The Licensor shall indemnify and hold the Licensee harmless from and against any and all damages, liabilities, costs and expenses incurred by the Licensee in connection with any final judgment arising out of or resulting from any breach by the Licensor of its representations and warranties contained in 5.1 to the extent any such claim, proceeding or judgment relates to aspects of Licensed Products as originated by the Licensor; provided, however, that the Licensor's total liability pursuant to this paragraph shall be limited to the aggregate amount of royalties paid to the Licensor hereunder during the term of this Agreement. In the event such a claim is asserted against the Licensee, the Licensee may suspend payment of the royalties due to the Licensor hereunder and apply such royalties toward the reasonable costs and legal expenses of defending such claim and the payment of any ensuing settlement or judgment. Within 30 days after the resolution of any such claim, the Licensee shall remit to the Licensor the amount, if any, of royalties withheld from the Licensor and not applied to the defense or payment of such claim, together with a statement setting forth all costs and legal expenses to which such royalties were applied. The provisions of this paragraph shall survive the termination of this Agreement. Such indemnification shall be in addition to any other remedies available to the Licensee.

5.3 The Licensee represents and warrants to the Licensor that this Agreement constitutes the legal, valid and binding obligation of the Licensee enforceable against the Licensee in accordance with its terms.

Note: In the event that the Licensee breaches its warranties, uses the property in an unauthorized manner, or manufactures the Products incorrectly, it will indemnify the Licensor, i.e., it will pay any and all damages and expenses resulting from that breach.

5.4 The Licensee shall indemnify and hold the Licensor harmless from and against any and all damages, liabilities, costs and expenses incurred by the Licensor in connection with any final judgment arising out of or resulting from:
(1) the breach by the Licensee of its representations and warranties contained in Section 5.3; (2) the manufacture, distribution or sale of Licensed Products (except insofar as such claims relate to the Licensor's representations and warranties contained in Section 5.1); (3) any unauthorized use by the Licensee or any Affiliate, Subsidiary or sublicensee of the Property; and (4) any defects (design or otherwise) or inherent dangers in the Property. The provisions of this paragraph shall survive the termination of this Agreement. Such indemnification shall be in addition to any other remedy available to the Licensor.

6. Product Liability Insurance

Note: Insert the minimum product liability insurance to be obtained by the Licensee, generally $1,000,000.00.

Promptly after the date this Agreement is executed (but in no event later than the date the Licensed Products are first manufactured), the Licensee shall obtain and keep in effect during the term of this Agreement, at its sole cost and expense, all risk product liability insurance in an aggregate amount of not less than $[x] naming the Licensor as an additional insured, and shall promptly provide the Licensor with evidence. Each insurance policy shall provide that if such insurance is canceled for any reason whatsoever, or if any substantial change is made in the coverage that affects the Licensor, or if such insurance is allowed to lapse for non-payment of any premium, such cancellation, change or lapse shall not be effective as to the Licensor until 30 days after receipt by the Licensor of written notice from the insurance Licensee.

7. Similar Products

Note: The Licensee is agreeing not to sell, manufacture or distribute competitive Products. Depending on the nature of your Products, you may need to clarify the bracketed words so they apply.

The Licensee agrees that throughout and after the term of this Agreement it will not manufacture, distribute or sell any product (other than Licensed Products manufactured, distributed or sold during the term of this Agreement) that [employs the basic principles or the basic concept of design of the Property). In the event that the Licensee does manufacture, distribute or sell any such product, the same shall be governed by the terms and conditions of this Agreement including, without limitation, the obligation to pay royalties in accordance with Section 4.

8. Patent, Copyright & Trademark

Note: The Licensor may, at its option, elect to seek a patent for the Product(s). Section 8 sets forth a number of formalities regarding patents.

8.1 Acquisition of Patent

8.1.1 The Licensor shall keep the Licensee apprised of the status of all patent applications, if any, filed by the Licensor with the United States Patent and Trademark Office, and shall promptly provide the Licensee with copies of any pending patent applications and patents issued. If the Licensor elects not to file and / or prosecute any such patent applications, the Licensee may do so at its sole cost and expense.

8.1.2 The Licensee in its sole discretion and at its sole cost and expense may apply for patents covering the Property in any foreign country in the Territory. At the Licensee's request, the Licensor shall assist the Licensee to the extent reasonably necessary in connection with any such patent applications.

8.1.3 Despite anything to the contrary contained in Section 8.1 and Section 8.2, all patent applications filed and patents issued in connection with Licensed Products shall be solely in the name of the Licensor; provided, however, that, at the request of the Licensee, all such patents issued shall be assigned to the Licensee for the term of this Agreement.

Note: The Licensor is also the owner of all copyrights and trademarks relating to the Products; the Licensee is required to include notices of any applicable patent, copyright or trademarks on the Products.

8.2 The Licensor shall be designated by the Licensee as the owner of all patents, and all copyrights and trademarks originated by the Licensor, used in connection with the sale of Licensed Products. The Licensee shall affix patent, copyright and trademark notices on all Licensed Products and all materials related thereto including, without limitation, all advertising, packaging, promotional display, printed and other materials indicating the Licensor's ownership of all such patents, copyrights and trademarks.

8.3 As the exclusive Licensee in the Territory, the Licensee shall assist the Licensor throughout the term of this Agreement, at the Licensor's sole cost and expense, in obtaining protection of any patent, and any copyright or trademark originated by the Licensor, used in connection with the sale of Licensed Products.

Note: The Licensee is required to get the Licensor's approval before using any of its Trademarks.

8.4 The Licensee shall not utilize any trademark in connection with any advertising, packaging, promotional display, printed or other material used in connection with the sale of Licensed Products without first submitting the same, together with production samples to the Licensor for its approval, which shall not be unreasonably withheld. The Licensor's approval shall be deemed given if it does not notify the Licensee of its disapproval within 10 days after each such submission.

9. Licensing Outside Territory

Note: The Licensor can license the Property outside the Territory so long as that Licensee has no rights within the Licensee's Territory.

The Licensor intends to license the Property to third parties for manufacture, distribution and sale outside the Territory. Each such license shall specifically limit such third party's right to manufacture, distribute and sell the Property and any products derived therefrom to the territory specified in such license, which in no event shall include any part of the Territory. The Licensor shall cooperate with the Licensee to the extent reasonably necessary to prevent any such third party from manufacturing, distributing or selling the Property and any products derived therefrom in the Territory.

10. Infringement

Note: If there is an infringement and the Licensor chooses to file an infringement suit, then it will keep the first bracketed percentage of any proceeds and give the

Licensee the second bracketed percent less its costs. If the Licensor elects not to pursue an action, the Licensee may. In that event, the Licensee keeps the third bracketed percentage of the proceeds plus its costs, with the final bracketed percentage going to the Licensor.

The Licensee and the Licensor agree to promptly notify each other of any suspected infringement of their respective interests in and to the Property by any third party. In the event that any legal action against any third party is deemed necessary by either the Licensee or the Licensor for the protection of their respective interests in and to the Property in the Territory, the Licensee and the Licensor shall cooperate with each other and render all reasonably necessary assistance in connection with any such legal action; provided, however, that neither party shall settle any such action without the prior written consent of the other, which shall not be unreasonably withheld. Within 30 days after notice from the Licensee of a suspected infringement, the Licensor shall advise the Licensee of whether or not it shall prosecute a suit for infringement. If the Licensor elects to prosecute such a suit, it may select legal counsel and shall bear all legal fees and other costs and expenses incurred in connection therewith. Any money recovered after such costs and expenses are reimbursed shall be shared as follows: [x]% to the Licensor; and [x]% to the Licensee. If the Licensor chooses not to prosecute any such suit for infringement, then the Licensee may do so after notice to the Licensor, and the Licensee may select legal counsel and shall bear all legal fees and other costs and expenses incurred in connection therewith. Any money recovered after such costs and expenses are reimbursed shall be shared as follows: [x]% to the Licensor; and [x]% to the Licensee.

11. Merchandising Rights

Note If the Licensor designates an Agent to do those things that the Licensee is not licensed to do, then the Licensor and Note: he Licensee will share equally in the proceeds.

The Licensor may designate an agent (the "Agent") to exploit all rights in and to the Property in the Territory (other than the right to manufacture, distribute and sell Licensed Products in the Territory) including, without limitation, book, television, cable, disc, videocassette, clothing and film rights and all other related media rights (collectively, the "Merchandising Rights") by sublicensing to third parties the right to manufacture, distribute and sell any products based on the Merchandising Rights. All amounts paid to the Licensor by the Agent from the exploitation of the Merchandising Rights shall be shared equally between the Licensee and the Licensor after deduction of the Agent's fees and commissions including any fees and commissions paid by the Agent to its agents.

12. General Provisions

Note: The General Provisions that follow are fairly standard. These provisions enhance the balance of the Agreement by defining certain common issues such as notice, assignment, legal remedies, waiver, and attorney fees, etc..

12.1   Independent Contractors. The relationship between both parties established by this Agreement is that of independent contractors, and nothing contained in this Agreement shall be construed to give either party the power to direct and control the day-to-day activities of the other. Neither party is an agent, representative or partner of the other party. Neither party shall have any right, power or authority to enter into any agreement for, or on behalf of, or incur any obligation or liability of, or to otherwise bind, the other party. This Agreement shall not be interpreted or construed to create an association, agency, joint venture or partnership between the parties or to impose any liability attributable to such relationship upon either party.

Note: You may or may not want to make this deal public – at least limit that event by this agreement and work out if/how/when you want to do that later.

12.2   Publicity. Neither party will make any public announcement or issue any press release concerning the terms of this Agreement without the prior approval of both parties.

Note: Make it clear that you will not try to hire away each others employees. If you do or it happens then there is compensation built-in and you can avoid further legal proceedings.

12.3   Non-Solicitation. Neither party shall solicit for employment or hire the other's current or future employees, either directly or indirectly, during the Term of this Agreement, without obtaining the other's prior written approval. Should an employee change employment from one party to the other, the new employer shall pay the old employer a fee equivalent to Twenty Percent (20%) of the employee's new compensation, annualized for the first year.

Note: You must decide which state governs this Agreement and where any legal action would be taken. Generally, it is your (company's) state of residence.

12.4   Governing Law Jurisdiction. This agreement and the parties' actions under this Agreement shall be governed by and construed under the laws of the state of [State], without reference to conflict of law principles. The parties hereby expressly consent to the jurisdiction and venue of the federal and state courts within the state of [State]. Each party hereby irrevocably consents to the service of process in any such action or proceeding by the mailing of copies thereof by registered or certified mail, postage prepaid, to such party at its address set forth in the preamble of this Agreement, such service to become effective thirty (30) days after such mailing.

Note: This Agreement is intended to be the only Agreement and that no other documents or communications are binding. Therefore, it is very important to make sure that everything [Company] and [Client] have agreed to be included in this Agreement. Otherwise, it is as if it were not agreed to.

12.5   Entire Agreement. This Agreement, including the attached exhibits, constitutes the entire Agreement between both parties concerning this transaction, and replaces all previous communications, representations, understandings, and Agreements, whether verbal or written between the parties to this Agreement or their representatives. No representations or statements of any kind made by either party, which are not expressly stated in this Agreement, shall be binding on such parties.

Note: Any changes to this Agreement must be in writing and signed by the party against whom that writing is to be used.

12.6   All Amendments in Writing. No waiver, amendment or modification of any provisions of this Agreement shall be effective unless in writing and signed by a duly authorized representative of the party against whom such waiver, amendment or modification is sought to be enforced. Furthermore, no provisions in either party's purchase orders or in any other business forms employed by either party will supersede the terms and conditions of this Agreement.

Note: All notices between the parties must be in writing and either delivered in person or by certified or registered mail, return receipt requested.

12.7   Notices. Any notice required or permitted by this Agreement shall be deemed given if sent by registered mail, postage prepaid with return receipt requested, addressed to the other party at the address set forth in the preamble of this Agreement or at such other address for which such party gives notice hereunder. Delivery shall be deemed effective three (3) days after deposit with postal authorities.

Note: In the event of a lawsuit or any legal proceeding involving this Agreement, the losing party will have to pay the winning party his or her costs and expenses, including reasonable attorney fees.

12.8   Costs of Legal Action. In the event any action is brought to enforce this Agreement, the prevailing party shall be entitled to recover its costs of enforcement including, without limitation, attorneys' fees and court costs.

Note: Legal remedies, i.e., money damages, may not be sufficient; therefore, both parties agree to equitable remedies such as an injunction where the breaching party would be required to do or not to do something.

12.9   Inadequate Legal Remedy. Both parties understand and acknowledge that violation of their respective covenants and Agreements may cause the other irreparable harm and damage, that may not be recovered at law, and each agrees that the other's remedies for breach may be in equity by way of injunctive relief, as well as for damages and any other relief available to the non-breaching party, whether in law or in equity.

12.10   Arbitration. Any dispute relating to the interpretation or performance of this Agreement shall be resolved at the request of either party through binding arbitration. Arbitration shall be conducted in [County], [State] in accordance with the then-existing rules of the American Arbitration Association. Judgment upon any award by the arbitrators may be entered by any state or federal court having jurisdiction. Both parties intend that this Agreement to arbitrate be irrevocable.

12.11   Delay is Not a Waiver. No failure or delay by either party in exercising any right, power or remedy under this Agreement, except as specifically provided in this Agreement, shall operate as a waiver of any such right, power or remedy.

12.12   Force Majeure. In the event that either party is unable to perform any of its obligations under this Agreement or to enjoy any of its benefits because of any Act of God, strike, fire, flood, governmental acts, orders or restrictions, Internet system unavailability, system malfunctions or any other reason where failure to perform is beyond the reasonable control and not caused by the negligence of the non-performing party (a "Force Majeure Event"), the party who has been so affected shall give notice immediately to the other party and shall use its reasonable best efforts to resume performance. Failure to meet due dates resulting from a Force Majeure Event shall extend such due dates for a reasonable period. However, if the period of nonperformance exceeds sixty (60) days from the receipt of notice of the Force Majeure Event, the party whose ability to perform has not been affected may, by giving written notice, terminate this Agreement effective immediately upon such notice or at such later date as is therein specified.

Note: CHOOSE one or the other of these two following paragraphs.

12.13   Assignability & Binding Effect. Except as expressly set forth within this Agreement, neither party may transfer or assign, directly or indirectly, this Agreement or its rights and obligations hereunder without the express written permission of the other party, not to be unreasonably withheld; provided, however, that both parties shall have the right to assign or otherwise transfer this Agreement to any parent, subsidiary, affiliated entity or pursuant to any merger, consolidation or reorganization, provided that all such assignees and transferees agree in writing to be bound by the terms of this Agreement prior to such assignment or transfer. Subject to the foregoing, this Agreement shall be binding upon and inure to the benefit of the parties hereto, their successors and assigns.

Or

Note: This paragraph DOES NOT ALLOW either party to transfer its rights to a successor company without prior approval.

12.13   Non-Assignability & Binding Effect . Except as otherwise provided For within this Agreement, neither party may assign any of its rights or delegate any of its obligations under this Agreement to any third party without the express written permission of the other. Any such assignment is deemed null and void.

Note: If any part of this Agreement is unenforceable or invalid, the balance of the Agreement should still be enforced. Basically, ignore any sections that are invalid.

12.14   Severability. If any provisions of this Agreement are held by a court of competent jurisdiction to be invalid under any applicable statute or rule of law, they are to that extent to be deemed omitted and the remaining provisions of this Agreement shall remain in full force and effect.

Note: The headings of the various sections are meant to explain or otherwise give meaning to those sections; they are for convenience only.

12.15   Cumulative Rights. Any specific right or remedy provided in this Agreement will not be exclusive but will be cumulative upon all other rights and remedies described in this section and allowed under applicable law.

12.16   Headings. The titles and headings of the various sections and sections in this Agreement are intended solely for convenience of reference and are not intended for any other purpose whatsoever, or to explain, modify or place any construction upon or on any of the provisions of this Agreement.

Note: Every copy shall be just as valid as the original.

<u>License Agreement - Trademarks</u>

Trademark License Agreement

Note: This is a standard introductory paragraph that lists the parties to the Agreement and the date the Agreement is being entered into. You need to enter the date of the Agreement, the names of the parties, the specific type of organization, and their addresses.

Note: Not knowing which party you will be in this deal, we have inserted the variables as if you are the licensor – to reverse this position, simply reverse the data in this top section.

Project Title **[Trademark Name]** Effective Date **[Date]** BETWEEN **[Company Legal Name]** ("[Company]" or "Licensor") a•*[Corporation / Partnership / Sole Proprietorship / Individual]* Located at **[Address] [City], [State] [Zip Code]** ("Licensor") AND **[Licensee],** ("Licensee") a *[Corporation / Partnership / Sole Proprietorship / Individual]* Located at **[Licensee Address] [City, State• Zip Code]**

Summary

The Licensor is the owner of all right, title and interest in and to the trademarks and the trade dress, labels and designs associated with the trademarks, that are described and listed in Exhibit A (the "Licensed Marks"), together with the goodwill of the [product / business] symbolized thereby in connection with the Products (defined below) in the Territory.

Note: Will the License be exclusive, meaning that the Licensee will be the only entity entitled to use the Licensed Marks in the Territory, or will the License be non-exclusive?

The Licensee desires to license from the Licensor, and the Licensor is willing to license to the Licensee, a (non-)exclusive license in the Territory for use of the Licensed Marks.

In consideration for the mutual promises, covenants, and agreements made below, the parties, intending to be legally bound, agree as follows:

Definitions

For purposes of this Agreement, the following terms will have the indicated definitions:

"Agreement" This Agreement is by and between the Licensor and the Licensee.

"License Fees" The gross License Fees billed by the Licensee (or any of its affiliates or sub-licensees) to customers for the Products, less trade discounts and allowances, returns, and any other deductions generally allowed by its customers, as normally deducted from license fee revenues. The amount of License Fees for any period is determined on the basis of transactions actually completed and recorded on the books and records of the Licensee (or any of its affiliates or sub- licensees) during such period consistent with past practice, without reference to the effects of any subsequent audit adjustments that result in any of such transactions being recognized by the Licensee (or any of its affiliates or sub- licensees) in another period.

Note: For both inserts in the paragraph below, enter the category of products, for example software or hardware.

"Products" All of the (Enter category) products described in Exhibit B. The list comprising these Products is expected to expand during the term of this Agreement to include additional [Enter category] products that represent an extension of the line of items constituting the Products, but any such expansion will not take place without the written consent of both the Licensor and the Licensee.

Note: Define the area where the License will be granted, for example, the United States and its territories and possessions.

"Territory" [Worldwide / Define Territory].

Note: The Licensee can pretty much do anything with the Products in the Territory. While it may sell the Products outside the Territory, it can not sell or distribute them there.

1. Grant of License. For the term of this Agreement, the Licensor hereby grants to the Licensee a (non-)exclusive license (the "License") to use and sublicense the Licensed Marks for and in connection with all activities relating to the packaging, marketing, distribution, selling, and licensing of the Products in the Territory.

Note: Section 2 sets forth the standards required of the Licensee and its sub- licensees regarding the Licensed Marks. Those standards and specifications are specifically set forth in Exhibit C that should be completed.

2. Quality Standards

2.1 Maintenance of Quality. The Licensee will maintain, and require its sub- licensees to maintain, the standards of quality and technical specifications, including packaging standards described in Exhibit C ("Standards and

Specifications"), or such other standards or specifications that the Licensor may adopt or approve during the term of this Agreement. If the Licensee sublicenses or otherwise authorizes use of any of the Licensed Marks, it will require those entities to maintain and adhere to the Standards and Specifications.

Note: Insert the period after which acceptance of any New Standards and Specifications will be deemed given (if no response).

2.2 Changes & Additions. Before adding a new item to the Products or changing the Standards and Specifications to an existing product, the Licensee agrees to provide the Licensor with the proposed Standards and Specifications and, if approved and adopted by the Licensor, such Standards and Specifications will become effective (the "New Standards and Specifications"). The Licensor will be deemed to have approved and adopted the New Standards and Specifications unless it advises the Licensee in the writing of its objections to such New Standards and Specifications within (Fifteen) days of their receipt.

Note: The Licensor is agreeing to treat all Standards and Specifications as confidential for the term of this Agreement and for the bracketed period of time thereafter (generally 10 years).

2.3 Procedure for Disclosure of New Standards Specifications.
The Licensee's disclosure of the New Standards and Specifications is solely for the purpose of enabling the Licensor to establish, enforce, and maintain quality standards and technical specifications respecting the Products. The Licensor acknowledges that the New Standards and Specifications, as well as the Standards and Specifications, are proprietary information constituting trade secrets owned by the Licensee, or disclosed to the Licensee in confidence by its sub-licensees. The Licensor agrees to treat all Standards and Specifications (including the New Standards and Specifications) as confidential during the term of this Agreement and for (Enter time) subsequent to its termination. Except as permitted by this Agreement, the Licensor will not disclose the Standards and Specifications (including any New Standards and Specifications) except in circumstances when disclosure is necessary for quality control purposes. Such restriction against disclosure will not apply to (1) any disclosure of information that is generally known in the trade or (2) any disclosures required by law or judicial or governmental order after notice by the Licensor to Licensee informing of the required disclosure and providing the Licensee the right to object.

Note: The Licensor may inspect the Licensee's and any sub-licensee's facilities to make sure they are complying with the Standards and Specifications set forth above.

2.4 Rights of Inspection. With prior notice to the Licensee or its sub-licensee, the Licensor and its authorized agents and representatives may enter the offices and facilities of the Licensor and its sub-licensees at all reasonable times, to inspect reasonable samples of the Products and to inspect the books and records, as they relate to compliance with the Standards and Specifications.

322

2.5 Submission or Selection of Samples. At the Licensor's request, the
Licensee will furnish, or cause each sub-licensee to furnish, in either case without cost to the Licensor, a reasonable number of samples of the Products; the Licensor may either select these samples at random or pursuant to a reasonable sampling procedure established by it.

3.   Term Termination

3.1 Term. The term of this Agreement will commence on the date stated above and will continue until terminated as provided below.

Note: Obviously, it is much easier for the Licensee to terminate the Agreement than the Licensor. You should carefully review these termination provisions deleting and / or adding where appropriate. Most of the following sections are not commented on, as they are fairly straightforward.

Note: Insert the termination notice required by the Licensee, generally 30 days.

3.2 Termination. This Agreement may be terminated by the Licensee at any time upon (Insert time period) prior notice to the Licensor, and by the Licensor:

3.2.1   Upon any material breach of this Agreement by the Licensee that is not remedied within 30 days after the Licensee's receipt of notice of such breach;

3.2.2   If the Licensor does not receive payment of the Minimum Royalty Installment as defined in 4.1

Note: Insert the date on or before that the Licensee must ship Products to its customers.

3.2.3   If the Licensee does not ship the Products to its customers on or before (Enter date);

Note: Insert a time frame, for example, during 1996.

3.2.4   The Licensee notifies the Licensor of its intent not to manufacture Products during (Enter time frame);

Note: Insert the time period, for example 12 months. If the Licensee doesn't manufacture or sell during this period, then the Licensor can terminate the Agreement.

3.2.5   If the Licensee does not manufacture and sell the Products for any consecutive (Enter time) period; or

3.2.6   If the Licensee files a petition in bankruptcy, is adjudicated a bankrupt, becomes insolvent, makes an arrangement or assignment for the benefit of creditors, or discontinues its business, or if a receiver or custodian is appointed for the Licensee or its business, or if a petition in bankruptcy is filed against the Licensee that is not dismissed within 60 days after the date of such filing.

Note: These termination provisions are fairly routine. Rather than comment all of the time periods, we have inputted standards for you; of course you can change them if you so desire. Basically, they all relate to when money is due the Licensor by Licensee; depending on the nature of those moneys, the due times will vary.

3.3 Effect of Termination. Upon termination of this Agreement by either party:

Note: Upon termination the Licensee gets 120 days to sell its existing inventory; after that all rights revert to the Licensor.

3.3.1 All rights granted to the Licensee hereunder will revert to the Licensor free and clear of any lien, security interest or other encumbrance, and the Licensee and its affiliates and subsidiaries will as soon as practicable cease the manufacture, distribution, sale, promotion, advertising and marketing of Products; provided, however, that for a period of 120 days after termination of this Agreement the Licensee and its affiliates and subsidiaries may complete any work in process and sell their existing inventories of Products;

3.3.2 All of the Advance Against Royalties described in section 4.2 that have not been paid will be immediately due and payable;

3.3.3 All royalty payments due pursuant to Section 4 (other than royalty payments, if any, for the 120 day period during which time the Licensee and its Affiliates and Subsidiaries may complete their work in process and sell their existing inventories of Products) will be paid to the Licensor within 30 days after the date this Agreement is terminated;

3.3.4 All other amounts due under this Agreement from either party to the other (except for amounts due from the Licensee's sub-licensees that will continue to be collected by the Licensee and paid to the Licensor in accordance with Sections 5) will be paid within 150 days after the date this Agreement is terminated, at that time the Licensee will submit to the Licensor a final account statement in accordance with Section 5.1.

4. License Fee

Note: Section 4.1 sets forth a Royalty Payment that is the greater of the Minimum Royalty Installment provided in Exhibit D or the sum of the License Fees for the Royalty Bearing Products multiplied by the Royalty Rate set forth in Exhibit D.

4.1 Royalty Rate and Payment Requirements. Thirty (30) days
following the end of each fiscal quarterly period, the Licensee will pay the Licensor a "Net License Fees Royalty Payment" that will be equal to the greater of (1) the amount

set forth as the "Minimum Royalty Installment" in Exhibit D for the immediately preceding fiscal quarterly period; and (2) an amount equal to the sum of the respective License Fees for each of the Products distributed under the Licensed Marks in the Territory, for the immediately preceding fiscal quarterly period (the Products referred to in this Section are referred to as "Royalty Bearing Products"), multiplied by, the royalty rate set forth under the heading "Net License Fees Royalty Payment" in Exhibit D. If the Net License Fees Royalty Payment is to be calculated for a period consisting of less than a full fiscal quarter, the Net License Fees Royalty Payment will be equal to the amount calculated in accordance with clause (2) of the immediately preceding sentence (that is, the Net License Fees Royalty Payment will be determined without reference to the Minimum Royalty Installment).

Note: Insert the advance payment, if any, to be paid to Licensor, along with a schedule of payments.

4.2 Advance Against Royalties. The Licensee will pay to the Licensor the sum of $(enter amount) as a non-refundable advance against royalties from the sale of Products in accordance with the following schedule: (Insert schedule of payments).

Note: While Licensee is agreeing on behalf of itself and its sub-licensees to use its best efforts to promote the Products and generate royalties, it reserves the right to discontinue the distribution of certain categories of the Products so long as it continues to sell at least the bracketed number of categories or products.

4.3 Best Efforts Commitment. The Licensee acknowledges that the Licensor expects to receive royalty payments pursuant to this Agreement and that this expectancy constitutes a material inducement to the Licensor to enter into this Agreement. As such, the Licensee will employ its reasonable efforts to promote the distribution of the Products under the Licensed Marks. The Licensee (for itself and its sub-licensees) expressly reserves the right to discontinue the distribution of any of the categories of products included within the Products as long as the Licensee (or one or more sub-licensees) continues to sell under the Licensed Marks at least (Enter number) of the categories of products constituting the Products.

4.4 Access to Books Records. The Licensee will keep complete and accurate books and records with respect to the manufacture, distribution and sale of Products. The Licensor will have the right, through an independent accountant retained by the Licensor, to inspect the Licensee's books and records relating to the subject matter of this Agreement once per year during the term of this Agreement and for a period of two years thereafter on reasonable notice to the Licensee, during regular business hours at the place where such books and records are normally kept and to the extent reasonably necessary to determine the accuracy of any royalty payments to be made under this Agreement.

The Licensee will be entitled to rely on the financial reports submitted to it by its sub-licensees' and the Licensee will not be required to verify such reports by actual inspection of its sub-licensees, books and records. However, the Licensee will require its sub-licensees to keep complete and accurate books and records with respect to the manufacture, distribution and sale of Products. The Licensee will make available to the Licensor the results of any audit it conducts of its sub-licensees. Any and all information obtained by the Licensor in such inspections and in the royalty reports provided under Section 4.1 will be considered strictly confidential and will not be released or disclosed to any person, except in connection with any action to enforce the rights of the Licensor under this Agreement.

5 Representations & Warranties; Indemnification

Note: Section 5 contains a number of fairly typical representations and warranties by both parties, along with standard indemnification provisions in the event of a breach of warranty or misrepresentation.

5.1 The Licensor represents and warrants to the Licensee that: (1) it is the owner of the Products and the Licensed Marks and has the power to grant the License to the Licensee; (2) it has not granted to any other person a license to manufacture, distribute or sell the Products in the Territory; and (3) to the best of its knowledge, the Products and the Licensed Marks do not infringe any patent, copyright, trademark, or other proprietary right of any third party.

Note: In the event that the Licensor breaches any of the warranties contained in 5.1 to the Licensee, it will indemnify the Licensee, i.e., it will pay any and all damages and expenses resulting from that breach. In the event of such a claim, the Licensor can suspend payment of royalties.

5.2 The Licensor will indemnify and hold the Licensee harmless from and against any and all damages, liabilities, costs and expenses incurred by the Licensee in connection with any final judgment arising out of or resulting from any breach by the Licensor of its representations and warranties contained in 5.1 to the extent any such claim, proceeding or judgment relates to aspects of Products or Licensed Marks as originated by the Licensor; provided, however, that the Licensor's total liability pursuant to this paragraph will be limited to the aggregate amount of royalties paid to the Licensor under this Agreement during the term of this Agreement.

In the event such a claim is asserted against the Licensee, the Licensee may suspend payment of the royalties due to the Licensor hereunder and apply such royalties toward the reasonable costs and legal expenses of defending such claim and the payment of any ensuing settlement or judgment. Within 30 days after the resolution of any such claim, the Licensee will remit to the Licensor the amount, if any, of royalties withheld from the Licensor and not applied to the defense or payment of such claim, together with a statement setting forth all costs and legal expenses to which such royalties were applied. The provisions of this paragraph will survive the termination of this Agreement. Such indemnification will be in addition to any other remedies available to the Licensee.

5.3 The Licensee represents and warrants to the Licensor that this Agreement constitutes the legal, valid and binding obligation of the Licensee enforceable against the Licensee in accordance with its terms.

Note: In the event that the Licensee breaches its warranties, uses the Products in an unauthorized manner, or manufactures the Products incorrectly, it will indemnify the Licensor, i.e., it will pay any and all damages and expenses resulting from that breach.

5.4 The Licensee will indemnify and hold the Licensor harmless from and against any and all damages, liabilities, costs, and expenses incurred by the Licensor in connection with any final judgment arising out of or resulting from:

(1) the breach by the Licensee of its representations and warranties contained in 5.3;

(2) the manufacture, distribution or sale of Products (except insofar as such claims relate to the Licensor's representations and warranties contained 5.1);

(3) any unauthorized use by the Licensee or any affiliate, subsidiary or sub-licensee of the Products or the Licensed Marks;

(4) any unfair or fraudulent advertising claims pertaining to the Products;

(5) any claims for unauthorized use or misuse of any patent, trademark, copyright or other proprietary right owned, used or controlled by any third party pertaining to the production, distribution, licensing, or marketing of the Products and

(6) any defects (design or otherwise) or inherent dangers in the Products caused by the Licensee.

The provisions of this paragraph will survive the termination of this Agreement. Such indemnification will be in addition to any other remedy available to the Licensor.

Note: The Licensor can license the Products outside the Territory so long as the third party has no rights within the Licensee's Territory.

6. Licensing Outside Territory.

The Licensor intends to license the Products and the Licensed Marks to third parties for use outside the Territory. Each such license will specifically limit such third party's right to use the Licensed Marks and sell the Products and any products derived therefrom to the territory specified in such license, which in no event will include any part of the Licensee's Territory. The Licensor will cooperate with the Licensee to the extent reasonably necessary to prevent any such third party from manufacturing, distributing or selling the Products and any products derived therefrom in the Territory.

7. Infringement

7.1 The Licensee and the Licensor agree to promptly notify each other of any suspected infringement of their respective interests in and to the Licensed Marks by any third party, as well as any petition to cancel any registration of any of the Licensed Marks, or any attempted use or any application to register any mark confusingly similar to, or a colorable imitation of, any of the Licensed Marks within the Territory of which they become aware. In the event that any legal action against any third party is deemed necessary by either party for the protection of their respective interests, they agree to cooperate with each other and render all reasonably necessary assistance in connection with any such legal action.

Note: If there is an infringement and the Licensor chooses to file an infringement suit, then it will keep the first bracketed percentage of any proceeds and give the Licensee the second bracketed percent, less its costs. If the Licensor elects not to pursue an action, the Licensee may. In that event, the Licensee keeps the third bracketed percentage of the proceeds plus its costs, with the final bracketed percentage going to the Licensor.

7.2 In the event Licensor does not institute and prosecute any action for infringement of the Licensed Marks within the Territory, defend any petition to cancel any registration of any of the Licensed Marks, or oppose any attempted use of or any application to register any mark confusingly similar to, or a colorable imitation of, any of the Licensed Marks within the Territory within 30 days after notice from the Licensee of a suspected infringement, Licensee will have the right to do so, but will not be obligated to, either in its own name or in the name of Licensor. If the Licensor elects to prosecute such a suit, it may select legal counsel and will bear all legal fees and other costs and expenses incurred in connection therewith. Any money recovered after such costs and expenses are reimbursed will be shared as follows: [enter percentage]% to the Licensor; and [enter percentage]% to the Licensee. If the Licensor chooses not to prosecute any such suit for infringement, then the Licensee may do so after notice to the Licensor, and the Licensee may select legal counsel and will bear all legal fees and other costs and expenses incurred in connection therewith. Any money recovered after such costs and expenses are reimbursed will be shared as follows: [enter percentage]% to the Licensor; and [enter percentage]% to the Licensee.

8. Undertakings of Licensor Respecting the Licensed Marks

8.1 Ownership and Right to License. The Licensor owns all rights with respect to the   Licensed Marks and has the full right to grant to the Licensee the license rights set forth herein.

Note: This section only applies to Exclusive licenses. If this is a non-exclusive license, then delete it.

8.2 No Licensor Use of Marks. The Licensor agrees not to use or license others to use the Licensed Marks in the Territory during the term of this Agreement except for such use as may be required in connection with the performance by the

Licensor of this Agreement. The Licensor reserves all rights with respect to all trademarks or service marks that may be owned by it or licensed to it that are not subject to this Agreement.

9. Ownership of the Licensed Marks; Modifications

Note: This is a routine section. Basically, the Licensee has no ownership rights nor will it acquire any ownership rights to the Licensed Marks.

9.1 Licensor's Ownership Rights. The Licensee acknowledges the Licensor's exclusive right, title, and interest in and to the Licensed Marks and further acknowledges that except as expressly provided, nothing in this Agreement grants the Licensee any rights in any of the Licensed Marks. The Licensee acknowledges that its use of the Licensed Marks will not give it any right, title, or interest in the Licensed Marks and that its use of the Licensed Marks in the Territory and the goodwill generated inures to the benefit of the Licensor. The Licensee warrants and represents with respect as follows:

9.1.1 The Licensee will not challenge the Licensor's right, title, or interest in the Licensed Marks or their validity or any registration;

9.1.2 The Licensee will not do or cause to be done or omit to do anything that would contest or in any way impair the Licensor's rights in the Licensed Marks;

9.1.3 The Licensee will not represent that it has any ownership in or rights to the Licensed Marks in the Territory other than the rights conferred by this Agreement; and

9.1.4 Either during or subsequent to the term of this Agreement, the Licensee will not use any trademark, service mark, trade name, insignia or logo that is similar to or a colorable imitation of any of the Licensed Marks.

Note: The Licensor may make changes to the Licensed Marks; once such changes are made, the Licensed Marks, as modified, are to be treated in the same way as the Licensed Marks.

9.2 Changes and Modifications to the Licensed Marks.

The Licensor expressly reserves the right to modify and change the Licensed Marks. As modified, the Licensed Marks are deemed to be the Licensed Marks referred to in this Agreement. All such modifications or changes developed or adopted by the Licensor will be the sole property of the Licensor, and the Licensor may incorporate them in the Licensed Marks and will have the exclusive right to register in the Territory such modified or changed marks as trademarks and / or service marks. The Licensee may propose changes to the Licensed Marks for adoption and approval by the Licensor.

Note: Section 10 sets forth numerous requirements that the Licensee must satisfy in its use of the Licensed Marks.

10. Undertakings of Licensee Respecting the Licensed Marks

10.1 Marking; Compliance with Trademark Laws.

The Licensee will, and will require each of its sub-licensees to (1) cause the appropriate designation "TM" or the registration symbol "®" to be placed adjacent to the Licensed Marks in connection with each use or display of the Licensed Marks and to indicate such additional information as the Licensor will reasonably specify concerning the license rights; and (2) comply with all laws pertaining to trademarks in force.

10.2 Display of the Marks. The Licensee will, and will require each of its sub- licensees to, display, in a manner consistent with the Licensor's standards, the Licensed Marks on packaging for each of the Products, visual displays on initial computer screens, and in marketing activities respecting the Products.

10.3 No Use Objectionable to Licensor. The Licensee will not, and the Licensee will not permit its sub-licensees to, use the Licensed Marks on or in connection with any screen display, packaging, or marketing material to which the Licensor objects.

10.4 Maintenance of Registrations. The Licensee will pay any continuing maintenance or filing fees respecting state or federal registrations of the Licensed Marks.

11. General Provisions

Note: The General Provisions that follow are fairly standard. These provisions enhance the balance of the Agreement by explaining issues such as notice, assignment, legal remedies, waiver, and attorney fees.

11.1 Independent Contractors. The relationship between both parties established by this Agreement is that of independent contractors, and nothing contained in this Agreement shall be construed to give either party the power to direct and control the day-to-day activities of the other. Neither party is an agent, representative or partner of the other party. Neither party shall have any right, power or authority to enter into any agreement for, or on behalf of, or incur any obligation or liability of, or to otherwise bind, the other party. This Agreement shall not be interpreted or construed to create an association, agency, joint venture or partnership between the parties or to impose any liability attributable to such relationship upon either party.

Note: You must decide which state governs this Agreement and where any legal action would be taken. Generally, it is your (company's) state of residence.

11.2 Governing Law• •Jurisdiction. This agreement and the parties' actions under this Agreement shall be governed by and construed under the laws of the state of [State], without reference to conflict of law principles. The parties hereby expressly consent to the jurisdiction and venue of the federal and state courts within the state of [State]. Each party hereby irrevocably consents to the service of process in any such action or proceeding by the mailing of copies thereof by registered or certified mail, postage prepaid, to such party at its address set forth in the preamble of this Agreement, such service to become effective thirty (30) days after such mailing.

Note: This Agreement is intended to be the only Agreement, and that no other documents or communications are binding. Therefore, it is very important to make sure that everything [Company] and [Client] have agreed to be included in this Agreement. Otherwise, it is as if it was not agreed to.

11.3   Entire Agreement. This Agreement, including the attached exhibits, constitutes the entire Agreement between both parties concerning this transaction, and replaces all previous communications, representations, understandings, and Agreements, whether verbal or written between the parties to this Agreement or their representatives. No representations or statements of any kind made by either party, which are not expressly stated in this Agreement, shall be binding on such parties.

Note: Any changes to this Agreement must be in writing and signed by the party against whom that writing is to be used.

11.4   All Amendments in Writing. No waiver, amendment or modification of any provisions of this Agreement shall be effective unless in writing and signed by a duly authorized representative of the party against whom such waiver, amendment or modification is sought to be enforced. Furthermore, no provisions in either party's purchase orders, or in any other business forms employed by either party will supersede the terms and conditions of this Agreement.

Note: All notices between the parties must be in writing and either delivered in person or by certified or registered mail, return receipt requested.

11.5   Notices. Any notice required or permitted by this Agreement shall be deemed given if sent by registered mail, postage prepaid with return receipt requested, addressed to the other party at the address set forth in the preamble of this Agreement or at such other address for which such party gives notice hereunder. Delivery shall be deemed effective three (3) days after deposit with postal authorities.

Note: In the event of a lawsuit or any legal proceeding involving this Agreement, the losing party will have to pay the winning party his or her costs and expenses, including reasonable attorney fees.

11.6   Costs of Legal Action. In the event any action is brought to enforce this Agreement, the prevailing party shall be entitled to recover its costs of enforcement including, without limitation, attorneys' fees and court costs.

Note: Legal remedies, i.e., money damages, may not be sufficient; therefore, both parties agree to equitable remedies such as an injunction where the breaching party would be required to do or not to do something.

11.7 Inadequate Legal Remedy. Both parties understand and acknowledge that violation of their respective covenants and Agreements may cause the other irreparable harm and damage, that may not be recovered at law, and each agrees that the other's remedies for breach may be in equity by way of injunctive relief, as well as for damages and any other relief available to the non-breaching party, whether in law or in equity.

Note: Assuming the parties wish to use Arbitration in the event of a dispute, the following section should be included. You take your chances with an arbitrator, but it keeps legal costs down and keeps you out of a drawn out legal process.

11.8 Arbitration. Any dispute relating to the interpretation or performance of this Agreement shall be resolved at the request of either party through binding arbitration. Arbitration shall be conducted in [County], [State] in accordance with the then-existing rules of the American Arbitration Association. Judgment upon any award by the arbitrators may be entered by any state or federal court having jurisdiction. [Company] and [Client] intend that this Agreement to arbitrate be irrevocable.

Note: Merely delaying to bring an action that one party has a right to bring does not cause that party to lose or waive his right to pursue that action.

11.9 Delay is Not a Waiver. No failure or delay by either party in exercising any right, power or remedy under this Agreement, except as specifically provided in this Agreement, shall operate as a waiver of any such right, power or remedy.

Note: Neither party will be blamed if there is a problem resulting from something beyond its control, such as an earthquake, flood, war.

11.10 Force Majeure. In the event that either party is unable to perform any of its obligations under this Agreement or to enjoy any of its benefits because of any Act of God, strike, fire, flood, governmental acts, orders or restrictions, Internet system unavailability, system malfunctions or any other reason where failure to perform is beyond the reasonable control and not caused by the negligence of the non-performing party (a "Force Majeure Event"), the party who has been so affected shall give notice immediately to the other party and shall use its reasonable best efforts to resume performance. Failure to meet due dates resulting from a Force Majeure Event shall extend such due dates for a reasonable period. However, if the period of nonperformance exceeds sixty (60) days from the receipt of notice of the Force Majeure Event, the party whose ability to perform has not been affected may, by giving written notice, terminate this Agreement effective immediately upon such notice or at such later date as is therein specified.

Note: This section limits the ability of either party to transfer any of its rights or delegate any of its duties to third parties.

Note: You want to make sure that you can sell your business along with all of the relationships you have developed along the way. (Often these relationships can add tremendous value to your business and you want to make sure that all of your agreements can be transferred to the new owners.) I wouldn't want to seek (let alone pay for) permission to sell my company. Generally, neither party may assign their respective rights to a third party; however, with the possible exception of assignment to a successor corporation or partnership, either party may transfer its rights or obligations under this Agreement without the approval of the other party. However, you may want to limit each other's ability to pass along this deal to another possibly unknown and possibly unfriendly entity. The second paragraph prevents unauthorized transfer of responsibilities.

Note: CHOOSE one or the other of these two following paragraphs.

11.10 Assignability & Binding Effect. Except as expressly set forth within this Agreement, neither party may transfer or assign, directly or indirectly, this Agreement or its rights and obligations hereunder without the express written permission of the other party, not to be unreasonably withheld; provided, however, that both parties shall have the right to assign or otherwise transfer this Agreement to any parent, subsidiary, affiliated entity or pursuant to any merger, consolidation or reorganization, provided that all such assignees and transferees agree in writing to be bound by the terms of this Agreement prior to such assignment or transfer. Subject to the foregoing, this Agreement shall be binding upon and inure to the benefit of the parties hereto, their successors and assigns.

Note: This paragraph DOES NOT ALLOW either party to transfer its rights to a successor company without prior approval.

11.11 Non-Assignability & Binding Effect. Except as otherwise provided for within this Agreement, neither party may assign any of its rights or delegate any of its obligations under this Agreement to any third party without the express written permission of the other. Any such assignment is deemed null and void.

Note: If any part of this Agreement is unenforceable or invalid, the balance of the Agreement should still be enforced. Basically, ignore any sections that are invalid.

11.12 Certain Sections Invalid. If any provisions of this Agreement are held by a court of competent jurisdiction to be invalid under any applicable statute or rule of law, they are to that extent to be deemed omitted and the remaining provisions of this Agreement shall remain in full force and effect.

Note: The headings of the various sections are meant to explain or otherwise give meaning to those sections; they are for convenience only.

11.13 Headings. The titles and headings of the various sections and sections in this Agreement are intended solely for convenience of reference and are not intended for any other purpose whatsoever, or to explain, modify or place any construction upon or on any of the provisions of this Agreement.

Note: Even after the termination of the Agreement, the parties may still have certain responsibilities such as keeping information confidential.

11.14   Survival of Certain Provisions. The warranties and the indemnification and confidentiality obligations set forth in the Agreement shall survive the termination of the Agreement by either party for any reason.

Understood, Agreed & Approved

We have carefully reviewed this contract and agree to and accept all of its terms and conditions. We are executing this Agreement as of the Effective Date above.

<table>
<tr><td>_________________________
[Company]</td><td>_________________________
[Licensee]</td></tr>
<tr><td>

____
[Owner / Founder]</td><td>

____
[Licensee Name]</td></tr>
<tr><td>

____
[Title]</td><td>

____
[Title]</td></tr>
</table>

Exhibit A

Licensed Marks

*   xxx

*   xxx

*   xxx

Exhibit B

Products

* xxx

* xxx

* xxx

Exhibit C

Standards & Specifications

* [The color for the "[Company]" text shall be PMS 327]

(See Pantone Matching System for a reference to color codes.)

* xxx

* xxx

Exhibit D

Minimum Royalty Installment & Royalty Rate

* xxx

* xxx

* xxx

Release Agreement - Model / Talent

Talent / Model Release

Note: This introductory paragraph lists the date and the parties to this Agreement. We formatted this agreement uniquely to make it easy on others (judge, arbitrator(s), etc. God forbid) to readily understand who is involved, when the agreement begins and some basic summary background information.

Effective Date_____________________ between **[Company Legal Name]**, ("Company") a **[State]** *[Corporation/Partnership/Sole Proprietorship / Resident]*, located at **[Address] [City], [State] [Zip Code]** and Model / Talent name:

_______________________________________ residing at

____

[Address, City, State Zip Code]

Release

For valuable consideration, the receipt and sufficiency of which are hereby acknowledged, I hereby agree as follows:• I hereby give and forever grant to **[Company]**, its advertising agency, licensees and producers or publishers of its promotional materials and their successors and assigns, the right to use, publish and copyright my picture, portrait and likeness, in whole or part, including alterations, modifications, derivations and composites thereof, in advertising and promotion of [Name of Product or Service] throughout the world.

This right shall include the right to combine my likeness with others and to alter my likeness, by digital means or otherwise, for the purposes set forth herein.

Understood, Agreed & Approved.

_______________________________   _______________________________
Talent / Model   Date

If Model / Talent Under 18

If model/talent is not yet eighteen (18) years old, the child's parent or guardian must complete and sign the following form:

Parent or Guardian hereby warrants that s/he is the Parent or Guardian of the

above named Talent/Model, a minor, and has full authority to authorize the above Release and indemnifies the licensed parties and their respective successors and assigns, from and against any and all liability arising out of the
exercise of the rights granted by the above Talent/Model Release.

_______________________________   _______________________________
Parent or Guardian Signature   Date

____

Release Agreement - Mutual

Mutual Release Agreement

Note: You have been engaged in a dispute, you have reached an agreement to resolve it. Here is a sample contract to use to release each other according to the terms of your mutual agreement.

Note: The first part of the Memorandum should be completed and distributed along with a copy of the Mutual Release.

Mutual Release Memorandum

Date **[Date]**

To **[Releasee]**

From **Owner/Founder]**

[Company]

Subject: **Mutual Release**

Note: While expressing some honest feeling to acknowledge your pain felt during the dispute, you want to avoid using the word "apologize" because it implies that you are admitting guilt or responsibility. Instead, we recommend that you use the word, "regret" since it connotes a somewhat similar emotion, yet it does not admit guilt.

I regret that we have engaged in this dispute as long as we have and I am delighted that we have come to a resolution that works for both of us.

Attached is a "Mutual Release" to discharge both of the parties to this Agreement from its obligations to the other regarding [Describe the exact obligation].

In addition to agreeing to a mutual release, **[Releasee]** agrees to pay $**[x]** to **[x] [Releasor]**. I believe that it embodies everything we discussed. Please read the agreement carefully.

We recommend that you also have it reviewed by your own qualified legal counsel. Time is of the essence.

Please sign and return it to me asap.

Thank you very much!

Mutual Release Agreement

Note: You need to enter the date you are executing the Release and the names and address of both parties.• Since both parties are both Releasors and Releasees, we will refer to them as Releasor 1 and Releasor 2.• Generally the Releasor is the party who has the claim or is owed the obligation, and the Releasee is the party paying the Releasor some form of consideration so that it is no longer obligated or indebted.

Effective Date **[Date]** between **[Company Legal Name]**, ("Company") located at **[Address] [City]. [State] [Zip Code]** and **[Releasor]**, ("Releasor") located / residing at **[Address] [City]. [State] [Zip Code]**.

1. Agreement

Note: The two parties agree to eliminate the liabilities and / or obligations described.

We voluntarily and knowingly execute this Mutual Release with the express intention of eliminating the liabilities and obligations described below.

2. Dispute Resolution

Note: This paragraph sets forth the matter that is being settled.

Note: You should describe in as much detail as possible the specific matter(s) that the two parties are releasing the other from.

Disputes and differences that we mutually desire to settle have arisen between us with respect to the following:•

*   [xxx]

*   [xxx]

*   [xxx]

3. Consideration

Note: Section 4 states what each of the Releasors will be getting for his or her release.• Generally, with a Mutual Release, each party will be released from something.• Sometimes, in addition to the release itself, money or other considerations might be transferred.

The consideration for this Mutual Release is as follows:

Note: The is the first part of the consideration, the mutual release.

3.1 Mutual relinquishment of our respective legal rights with reference to the disputes and differences described above; and

Note: This is the other part of the consideration. If there is nothing more than a mutual exchange of releases, then delete 4.2.

Note: Describe the other consideration and indicate who is giving what to whom.

3.2 Other valuable consideration is as follows:•

*   A one time payment by [Company] to [Other] in the amount of $[xxx]

*   **[Describe other consideration].**

Note: Not only do the Releasors grant releases on their own behalf, but they bind any other individuals or entities that might claim under them. Each Releasor also warrants or promises that it has not assigned any of its claims to other parties.

4.   Mutual Release

In exchange for this consideration, each of us expressly releases the other, and his heirs, insurers, and legal representatives from all claims known or unknown to us that have arisen or may arise from the transaction described in Section 3. In executing this Release we intend to bind our spouses, heirs, legal representatives, assigns, and anyone else claiming under us, in addition to ourselves. Neither of us has assigned a claim arising from the transaction described in Section 3 to another party.

5.   General Provisions

Note: The General Provisions that follow are fairly standard. These provisions enhance the balance of the Agreement by explaining issues such as notice, assignment, legal remedies, waiver, and attorney fees.

5.1 Independent [Company]s. The relationship between both parties established by this Agreement is that of independent [Company]s, and nothing contained in this Agreement shall be construed to give either party the power to direct and control the day-to-day activities of the other. Neither party is an agent, representative or partner of the other party. Neither party shall have any right, power or authority to enter into any agreement for, or on behalf of, or incur any obligation or liability of, or to otherwise bind, the other party. This Agreement shall not be interpreted or construed to create an association, agency, joint venture or partnership between the parties or to impose any liability attributable to such relationship upon either party.

Note: You must decide which state governs this Agreement and where any legal action would be taken. Generally, it is your (company's) state of residence.

5.2 Governing Law Jurisdiction. This agreement and the parties' actions under this Agreement shall be governed by and construed under the laws of the state of [State], without reference to conflict of law principles. The parties hereby expressly consent to the jurisdiction and venue of the federal and state courts within the state of [State]. Each party hereby irrevocably consents to the service of process in any such action or proceeding by the mailing of copies thereof by registered or certified mail, postage prepaid, to such party at its address set forth in the preamble of this Agreement, such service to become effective thirty (30) days after such mailing.

Note: This Agreement is intended to be the only Agreement, and that no other documents or communications are binding. Therefore, it is very important to make sure that everything [Company] and [Client] have agreed to is included in this Agreement. Otherwise, it is as if it was not agreed to.

5.3 Entire Agreement. This Agreement, including the attached exhibits, constitutes the entire Agreement between both parties concerning this transaction, and replaces all previous communications, representations, understandings, and Agreements, whether verbal or written between the parties to this Agreement or their representatives. No representations or statements of any kind made by either party, which are not expressly stated in this Agreement, shall be binding on such parties.

Note: Any changes to this Agreement must be in writing and signed by the party against whom that writing is to be used.

5.4 All Amendments in Writing. No waiver, amendment or modification of any provisions of this Agreement shall be effective unless in writing and signed by a duly authorized representative of the party against whom such waiver, amendment or modification is sought to be enforced. Furthermore, no provisions in either party's purchase orders, or in any other business forms employed by either party will supersede the terms and conditions of this Agreement.

Note: All notices between the parties must be in writing and either delivered in person or by certified or registered mail, return receipt requested.

5.5 Notices. Any notice required or permitted by this Agreement shall be deemed given if sent by registered mail, postage prepaid with return receipt requested, addressed to the other party at the address set forth in the preamble of this Agreement or at such other address for which such party gives notice hereunder. Delivery shall be deemed effective three (3) days after deposit with postal authorities.

Note: In the event of a lawsuit or any legal proceeding involving this Agreement, the losing party will have to pay the winning party his or her costs and expenses, including reasonable attorney fees.

5.6 Costs of Legal Action. In the event any action is brought to enforce this Agreement, the prevailing party shall be entitled to recover its costs of enforcement including, without limitation, attorneys' fees and court costs.

Note: Legal remedies, i.e., money damages, may not be sufficient; therefore, both parties agree to equitable remedies such as an injunction where the breaching party would be required to do or not to do something.

5.7 Inadequate Legal Remedy. Both parties understand and acknowledge that violation of their respective covenants and Agreements may cause the other irreparable harm and damage, that may not be recovered at law, and each agrees that the other's remedies for breach may be in equity by way of injunctive relief, as well as for damages and any other relief available to the non-breaching party, whether in law or in equity.

Note: Assuming the parties wish to use Arbitration in the event of a dispute, the following section should be included. You take your chances with an arbitrator, but it keeps legal costs down and keeps you out of a drawn out legal process.

5.8 Arbitration. Any dispute relating to the interpretation or performance of this Agreement shall be resolved at the request of either party through binding arbitration. Arbitration shall be conducted in [County], [State] in accordance with the then-existing rules of the American Arbitration Association. Judgment upon any award by the arbitrators may be entered by any state or federal court having jurisdiction. [Company] and [Client] intend that this Agreement to arbitrate be irrevocable.

Note: Merely delaying to bring an action that one party has a right to bring does not cause that party to lose or waive his right to pursue that action.

5.9 Delay is Not a Waiver. No failure or delay by either party in exercising any right, power or remedy under this Agreement, except as specifically provided in this Agreement, shall operate as a waiver of any such right, power or remedy.

Note: Neither party will be blamed if there is a problem resulting from something beyond its control, such as an earthquake, flood, war.

5.10 Force Majeure. In the event that either party is unable to perform any of its obligations under this Agreement or to enjoy any of its benefits because of any Act of God, strike, fire, flood, governmental acts, orders or restrictions, Internet system unavailability, system malfunctions or any other reason where failure to perform is beyond the reasonable control and not caused by the negligence of the non-performing party (a "Force Majeure Event"), the party who has been so affected shall give notice immediately to the other party and shall use its reasonable best efforts to resume performance.• Failure to meet due dates resulting from a Force Majeure Event shall extend such due dates for a reasonable period.• However, if the period of nonperformance exceeds sixty (60) days from the receipt of notice of the Force Majeure Event, the party whose ability to perform has not been affected may, by giving written notice, terminate this Agreement effective immediately upon such notice or at such later date as is therein specified.

Note: You want to make sure that you can sell your business along with all of the relationships you have developed along the way. (Often these relationships can add tremendous value to your business and you want to make sure that all of your agreements can be transferred to the new owners.) I wouldn't want to seek (let alone pay for) permission to sell my company.

5.11   Assignability & Binding Effect. Subject to the foregoing, this Agreement shall be binding upon and inure to the benefit of the parties hereto, their successors and assigns.•

Note: If any part of this Agreement is unenforceable or invalid, the balance of the Agreement should still be enforced. Basically, ignore any sections that are invalid.

5.12   Certain Sections Invalid. If any provisions of this Agreement are
held by a court of competent jurisdiction to be invalid under any applicable statute or rule of law, they are to that extent to be deemed omitted and the remaining provisions of this Agreement shall remain in full force and effect.

Note: The headings of the various sections are meant to explain or otherwise give meaning to those sections; they are for convenience only.

5.13   Headings. The titles and headings of the various sections and sections in this Agreement are intended solely for convenience of reference and are not intended for any other purpose whatsoever, or to explain, modify or place any construction upon or on any of the provisions of this Agreement.

Note: Even after the termination of the Agreement, the parties may still have certain responsibilities such as keeping information confidential.

5.14   Survival of Certain Provisions. The warranties and the indemnification and confidentiality obligations set forth in the Agreement shall survive the termination of the Agreement by either party for any reason.

Understood, Agreed & Approved

We have carefully reviewed this contract and agree to and accept all of its terms and conditions. We are executing this Agreement as of the Effective Date above.

Note: Both parties and their spouses, if any, should sign below, along with two witnesses.

____
[Owner/Founder]

____
[Releasor's Spouse]

____
[Releasee]

____
[Releasee's Spouse's Name]

Witnesses:

____
[Name]

____
Address

____
[Name]

____
Address

Letter of Intent - Business Purchase

Letter of Intent for Purchase of Business

Note: Use this sample "Letter of Intent" to establish the basic terms for entering into negotiations to acquire a business.

Note: The first part of the Memorandum should be completed and distributed to the Board of Directors or a Senior Officer of the Seller along with a copy of the Letter of Intent for Purchase of Business.

Memorandum of Intent for Purchase of Business

Date:**[Month, Day, Year]**

To:**[Board of Directors or Senior Officer of Seller]**

From:**[Owner/Founder]**

[Company]

Subject:**Letter of Intent for Sale of Business**

Attached is a "Letter of Intent for Sale of Business" In order to establish the mutual intention of the Seller and the Buyer.

I believe that it embodies everything we discussed. Please read the agreement carefully.

We recommend that you also have it reviewed by your own qualified legal counsel. Time is of the essence.

Please sign and return it to me as soon as possible.

Thank you very much,

[Company Legal Name]

[Address] * [City], [State] [Zip Code]

[Telephone] * [WebSite Address]

Letter

Note: This letter of intent should be addressed to the Board of Directors or a Senior Officer of the Seller.

[Date]

[Board of Directors / Officer]
[Company Name]
[Address)
[City, State and Zip)

Dear [Name]

Re: Letter of Intent for Sale of Business

Note: The introductory sentence states the general intention of the parties. Two originals of this letter should be sent to the Purchaser.

This letter of intent executed in duplicate, establishes the mutual intention of [Company Name] the ("Seller"), and [Company Legal Name] the ("Buyer"), that the Buyer acquire the Seller's business under the following terms:

Note: There are various ways one corporation can acquire another. In the following section, the parties agree that the corporations will be merged and that the parties will decide upon the type of merger at a later date. Take note that there are several different types of mergers, each of which is subject to special rules. You should discuss these rules with an attorney if you intend to engage in a corporate merger.

1.   The parties intend to accomplish the acquisition through a merger of the two corporations. The type of merger will be determined by mutual Agreement between the parties.
Note: In Section 2, the Purchaser places conditions on its obligation to complete the transaction. The Purchaser will require: (1) a complete written Agreement; (2) approval by the Board of Directors of both companies; (3) verification of the Seller's financial statements; (4) compliance with all laws and regulations; and (5) an opinion from counsel of the Seller that the Seller's securities have been issued in compliance with state and federal laws.

2.   Closing of the transaction will be subject to certain conditions, including the following:

*   the preparation and execution of a definitive Agreement setting forth the terms of the transaction;

*   the approval of that Agreement by the Board of Directors of both the Buyer and the Seller;

*   (the purchaser's verification and approval of the Seller's financial statements. The Purchaser may elect to have third party consultants perform a confidential audit of the Seller's financial records;

*   compliance with all applicable laws and regulations; and

*   An opinion from the Seller's counsel that issuance of securities of the Seller has been made in compliance with state and federal laws.

Note: The Seller is prepared to forestall negotiations with other potential purchasers while this deal is being negotiated.

3.   The Seller agrees that it will not negotiate or agree to negotiate, whether directly or indirectly, with any other party concerning the sale of its business.

Note: The Seller agrees not to do anything that would significantly decrease the value of the Seller's business.

4.   The Seller agrees that it will not engage in any practices or transactions during the period of negotiating and consummating the transaction contemplated herein that would adversely affect the value of the Seller's business on assets.

Note: In the following section, the parties agree to keep their deal confidential unless they are required by law to disclose their involvement.

5.   The parties agree that any information concerning the transaction contemplated within this Agreement shall remain confidential; provided, however, that the parties may disclose information concerning the transaction to the public or governmental agencies if, in the judgment of their respective legal counsels, such disclosure is necessary to comply with applicable law.

Note: In this next section the parties agree that this is not an agreement for the sale of the Seller's business, but a non-binding discussion of some of the particulars of the contemplated transaction. However, the parties agree that the provisions concerning confidentiality and restriction on the Seller's power to negotiate with other potential purchasers are binding to the parties through this document.

6.   The parties agree to be bond by Sections 3 and 4 above. However, the parties are not bound or otherwise obligated by any other term herein and that no such term creates any rights or obligations whatsoever.

Note: In this last section, the Purchaser requests that the Seller sign this letter if the Seller agrees with its terms.

Please sign where indicated on each copy of this Letter of Intent and return one copy to us.

Very truly yours,

____

[Owner / Founder], [Title]

____

[Company]

Understood, Agreed & Accepted

____

[Seller Corporation]

____

Date

<u>**Letter of Intent - Negotiations**</u>

Memorandum of Intent for Negotiation & Information Exchange

Note: This is an NDA on steroids – it presumes that you are going to go deeply into negotiations toward a definite agreement for some kind of joint venture.

Note: The first part of the Memorandum should be completed and distributed to the other party along with a copy of the Letter of Intent for Negotiation and Information Exchange.

Date **[Date]**

To **[Name of other party]**

From **Owner/Founder]**

[Company]

Subject: **Letter of Intent for Negotiation & Information Exchange**

Attached is a "Letter of Intent for Negotiation   Information Exchange" in order to outline the procedures for our discussions and negotiations and to set forth certain restrictions regarding materials we will be exchanging in the course of those negotiations.

I believe that it embodies everything we discussed. Please read the agreement carefully.

We recommend that you also have it reviewed by your own qualified legal counsel. Time is of the essence.

Please sign and return it to me as soon as possible.

Thank you very much!

Letter of Intent for Negotiation Information Exchange

Note: This is a standard introductory paragraph that lists the parties to the Agreement and the date the Agreement is being entered into. You need to enter the date of the Agreement, the names of the parties, the specific type of organization they are and their addresses.

Effective Date **[Date]** between **[Company   Legal Name]**, ("Company")
a**[State of organization]** **[Corporation / Partnership / Sole
Proprietorship , Located at [Address] [City],   [State] [Zip
Code]** and **[Party 2]**, ("Party 2") a **[State   of organization]**
**[Corporation   /   Partnership   /   Sole   Proprietorship
/
Resident]** located at **[Address]**.

Note: The following section is like an introduction.

Summary

*Note: For the first insert explain what [Company] does (for example,
manufacturing). For the second insert describe the specific Products that
[Company] does this to (manufactures).*

[Company] is engaged in the **[Describe   business]** of **[Describ
e
specific Products]** (the "Products/Services").

Note: Explain exactly what Party 2 does as it is related to [Company].

Party 2 is engaged in **[Describe   what Party 2 does]**.

*Note: Describe the desired scope or purpose of the proposed Agreement. For
example, the development of certain computer accounting software functions,
and related technical end-user documentation, and (2) the terms of the ownership,
and subsequent marketing and maintenance, of such programming and
documentation.*

The parties propose entering into an Agreement concerning:

* **[Describe purpose]** (the "Deal").

* xxx

* xxx

On **[Month, Day, Year]**, the parties had discussions concerning the Deal
during which they determined that further negotiations would be appropriate. As
it is expected that these subsequent negotiations will involve frequent
communications, including the exchange of proprietary information, they agree
as follows.

Agreement

Except for Sections 2.3, 3, 4, 5, 7 and this section that are legally binding, and survive any cessation of negotiations or termination of this Agreement, this Agreement is only a statement of intent to conduct further negotiations and does not constitute a binding Agreement in any respect. Such a binding Agreement will arise only when all material terms have been set forth in a conclusive written Agreement, or sets of Agreements, executed by both parties (the "Final Agreement"). All drafts, "term sheets," memoranda, and other communications prepared or exchanged in the course of negotiations, even if signed by one or both Contacts (defined below), are preliminary and have no legal effect unless subsequently incorporated into a Final Agreement.

1. Negotiations

Note: Enter the names of the principal contacts for each of the parties.

1.1 Designation of Negotiators. The following persons (the "Contacts") shall represent the parties in the negotiations:

*   For **[Company], [Owner/Founder].**

*   For Party 2, **[Name]**.

*   Either party may replace their Main Contact by giving written notice to the other party.

2. Conduct of Negotiations

Note: We have tried to be as thorough as possible as to the Conduct of the Negotiations; you may wish to add or delete information where appropriate.

Note: Enter a date that you desire to execute the Final Agreement. You should prepare a timetable that sets forth the schedule of negotiations (to be included as Exhibit A).

2.1 The parties desire to execute a Final Agreement by **[Month, Day, Year]** (the "Target Date"). The Contacts will talk regularly, schedule negotiations, and coordinate all exchanges of information, including recommendations, drafts, and proposals. A Timetable setting forth the preliminary schedule of negotiations is attached as Exhibit A. A reasonable number of employees, agents and advisers may accompany the Contacts at meetings and negotiations.

2.2 No less than **[Enter number]** of executives of both parties will meet to review the progress of negotiations, and to identify and clarify issues. Following each meeting, the parties will decide whether to continue or terminate their negotiations.

Note: The parties should review the following list and add or delete information where appropriate with the goal being to set forth all of the items that you will need to address in the course of negotiating the Deal.

The parties will negotiate with the goal of including the following items in the Final Agreement:

1. Defining who contributes what, as well as who prepares specifications.

2. Setting forth ownership rights of the parties in past, present and future works.

3. The respective rights of the parties to use any developed works, including the right to license or sublicense others and the right to make derivative works.

4. Who pays for costs and expenses incurred.

5. Structure of royalty payments.

6. Defining obligations regarding future development, modifications and enhancements.

7. **Competitive restrictions.**

Note: Describe the particular nature of the Deal so that negotiations are not entered into with other parties that could possibly interfere or conflict with your negotiations.

2.3   No Simultaneous Negotiations. So long as the parties are actively engaged in negotiations with each other, both agree not to directly or indirectly enter into negotiations or arrangements with any third parties engaged in [Describe nature of the deal] that are the same as, or functionally equivalent to, the subject to these negotiations.

3.   Costs & Expenses of Negotiation

3.1 Each party shall bear its own costs and expenses.

3.2 In the event that the parties agree to select a location other than at their respective offices, the cost will be shared equally.

4. Protection of Information

Note: Section 4 is a fairly standard non-disclosure section. As there are numerous provisions set forth on how to treat any information received or disclosed by the parties, you ought to review it carefully. Basically, you should mark any information you provide as "Confidential Information." Such information may only be shared with others involved in the negotiations. You must get the other party's consent before issuing any press releases or making any public statements regarding the Confidential Information or the Negotiations themselves.

Note: Enter the period commencing with the receipt of the Confidential Information, during which the Recipient cannot reveal the Information.

4.1 The parties agree to conspicuously mark all information exchanged or created in the course of negotiations as "Confidential Information." The receiving party along with its affiliates, agents, and employees (collectively "Recipient"), may use this Confidential Information for any purpose, including the manufacture, design or sale of the Recipient's Products and services. The Recipient's use of the Information is subject only to:

(a) an obligation, for a **[Enter number]** year period commencing from the date of receipt, to refrain from revealing any Confidential Information to third parties not engaged in these negotiations by using the same care and discretion that the Recipient employs to protect its own documents that it does not want disclosed, and

(b) the originating party's trademarks, copyrights, and patent rights that it may not interfere or otherwise use.

4.2 Any copies of the Confidential Information should be marked and treated as such.

4.3 If a Final Agreement has not been executed, then upon termination of this Agreement, the parties agree to return the other's Confidential Information, including all copies.

4.4 The parties agree to use their best efforts to avoid disclosure of the fact or
object of their negotiations and to restrict all internal communications concerning the negotiations to those recipients to whom such information must be disclosed in order to effectively conduct the negotiations. Except as otherwise required by law, the parties agree not to issue any press releases or make any public announcements regarding the negotiations without the prior written approval of the other.

4.5 Despite any captions, headings, or restrictions regarding proprietary matters or any nondisclosure notices or policy statements contained in the Confidential Information, this Section 4 constitutes the sole and exclusive

Agreement of the parties concerning the Confidential Information and any information exchanged or disclosed in connection with the negotiations.

4.6 If the negotiations result in a Final Agreement, the Final Agreement may contain further terms and conditions respecting confidentiality.

5. Limitation of Liability

Note: If either party somehow suffers a loss related to the (termination of the) Negotiations or disclosure of the Confidential Information, the other party will not be liable for the resulting damages. You may wish to modify this at least with respect to the Confidential Information by starting the following paragraph with "Despite Section 4..." You would then delete Section 4 from the last sentence of the paragraph.

Neither party shall make a claim against, or be liable to, the other party or its affiliates or agents for any damages, including, without limitation, lost profits or injury to business reputation, resulting from the continuation or abandonment of negotiations and the consequences of that. Neither party shall make a claim against, or be liable to, the other party or its affiliates or agents for any special, incidental, or consequential damages, including, without limitation, lost profits, based on any breach, default, or negligence of such other party, its affiliates, or agents with respect to Sections 2.4 and 4 of this Agreement.

6. Term

This Agreement shall continue until either party gives written notice of its intention to abandon further negotiations, or until superseded by the execution of the Final Agreement.

7. General Provisions

Note: The General Provisions that follow are fairly standard. These provisions enhance the balance of the Agreement by defining certain common issues such as notice, assignment, legal remedies, waiver, and attorney fees, etc.

7.1 Independent Contractors. The relationship between both parties established by this Agreement is that of independent contractors, and nothing contained in this Agreement shall be construed to give either party the power to direct and control the day-to-day activities of the other. Neither party is an agent, representative or partner of the other party. Neither party shall have any right, power or authority to enter into any agreement for, or on behalf of, or incur any obligation or liability of, or to otherwise bind, the other party. This Agreement shall not be interpreted or construed to create an association, agency, joint venture or partnership between the parties or to impose any liability attributable to such relationship upon either party.

Note: You may or may not want to make this deal public – at least limit that event by this agreement and work out if/how/when you want to do that later.

7.2 Publicity. Neither party will make any public announcement or issue any press release concerning the terms of this Agreement without the prior approval of both parties.

Note: Make it clear that you will not try to hire away each others employees. If you do or it happens then there is compensation built-in and you can avoid further legal proceedings.

7.3 Non-Solicitation. Neither party shall solicit for employment or hire the other's current or future employees, either directly or indirectly, during the Term of this Agreement, without obtaining the other's prior written approval. Should an employee change employment from one party to the other, the new employer shall pay the old employer a fee equivalent to Twenty Percent (20%) of the employee's new compensation, annualized for the first year.

Note: You must decide which state governs this Agreement and where any legal action would be taken. Generally, it is your (company's) state of residence.

7.4 Governing Law Jurisdiction. This agreement and the parties' actions under this Agreement shall be governed by and construed under the laws of the state of [State], without reference to conflict of law principles. The parties hereby expressly consent to the jurisdiction and venue of the federal and state courts within the state of [State]. Each party hereby irrevocably consents to the service of process in any such action or proceeding by the mailing of copies thereof by registered or certified mail, postage prepaid, to such party at its address set forth in the preamble of this Agreement, such service to become effective thirty (30) days after such mailing.

Note: This Agreement is intended to be the only Agreement and that no other documents or communications are binding. Therefore, it is very important to make sure that everything [Company] and [Client] have agreed to is included in this Agreement. Otherwise, it is as if it were not agreed to.

7.5 Entire Agreement. This Agreement, including the attached exhibits, constitutes the entire Agreement between both parties concerning this transaction, and replaces all previous communications, representations, understandings, and Agreements, whether verbal or written between the parties to this Agreement or their representatives. No representations or statements of any kind made by either party, which are not expressly stated in this Agreement, shall be binding on such parties.

Note: Any changes to this Agreement must be in writing and signed by the party against whom that writing is to be used.

7.6 All Amendments in Writing. No waiver, amendment or modification of any provisions of this Agreement shall be effective unless in writing and signed by a duly authorized representative of the party against whom such waiver, amendment or modification is sought to be enforced.

Furthermore, no provisions in either party's purchase orders or in any other business forms employed by either party will supersede the terms and conditions of this Agreement.

Note: All notices between the parties must be in writing and either delivered in person or by certified or registered mail, return receipt requested.

7.7 Notices. Any notice required or permitted by this Agreement shall be deemed given if sent by registered mail, postage prepaid with return receipt requested, addressed to the other party at the address set forth in the preamble of this Agreement or at such other address for which such party gives notice hereunder. Delivery shall be deemed effective three (3) days after deposit with postal authorities.

Note: In the event of a lawsuit or any legal proceeding involving this Agreement, the losing party will have to pay the winning party his or her costs and expenses, including reasonable attorney fees.

7.8 Costs of Legal Action. In the event any action is brought to enforce this Agreement, the prevailing party shall be entitled to recover its costs of enforcement including, without limitation, attorneys' fees and court costs.

Note: Legal remedies, i.e., money damages, may not be sufficient; therefore, both parties agree to equitable remedies such as an injunction where the breaching party would be required to do or not to do something.

7.9 Inadequate Legal Remedy. Both parties understand and acknowledge that violation of their respective covenants and Agreements may cause the other irreparable harm and damage, that may not be recovered at law, and each agrees that the other's remedies for breach may be in equity by way of injunctive relief, as well as for damages and any other relief available to the non-breaching party, whether in law or in equity.

Note: Assuming the parties wish to use Arbitration in the event of a dispute, the following section should be included. You take your chances with an arbitrator, but it keeps legal costs down and keeps you out of a drawn out legal process.

7.10 Arbitration. Any dispute relating to the interpretation or performance of this Agreement shall be resolved at the request of either party through binding arbitration. Arbitration shall be conducted in [County], [State] in accordance with the then-existing rules of the American Arbitration Association. Judgment upon any award by the arbitrators may be entered by any state or federal court having jurisdiction. Both parties intend that this Agreement to arbitrate be irrevocable.

Note: Merely delaying to bring an action that one party has a right to bring does not cause that party to lose or waive his right to pursue that action.

7.11   Delay is Not a Waiver. No failure or delay by either party in exercising any right, power or remedy under this Agreement, except as specifically provided in this Agreement, shall operate as a waiver of any such right, power or remedy.

Note: Neither party will be blamed if there is a problem resulting from something beyond its control, such as an earthquake, flood, war.

7.12   Force Majeure. In the event that either party is unable to perform any of its obligations under this Agreement or to enjoy any of its benefits because of any Act of God, strike, fire, flood, governmental acts, orders or restrictions, Internet system unavailability, system malfunctions or any other reason where failure to perform is beyond the reasonable control and not caused by the negligence of the non-performing party (a "Force Majeure Event"), the party who has been so affected shall give notice immediately to the other party and shall use its reasonable best efforts to resume performance.• Failure to meet due dates resulting from a Force Majeure Event shall extend such due dates for a reasonable period.• However, if the period of nonperformance exceeds sixty (60) days from the receipt of notice of the Force Majeure Event, the party whose ability to perform has not been affected may, by giving written notice, terminate this Agreement effective immediately upon such notice or at such later date as is therein specified.

Note: This section limits the ability of either party to transfer any of its rights or delegate any of its duties to third parties.

Note: You want to make sure that you can sell your business along with all of the relationships you have developed along the way. (Often these relationships can add tremendous value to your business and you want to make sure that all of your agreements can be transferred to the new owners.) I wouldn't want to seek (let alone pay for) permission to sell my company.

Note: Generally, neither party may assign their respective rights to a third party; however, with the possible exception of assignment to a successor corporation or partnership, either party may transfer its rights or obligations under this Agreement without the approval of the other party. However, you may want to limit each other's ability to pass along this deal to another possibly unknown and possibly unfriendly entity. The second paragraph prevents unauthorized transfer of responsibilities…

Note: CHOOSE one or the other of these two following paragraphs.

7.13   Assignability & Binding Effect. Except as expressly set forth within this Agreement, neither party may transfer or assign, directly or indirectly, this Agreement or its rights and obligations hereunder without the express written permission of the other party, not to be unreasonably withheld; provided, however, that both parties shall have the right to assign or otherwise transfer this Agreement to any parent, subsidiary, affiliated entity or pursuant to any merger, consolidation or reorganization, provided that all such assignees and transferees agree in writing to be bound by the terms of this Agreement prior to such assignment or transfer. Subject to the foregoing, this Agreement shall be binding upon and inure to the benefit of the parties hereto, their successors and assigns.•

~ OR ~

Note: This paragraph does not allow either party to transfer its rights to a successor company without prior approval.

7.13 Non-Assignability & Binding Effect. Except as otherwise provided for within this Agreement, neither party may assign any of its rights or delegate any of its obligations under this Agreement to any third party without the express written permission of the other. Any such assignment is deemed null and void.

Note: If any part of this Agreement is unenforceable or invalid, the balance of the Agreement should still be enforced. Basically, ignore any sections that are invalid.

7.14 Severability. If any provisions of this Agreement are held by a court of competent jurisdiction to be invalid under any applicable statute or rule of law, they are to that extent to be deemed omitted and the remaining provisions of this Agreement shall remain in full force and effect.

Note: The headings of the various sections are meant to explain or otherwise give meaning to those sections; they are for convenience only.

7.15 Cumulative Rights. Any specific right or remedy provided in this Agreement will not be exclusive but will be cumulative upon all other rights and remedies described in this section and allowed under applicable law.

7.16 Headings. The titles and headings of the various sections and sections in this Agreement are intended solely for convenience of reference and are not intended for any other purpose whatsoever, or to explain, modify or place any construction upon or on any of the provisions of this Agreement.

Note: Every copy shall be just as valid as the original.

7.17 Counterparts. This Agreement may be executed in multiple counterparts, any one of which will be considered an original, but all of which will constitute one and the same instrument.

Note: Even after the termination of the Agreement, the parties may still have certain responsibilities such as keeping information confidential.

7.18 Survival of Certain Provisions. The warranties and the indemnification and confidentiality obligations set forth in the Agreement shall survive the termination of the Agreement by either party for any reason.

Understood, Agreed & Approved

We have carefully reviewed this contract and agree to and accept all of its terms and conditions. We are executing this Agreement as of the Effective Date above.

____

[Company]

____

[Owner/Founder],

____

[Party 2],

____

Vendor

____

[Title]

____

[Title]

Exhibit A

Schedule of Negotiations

*

*

*

<u>Right of First Refusal - Real Estate</u>

Right of First Refusal to Purchase Property

Note: A First Right to Purchase a Property given by the Owner of the Property to a Party, in the event that the Owner receives an Offer from a third party to sell the Property to the third party.

TO: Name of Person Receiving Right of First Refusal (the "Purchaser")

RE: Property municipally known as Municipal Address of Property (ie. 123 Anywhere Street, Anyplace, USA and described as Brief Description of Property (ie. a 2.1 acre parcel of land with a detached three bedroom home) (the "Property")

In consideration of the sum of Amount being paid for this Right of First Refusal *(ie. $1,000.00)* or if nominal, state $10.00 paid by the Purchaser to the undersigned owner of the Property (the "Owner"), and for other good and valuable consideration, the receipt and sufficiency of which is hereby acknowledged, the Owner hereby agrees as follows:

1.   If, on or before Termination Date of Right of First Refusal (ie. January 1, 2003), the Owner receives an offer (a "Third Party Offer") from a third party to purchase the Property from the Owner, which the Owner is prepared to accept, the Owner shall deliver a true copy of the Third Party Offer to the Purchaser.

2.   The Purchaser shall have Specify Period Within Which Purchaser must Exercise Right of First Refusal (ie. 72 hours) following receipt of the Offer (the "Matching Period") to match the Third Party Offer, in which case the Purchaser shall deliver to the Owner, before expiry of the Matching Period, an offer (the "Matching Offer") which shall be on the same terms and conditions as the Third Party Offer.

3.   Upon receipt of the Matching Offer within the Matching Period, the Owner shall forthwith accept the same and deliver a copy of such acceptance to the Purchaser.

4.   In the event that the Purchaser does not submit a Matching Offer within the Matching Period, then the Purchaser shall be deemed to have waived its rights under this Agreement and the Owner shall be free to accept the Third Party Offer and sell the Property to the party submitting the Third Party Offer; provided however that such sale shall take place on the same terms and conditions contained in, and within the time provided in, the Third Party Offer, failing which this Agreement shall remain in full force and effect and the Owner shall be required to comply with the same in connection with any subsequent Third Party Offer it receives.

5.   This Agreement shall enure to the benefit of the Purchaser and his or her heirs, executors, administrators and other legal representatives and shall be binding upon the Owner and his or her heirs, executors, legal representatives, successors and assigns.

____

DATE:

____

Witness

____

Name of Property Owner (Seller)

<u>Marketing Partnership Agreement</u>

Effective Date: **[Date]** of this Agreement by and between **[Partner Legal Name]** (Partner) a **[State]** Corporation located at **[Address]** *AND* **[Company Legal Name]** ("Company") a **[State]** Corporation located at **[Address] [City], [State] [Zip Code]**

Summary

Partner wishes to obtain from [Company], and [Company] is willing to grant to Partner, the exclusive right to offer [Company]'s Products/Services and Product Components for sale as an add-on sale to other offers made through telemarketing call centers.

[Company] grants to Partner, and Partner accepts from [Company], a revocable, non-transferable, EXCLUSIVE right to promote its Products/Services and Product Components through call center entities provided that the price offered to our end-user customers is greater than $[xxx.00] each USD.

In consideration for the exclusivity and preferential pricing granted, partner agrees to pay an advance payment of [Fifteen Thousand ($15,000)] to be used solely for developing enhancements to [product/service], attached as Exhibit C.

In consideration for the mutual promises, covenants, and agreements made below, Partner and [Company], intending to be legally bound, agree as follows:

1. Definitions

For purposes of this Agreement, the following terms will have the indicated definitions:

* **"Agreement"** This Agreement is by and between Partner and [Company].

* **"End-User"** Any person or entity that purchases or licenses the Products/Services(s) from the call center.

* **"Personal Information"** includes personal identity, demographic, psychographic, and billing information and navigation of site visitors,

* **"Intellectual Property Rights"** The intangible legal rights or interests evidenced by or embodied in

(a) any idea, design, concept, technique, invention, discovery, or improvement regardless of patentability, but including patents, patent applications, trade secrets and know-how;

(b) any work of authorship, regardless of copyright-ability, but including copyrights and any moral rights recognized by law; and

(c) any other similar rights, in each case on a worldwide basis.

"Products / Services" The products and services owned by [Company] and Partner respectively and referred to by reference to their respective tradenames listed in Exhibit A attached to the bottom of this Agreement, along with all options to the Products / Services; all future versions of the Products / Services; and all enhancements, revisions, or modifications made to the Products / Services by Partner.

"Product Component" These may be a partial of the above product, or a single document, spreadsheet, database or other module that may be created separately and/or included with or within any of the above Products/Services.

Note: For example, we may offer just one agreement from the Agreement Builder product, or just the financial spreadsheets from BizPlan Builder as a product component.

"Term" The duration of this Agreement.

"Territory" For this agreement, the parties intend to focus strictly on selling products and services through companies whose principal business is that of a 'telemarketing call center'.

"Trademarks" The trademarks specified in Exhibit B (attached to the end of this Agreement).

2.   Relationship

2.1 EXCLUSIVE. [Company] grants to Partner, and Partner accepts from [Company], a revocable, non-transferable, EXCLUSIVE right to promote the product(s) listed in Exhibit A attached.

2.2 Independent Contractors. Partner and [Company] agree that their relationship is that of the seller and the representative (or the licenser and the licensee) and not that of joint venturers, principals or agents, or franchiser and franchisee. Both are independent contractors acting for their own accounts, and neither is authorized to make any commitment or representation, express or implied, on the other's behalf unless authorized to do so by the other in writing.

2.3 Use of Trademarks   Trade Names. No right, title or interest in or to any trademarks, trade names, slogans, labels and designs used by either Partner or [Company], nor the goodwill connected is conveyed by this Agreement. Both parties may, in connection with the promotion and sale of the other's Products / Services pursuant to the terms of this Agreement, refer to the other's applicable trade names or trademarks provided that all such references are in conformance with the other's requirements regarding such use, as such requirements are communicated to the other party in writing from time to time. Neither party may register the other's trademarks, or otherwise use the trademarks for any purpose except as explicitly provided in this Agreement.

3. Term

3.1 Term. This Agreement will commence on the date stated as the "Effective Date" above and will terminate in [one (1)] year, unless it terminates sooner according to the provisions of this Agreement. This Agreement will renew automatically for another [One (1)] year term unless either party communicates to the other, in writing, at least by 30 days of the termination date that it wishes to discontinue this Agreement.

3.2 Continuation or Survival of Certain Sections. Certain sections, as indicated below, will survive and remain effective even after the termination of this Agreement. All other rights and obligations of each party to the other will terminate upon the termination of this Agreement.

4. Power to Promote

Partner will use its best efforts to promote and distribute the Products / Services. Any promotions or discounts applied toward **[Company]** products/services as well as the terms and conditions of any sale must be pre-approved in writing by **[Company]**.

User Data. Partner agrees to share all End-User Personal Information as available with [Company] for [Company]'s marketing purposes.

However, Partner will not collect, use or disclose any personal information of site visitors, except:

*   as functionally necessary to process visitor instructions and transactions;

*   for efficient internal operation, subject to adequate data security;

*   for appropriate sharing between the two parties for their own marketing purposes;

*   for disclosure to and use by third parties with respect to visitors who consent after being notified of intended uses;

*   to enforce this Agreement or comply with legal process;

*   in emergencies when physical safety is believed at risk;

*   as according to the terms and conditions of the Partner Membership Agreement.

5. Product / Service Content

5.1 [Company] reserves the right at any time without liability or prior notice to

(a) determine the contents of its Products / Services and Product Components, including its specifications, features, and functions, as well as any documentation or related materials;

(b) discontinue distribution of any or all of its Products / Services and Product
Components in some or all markets or through some or all channels of distribution;

(c) change or terminate any of its specifications, features, or functions of the Products / Services or Product Components; or

(e) change or terminate the level or type of support or service that it makes available for its Products / Services. Any change or discontinuance of a Products / Services or Product Components will be indicated by an addition or deletion from [Company]'s web page, [Company] may cancel any orders for discontinued Products / Services or Product Components without liability.

5.2 Modifications. Partner agrees that it will not copy, reverse engineer, disassemble, decompile, translate, or modify any of the [Company] Products/Services or Product Components, nor combine such with other Products / Services or material to form derivative works—nor grant any other person or entity any right to do so.

5.3 Compliance with Laws. [Company] and Partner will comply with all material applicable present and future federal, state, county, local, and, where necessary, foreign laws, ordinances, and regulations relating to the sale of the Products / Services and Product Components.

5.4 Service Support. Neither party is responsible to the other for any customer service support for purchases and fulfillment including but not limited to, providing qualified personnel to receive End-User inquiries.

6. Compensation

Partner will pay [Company] according to the schedule in Exhibit A attached.

Complete products (as listed under the "Products / Services Offered" in the attached Exhibit A) for Electronic Software Distribution (ESD) – electronically downloaded from the Internet – will be managed by a third party fulfillment company [like CyberSource or another] of [Company]'s choosing. Such third party fulfillment company shall act as a "clearing house" and provide regular reports to both [Company] and Partner as to the actual results of sales activities. In the event of a dispute, these reports shall be deemed accurate and the sole basis for determining any monies due either party.

6.1 Suggested List Prices. A copy of [Company]'s current price schedule for the Products / Services is described on the website www.dot.com. [Company] may change the suggested list prices of any Products / Services at any time. In the event Partner wants to offer a special promotion on any of [Company]'s Products/Services or Product Components, it may do so through prior agreement, and amended to Exhibit A.

6.2 Taxes. Both [Company] and Partner are responsible for payment of any/all respective taxes.

6.3 Payment. Partner will pay [Company] its balances due for all Products / Services purchased, within Thirty (30) days after the close of the fiscal month in which purchases were made.

6.4 Interest. Interest will accrue on any delinquent amounts owed at the rate of 1.5% percent per month (18% APR), or the maximum rate permitted by applicable law, whichever is less.

Note: It makes sense to include something about auditing because you want to keep them honest – this deal is fair because it establishes the conditions for paying for the audit.

6.5 Auditing. [Company] has the right to audit Partner's records and may do so by sending or designating a CPA of [Company]'s choice. If the audit proves that there is an inaccuracy of less than Five Percent (5%), [Company] will pay for the audit, if there is an inaccuracy of more than Five Percent (5%), Partner will pay for the audit.

7. Ownership Warranty & Indemnification

7.1 Disclaimer, No Other Warranty

Neither [Company] nor Partner grant any warranties, express of implied, by statute or otherwise, regarding their respective Products / Services, its fitness for any purpose, its quality, its merchantability, or otherwise.

7.2 Limitation of Liability

[Company]'s liabilities under any warranties will be limited to replacement, repair or credit for the customer's purchase price. In no event will [Company] be liable for the cost of procurement of substitute goods by the customer or for any special, consequential or incidental damages for breach of warranty.

7.3 Ownership Warranty

[Company] represents and warrants to Partner that:

(a)   its Products / Services are original or under license with [Company];

(b)   its Products / Services do not infringe upon any patent, copyright, trade secret or other proprietary rights of others;

(c) [Company] has full power and authority to grant the rights granted within this Agreement to [Company]; and

(d) [Company] has not previously or otherwise granted any other rights in the Products / Services to any third party that conflict with the rights in this Agreement granted to [Company].

7.4 Indemnification Partner and [Company] will indemnify and hold each other harmless for damages or expenses resulting from any claim, suit or proceeding brought against the other party on any issue including, but not limited to product liability.

Both parties agree that the other has the right to defend, or at its option to settle any claim, suit or proceeding brought against it or its Customer at its own expense, subject to the limitations described in this Agreement. The party whose product(s) or action(s) are the subject of any legal action will have sole control of any such action or settlement negotiations, and agrees to pay, any final judgment entered against it and/or the other party or its Customer on such issue in any such suit or proceeding.

The party whose product is the primary subject of any legal action will bear all associated legal costs of both parties. For example, if Partner is named in a lawsuit due to its participation in a marketing program with [Company], but [Company]'s product, [product/service], is the subject of the legal action, then [Company] shall bear all associated legal costs of both parties.

The foregoing provisions state the entire liability and obligations of [Company] and Partner and the exclusive remedies with respect to any legal action and/or alleged product liability suit related to the product(s) promoted in this Co-Marketing Agreement.

7.5 Survival of Warranties. The warranties and indemnities stated in this section will survive the expiration or termination of this Agreement.

8. Termination

8.1 Termination Events. This Agreement may be terminated by either party upon the occurrence of any of the following circumstances:

8.1.1 Any assignment for the benefit of the creditors, or any bankruptcy, reorganization, or other proceeding under any bankruptcy or insolvency law is initiated by the other party, or is initiated against it and not dismissed or stayed within Sixty (60) days;

A material breach by the other party of any of the terms of this Agreement, which breach is not remedied by the other party within Thirty (30 days of the other party's receipt of notice of such breach; or

In the event [Company] or a substantial portion of [Company]'s assets are acquired, at any time, the acquiring party may terminate this Agreement unconditionally, at its option.

8.2 Fulfillment of Obligations. The termination of this Agreement will not otherwise release either party from its obligation to pay any sum that may be then or thereafter owing to the other party nor operate to discharge any liability that had been incurred by either party prior to any such termination. Except as qualified by the preceding sentence, neither party will, by reason of the termination of this Agreement, be liable to the other for any damages (whether direct, consequential or incidental to, and including loss of profit or prospective profits of any kind) sustained or arising out of any such termination.

8.3 Effect of Termination Survival. Upon termination of this Agreement, Partner will discontinue all further promotion of [Company]'s Products/Services. Without limiting the generality of the foregoing, both [Company] and Partner will cease all display, advertising, and use of all of the other party's respective names, trademarks, logos, and designations and will not thereafter use, advertise, or display any such names, trademarks, logos, or designations. Upon termination of this Agreement, the due date of all outstanding invoices for the Products/Services will automatically be accelerated and all such Commissions will become due and payable. Despite any termination of this Agreement, the provisions in Sections 7, 9, and 10 will remain in full force and effect.

9. General Provisions

Note: The General Provisions that follow are fairly standard. These provisions enhance the balance of the Agreement by explaining issues such as notice, assignment, legal remedies, waiver, and attorney fees.

Note: You must decide which state governs this Agreement and where any legal action would be taken. Generally, it is your (company's) state of residence.

9.1 Governing Law & Jurisdiction. This agreement and the parties' actions under this Agreement shall be governed by and construed under the laws of the state of [State], without reference to conflict of law principles. The parties hereby expressly consent to the jurisdiction and venue of the federal and state courts within the state of [State]. Each party hereby irrevocably consents to the service of process in any such action or proceeding by the mailing of copies thereof by registered or certified mail, postage prepaid, to such party at its address set forth in the preamble of this Agreement, such service to become effective thirty (30) days after such mailing.

Note: This Agreement is intended to be the only Agreement, and that no other documents or communications are binding. Therefore, it is very important to make sure that everything [Company] and [Client] have agreed to is included in this Agreement. Otherwise, it is as if it was not agreed to.

9.2 Entire Agreement. This Agreement, including the attached exhibits, constitutes the entire Agreement between both parties concerning this transaction, and replaces all previous communications, representations, understandings, and Agreements, whether verbal or written between the parties to this Agreement or their representatives. No representations or statements of any kind made by either party, which are not expressly stated in this Agreement, shall be binding on such parties.

Note: Any changes to this Agreement must be in writing and signed by the party against whom that writing is to be used.

9.3 All Amendments in Writing. No waiver, amendment or modification of any provisions of this Agreement shall be effective unless in writing and signed by a duly authorized representative of the party against whom such waiver, amendment or modification is sought to be enforced. Furthermore, no provisions in either party's purchase orders, or in any other business forms employed by either party will supersede the terms and conditions of this Agreement.

Note: All notices between the parties must be in writing and either delivered in person or by certified or registered mail, return receipt requested.

9.4 Notices. Any notice required or permitted by this Agreement shall be deemed given if sent by registered mail, postage prepaid with return receipt requested, addressed to the other party at the address set forth in the preamble of this Agreement or at such other address for which such party gives notice hereunder. Delivery shall be deemed effective three (3) days after deposit with postal authorities.

Note: In the event of a lawsuit or any legal proceeding involving this Agreement, the losing party will have to pay the winning party his or her costs and expenses, including reasonable attorney fees.

9.5 Costs of Legal Action. In the event any action is brought to enforce this Agreement, the prevailing party shall be entitled to recover its costs of enforcement including, without limitation, attorneys' fees and court costs.

Note: Legal remedies, i.e., money damages, may not be sufficient; therefore, both parties agree to equitable remedies such as an injunction where the breaching party would be required to do or not to do something.

9.6 Inadequate Legal Remedy. Both parties understand and acknowledge that violation of their respective covenants and Agreements may cause the other irreparable harm and damage, that may not be recovered at law, and each agrees that the other's remedies for breach may be in equity by way of injunctive relief, as well as for damages and any other relief available to the non-breaching party, whether in law or in equity.

Note: Assuming the parties wish to use Arbitration in the event of a dispute, the following section should be included. You take your chances with an arbitrator, but it keeps legal costs down and keeps you out of a drawn out legal process.

9.7 Arbitration. Any dispute relating to the interpretation or performance of this Agreement shall be resolved at the request of either party through binding arbitration. Arbitration shall be conducted in [County], [State] in accordance with the then-existing rules of the American Arbitration Association. Judgment upon any award by the arbitrators may be entered by any state or federal court having jurisdiction. Both parties intend that this Agreement to arbitrate be irrevocable.

Note: Merely delaying to bring an action that one party has a right to bring does not cause that party to lose or waive his right to pursue that action.

9.8 Delay is Not a Waiver. No failure or delay by either party in exercising any right, power or remedy under this Agreement, except as specifically provided in this Agreement, shall operate as a waiver of any such right, power or remedy.

Note: Neither party will be blamed if there is a problem resulting from something beyond its control, such as an earthquake, flood, war.

9.9 Force Majeure. In the event that either party is unable to perform any of its obligations under this Agreement or to enjoy any of its benefits because of any Act of God, strike, fire, flood, governmental acts, orders or restrictions, Internet system unavailability, system malfunctions or any other reason where failure to perform is beyond the reasonable control and not caused by the negligence of the non-performing party (a "Force Majeure Event"), the party who has been so affected shall give notice immediately to the other party and shall use its reasonable best efforts to resume performance. Failure to meet due dates resulting from a Force Majeure Event shall extend such due dates for a reasonable period. However, if the period of nonperformance exceeds sixty (60) days from the receipt of notice of the Force Majeure Event, the party whose ability to perform has not been affected may, by giving written notice, terminate this Agreement effective immediately upon such notice or at such later date as is therein specified.

Note: This section limits the ability of either party to transfer any of its rights or delegate any of its duties to third parties.

Note: You want to make sure that you can sell your business along with all of the relationships you have developed along the way. (Often these relationships can add tremendous value to your business and you want to make sure that all of your agreements can be transferred to the new owners.) I wouldn't want to seek (let alone pay for) permission to sell my company.

Note: Generally, neither party may assign their respective rights to a third party; however, with the possible exception of assignment to a successor corporation or partnership, either party may transfer its rights or obligations under this Agreement without the approval of the other party. However, you may want to limit each other's ability to pass along this deal to another possibly unknown and possibly unfriendly entity. The second paragraph prevents unauthorized transfer of responsibilities…

9.10•• Assignability   Binding Effect. Except as expressly set forth within this Agreement, neither party may transfer or assign, directly or indirectly, this Agreement or its rights and obligations hereunder without the express written permission of the other party, not to be unreasonably withheld; provided, however, that both parties shall have the right to assign or otherwise transfer this Agreement to any parent, subsidiary, affiliated entity or pursuant to any merger, consolidation or reorganization, provided that all such assignees and transferees agree in writing to be bound by the terms of this Agreement prior to such assignment or transfer. Subject to the foregoing, this Agreement shall be binding upon and inure to the benefit of the parties hereto, their successors and assigns.

Note: This paragraph DOES NOT ALLOW either party to transfer its rights to a successor company without prior approval.

- OR -

9.10•• Non-Assignability & Binding Effect. Except as otherwise provided for within this Agreement, neither party may assign any of its rights or delegate any of its obligations under this Agreement to any third party without the express written permission of the other. Any such assignment is deemed null and void.

Note: If any part of this Agreement is unenforceable or invalid, the balance of the Agreement should still be enforced. Basically, ignore any sections that are invalid.

9.11•• Certain Sections Invalid. If any provisions of this Agreement are held by a court of competent jurisdiction to be invalid under any applicable statute or rule of law, they are to that extent to be deemed omitted and the remaining provisions of this Agreement shall remain in full force and effect.

Note: The headings of the various sections are meant to explain or otherwise give meaning to those sections; they are for convenience only.

9.12•• Headings. The titles and headings of the various sections and sections in this Agreement are intended solely for convenience of reference and are not intended for any other purpose whatsoever, or to explain, modify or place any construction upon or on any of the provisions of this Agreement.

Note: Even after the termination of the Agreement, the parties may still have certain responsibilities such as keeping information confidential.

9.13•• Survival of Certain Provisions. The warranties and the indemnification and confidentiality obligations set forth in this Agreement shall survive the termination of the Agreement by either party for any reason.

Understood, Agreed & Approved

We have carefully reviewed this contract and agree to and accept all of its terms and conditions. We are executing this Agreement as of the Effective Date above.

____

[Company]

____

[Owner / Founder]

____

[President / CEO]

____

Partner

____

[Name]

____

[President / CEO]

Exhibit A

Products / Services Offered

*   [xXxx]

*   [xXxx]

*   [xXxx]

Exhibit B

Trademarks Owned by [Company]

*   [xXxx] ®

*   [xXxx] ®

*   [xXxx] ®

NOTES

<u>NOTES</u>

About The Author

Kyle Davis, a U.S. Air Force Veteran, is the groundbreaking author of "How to Build a New Black Wall Street". This non-fiction, published in 2016, is the first of it's kind, as to addressing the black community with a non-documentary abstract that presents proven business practices and sample contracts: shareholder agreements and Nondisclosure Agreements, for example.

At the same time of publishing "How to Build a New Black Wall Street", Kyle wanted to influence the Google Search Algorithm, that was presenting negative imagery of black children. With Kyle having experience in online advertising & SEO, he knew the only path was to flood Google's Search Algorithm with Meta-Data for black children and black children imagery. A flip on the idiom: cannot see the forest for the trees.

Thereafter, Kyle started "Black Children's Coloring Books" to address the needs of black children for coloring books that feature black children, as well as, titling the books "Black Children's Coloring Book" so that black parents and parents of black children would be able to find coloring books designed for them.